*Praise for the First Edition of*
# Not One Dollar More!

The following are excerpts from the hundreds of letters homebuyers have written in praise of the first edition of *Not One Dollar More!* Names have been withheld only to preserve confidentiality, but all are on file with the publisher.

## WHAT READERS SAID

"Thank you so much. We are grateful to you and your book for saving us $24,000. We will recommend *Not One Dollar More!* to other homebuyers. Many thanks!!!!"

*Peter and Diane, Pittsburgh, PA*

"So much better than anything else written on the subject."

*D. L. T., Attorney-at-Law, NC*

"*Not One Dollar More!* was definitely instrumental in helping us get $33,000 off the purchase price! Asking price was $275,000, we got it for $242,000. The book is such an incredible resource for first-time homebuyers like ourselves."

*Patti and Doug G., Cambridge, MA*

"With the confidence *Not One Dollar More!* gave me, I was able to buy the house I wanted for $11,500 below the list price. This is all the more incredible since I was dealing with two seasoned real estate agents (the seller was also an agent)! Proof positive that it can be done."

*K. M. K., Lower Burrell, PA*

"Joseph Éamon Cummins is sharp and so good to read, a wonderfully interesting writer. He should be writing in the *Los Angeles Times* or some big daily newspaper like that."

*R. T. H. Jr., San Diego, CA*

"The most important thing I can say about the book is that it gave me new confidence. *Not One Dollar More!* reminded me that I'm in charge, not the real estate agent, not the seller, but me and my cash."

*R. A. C., Rochester, PA*

"A fantastic book! Details I never saw or heard before. Everybody should read this book, buyers and sellers. Have recommended it to everyone."

*B. Y., Woburn, MA*

"I am in commercial real estate. I found the book fascinating, wonderful. A very well written book. Excellent negotiation tips and a wealth of great information. I couldn't have asked for a better book."

*B. R., Arlington Heights, IL*

"I'm older now but I was well pleased with this book. I wish I had this information 25 or 30 years ago. It would have made a big difference to my finances. One thing is for certain, I'll make sure my son reads it."

*G. D., Wedowee, AL*

"Creating wealth is hard. I have read all kinds of books searching for good answers. This book does a really good job. It fills a definite need, the know-how of creating personal wealth. It is reliable and down to earth. And best of all, it has great concrete examples. I especially enjoyed the anecdotes."

*J. I., Philadelphia, PA*

"Upon arriving in Indiana, we had only two weeks to find a place before I started working. We followed the book's suggestions (as we) looked at 34 homes. We offered $92,000 on a house listed at $110,000. We bought it at $97,000, a single-story rancher just two miles outside town. You saved us $13,000!"

*G. and D. R., Ft Wayne, IN*

"Thank you for a fascinating book!"

*Evelyn and Gil B., York, ME*

"EXCELLENT!! More than a book about negotiating to buy a home. Contains valuable life skills beneficial to everyone. Our kids should be learning these skills in school, something that would have a powerful impact on their whole lives. This book is inspirational, easy to read, and a great confidence builder, advice only your best friend would give you—if only they knew it. BRAVO!"

*Chris M., Mays Landing, NJ (from Amazon.com Website)*

"Don't be another real estate victim! Feeling like a lamb led to the slaughter? This book provides the tools with which to fight back. Mr. Cummins weaves concepts and real-life illustrations together to create an informative, inspiring book."

*E. L., Los Angeles, CA (from Amazon.com Website)*

"This is an excellent book, which we are reading every day while we are looking for a home. By using your suggestions, we have already been able to get reductions in asking prices."

*Sue T., New York, NY*

"Absolutely the best! *Not One Dollar More!* provides a unique perspective on homebuying. This text provides insight into the roles—and motivations—of the many individuals involved in a real estate transaction. Empowers you, the homebuyer, to select, negotiate and buy (or reject!) a home on YOUR terms."

*A reader from New York City, (from Amazon.com Website)*

"Your *Not One Dollar More!* is extraordinary as a resource for buyers. I am an attorney-broker providing essential negotiation and consulting services to residential real estate buyers. Your book has elevated the profession in my eyes, and certainly in the public's eyes. BRAVO!"

*M. R. LeB., Attorney-at-Law, St Paul, MN*

## WHAT THE CRITICS SAID

"This book is *extraordinary!*"

*Tony Robbins, Trainer,*
*Author: Unlimited Power, Awaken The Giant Within, etc.*

"*Not One Dollar More!* helps you CASH IN on savings!"

*Kiplinger's ("Worth Getting" column)*

"This book hands you the advantage—grasp it!"

*Barry M. Miller, Consumer Advocate*

"Helps the reader from the start. Shows how to hold on to your money—with GREAT anecdotes."

*Andrew Tobias,*
*Author: The Only Investment Guide You'll Ever Need, etc.*

"A wealth of detail as it takes you to right up to the settlement table."

*Philadelphia Daily News*

"A book with great promise for homebuyers."

*Dr. Wayne W. Dyer, Author: Your Erroneous Zones, Living Without*
*Limits, The Awakened Life, etc.*

"*Not One Dollar More!* is well written, and filled with valuable ammunition homebuyers need in their quest."

*Robert Bruss, National Syndicated Columnist*

"None of the complexity or tedious language of other "money" books. From the start the reader is helped along with examples and entertaining anecdotes that communicate important know-how."

*TV Review*

"Sound Advice!"

"A wonderful money guide for homebuyers and those who long to be."

"Shows clearly how to buy a home without paying too much for it."

"An indispensable book!"

"This *really is* a GREAT book!"

"No contest—*the* best! A consumer milestone. On-target, easy to understand. Puts power in the hands of the consumer."

"One of the great books on personal finance. Shows how to get a great deal and reads like a novel. A gift to consumers. Five stars!"

"Few book writers can put money in your pocket; here's one who can! Cummins is surely the new master of negotiation, and a gifted writer. Certainly *the best* and most enjoyable book on homebuying. Inspiring!"

"THE BIBLE! An invaluable resource and companion."

"An outrageously good book! Read well what Cummins writes, it could make all the difference."

"DON"T loan this book. You won't get it back!"

"Worth its weight in gold. Every house in the nation should have this book NOW!"

# NOT ONE DOLLAR more!

## How to Save $3,000 to $30,000 Buying Your Next Home

Second Edition

JOSEPH ÉAMON CUMMINS

JOHN WILEY & SONS, INC.

New York · Chichester · Weinheim · Brisbane · Singapore · Toronto

*Most especially…*

I dedicate this book to my mother and father,
Bridget and Joseph Cummins,
for their ever-present love
and their wise and inspired teaching.

*I dedicate it also…*

to the unsung heroes in all walks of life
who bring into reach
the knowledge that opens minds to human potential
and illuminates paths to joy and wisdom.

*And to the new bright-eyed flag bearers…*

Bridget, Keith, Colin, Claire, Eoin, Roy, Steven,
Christina, Aran, Andrew, Éamon.

Published by John Wiley & Sons, Inc.

Published simultaneously in Canada.

This publication is designed to provide accurate and authoritative information in regard to the subject matter covered. It is sold with the understanding that the publisher is not engaged in rendering professional services. If professional advice or other expert assistance is required, the services of a competent professional person should be sought.

*Library of Congress Cataloging-in-Publication Data:*

Cummins, Joseph Éamon.
    Not one dollar more! : how to save $3,000 to $30,000 buying your
next home / Joseph Éamon Cummins. — 2nd ed.
        p.   cm.
    Includes bibliographical references and index.
    ISBN 0-471-35726-X (paper : alk. paper)
    1. House buying—United States.   2. Negotiation in business—United States. I. Title.
HD255.C86 1999
643'.12—dc21                                                                99-23040
                                                                                    CIP

Printed in the United States of America.

10  9  8  7  6  5  4  3  2  1

# AUTHOR'S NOTE

When this book first appeared in the mid 1990s, few anticipated the impact it would make. But right away it became a major force for positive change in how the tradition-heavy real estate industry had always under-served homebuyers.

With the book's growing popularity, brokers and agents who had resisted fair and equal representation for buyers began to jump on the bandwagon. These professionals realized that the changes called for in *Not One Dollar More!* were overdue and inevitable. After all, the goal of a better-informed and better-served consumer is hard to argue with indefinitely.

Today, for example, it is not nearly so hard for a homebuyer to find and engage an exclusive buyer broker. Such a broker will pledge loyalty and confidentiality solely to the buyer's interests; this is the same standard and quality of representation sellers have always enjoyed.

For you, being an informed homebuyer means, first, preparing early and well for the task ahead. It means knowing the mistakes that are common—and costly!—and how to avoid them. It also means being able to shop wisely for a mortgage, an undertaking in which the benefits of a well-negotiated home purchase can be wiped out by going with the wrong loan. For that reason, this new edition includes a new and comprehensive chapter on shopping for the best mortgage.

You'll also find here a revised Resources section with one major change: the Internet. Much of the homebuyer's early research and leg-work can now be done online. This new section provides many useful Web addresses that can take much of the tedium out of your task. Included also are telephone numbers, street addresses, and a list of recommended services.

The reason I wrote this book in the first place was simple: to offer an honest resource for the homebuyer, a "mentor" to help you protect your money and your interests. That meant providing only reliable, unbiased advice, free and independent of any vested interests or real estate industry leaning. With this new edition, I have been guided by precisely those same goals.

When you learn ahead of time what to expect in the real estate marketplace, prepare well, and then apply simple negotiation skills, you are well ahead of the masses!

Fortune favors the brave, certainly, but even more, it favors the prepared.

*Joseph Éamon Cummins*

# ACKNOWLEDGMENTS

*Not One Dollar More!* is based on my own first-hand experience of buying and selling property, both as a real estate agent and as a private individual. In addition, it draws on my work as a communications lecturer, sales trainer, and journalist. Nonetheless, a project of this scale is rarely a completely solo accomplishment.

In three years of research, I traveled to many parts of the United States and received uplifting support and assistance from a number of sources. Along the way, I discovered that buyers everywhere face similar challenges. I was given opportunities to become an *insider;* to observe close-up the ways, typically, in which the average homebuyer is disadvantaged, outwitted, and outmaneuvered; the traps into which he or she is frequently led, pressured, or blindly walks. And I saw again and again how the odds are kept stacked against the buyer ever getting the lowest price or the best terms attainable.

From time to time, I received unanticipated cooperation from traditional real estate agents and brokers, and thus gained further insights into what happens day by day in home buying and selling.

These and other special individuals and groups made easier the hard work of researching and writing. All contributed to what I am convinced is the only book of its kind ever published—a dos and don'ts guide that is immediately usable and of countable financial benefit to homebuyers of all kinds, in all price ranges, and in all places.

The list is incomplete, but to the following people, I offer my special gratitude:

- For her reading and perceptive critiquing of the manuscript; for her intuitive thinking and uncommon wisdom; and most of all, for her love and her infectious sense of fun, I am especially grateful to my wife, Kathy Argenti-Cummins.

- To my brother Desi, for his wise counsel, his trust, and his challenging and uniquely insightful intellect, and, in particular, for his friendship.

- To my sister, Ann, for her astute suggestions, her encouragement, and her boundless enthusiasm for my work. I am also grateful for her rich wellspring of reachable and always-uplifting belief.

- To my brother, Paddy, one of my earliest teachers, for his loyalty and resourceful friendship. His search for truth and learning never bowed to convention or to popular political thought.

- To GFC, always inspiring.

- To the happy memory of Isabel and Tom.

- To all my students and teaching colleagues for keeping me learning and on my toes.

- To the thousands of people who helped in my research—homebuyers, sellers, investors, attorneys, consumer advocates, regulators, media professionals, educators, and the many agents and brokers—for their time, insights, honesty and openness.

- And in particular to the following for their generous help: Paul R. Roark of the U.S. Federal Trade Commission; the U.S. Office of Consumer Affairs, Washington, D.C.; Bill Wendel; Steven Kropper; Stephen Brobeck of the Consumer Federation of America; Joe Reddin and John Foley of Dublin Institute of Technology; Barry M. Miller; Marc Eisenson; and Christopher Weimar.

  Also: Jordan Clark; U.S. Dept. of Housing and Urban Development; The Council of Better Business Bureaus; Maureen Glasheen; Dr. Wayne Dyer; Raymond Stoklosa; Sloan Bashinsky; Bruce Hahn, President, American Homeowners Foundation; Jerilyn Coates; Tom Hathaway; George Rosenberg; Keith T. Gumbinger; Dr. Joyce Whitehead; Dr. Felix V. Malkiel.

- To my current and former colleagues, most resourceful and inspiring, Isteiki Kurosawa, Dr. Trevor Kedfradkis, Eswain Deives, and Jeremy Stone.

- To all whose names I've left out, through oversight or by design, my most sincere thanks.

- And last but not least, to all of the "old" Kells clan.

# CONTENTS

## PART FOUR
## TACTICS IN ACTION: BUYING DIRECTLY
## FROM A PRIVATE SELLER

# ABOUT THE AUTHOR

**Joseph Éamon Cummins** is a specialist in psychology and human learning, and a consultant to a broad spectrum of groups and individuals. He has taught critical thinking, negotiation, and other subjects at a number of universities, and has produced a series of acclaimed television documentaries.

A former licensed real estate agent, he spent three years researching and writing the clear, lively text for *Not One Dollar More!* The book has drawn countless accolades from readers and critics alike, is frequently hailed as "a classic", and has won a score of superlative honors.

The author is a member of The Authors Guild in New York City and is an affiliate of the American Psychological Association. A native of Dublin, Ireland, he is also an active fiction writer. He lives between New York City and Philadelphia.

# Introduction

*The real purpose of books is to trap the mind
into doing its own thinking.*
—Christopher Morley

Congratulations. The book you are holding can help make you richer by many thousands of dollars. It can, without question, put money *into* your pocket. And, just as certainly, it can stop others from taking money *out of* your pocket. It matters not whether you are a first-timer or an old hand at homebuying, *Not One Dollar More!* can be of immense value to you.

What you will learn in these pages has taken me more than 15 years of study, testing, and observation to acquire. I have refined, applied and proved these methods in the *real* world where they have worked time after time in thousands of business deals, real estate and otherwise. There is no other book like this—no substitute, and no competition.

The advice and suggestions, and the often jealously guarded secrets you'll learn, come directly from my own personal involvement in buying, selling, and negotiating; from the thinking of men and women who, as a rule, do *not* share their skill or opinions with others; and from extensive research and countless detailed notes I recorded over the years. To add to this, I have called on key insights I have learned, and successfully taught, in the fields of marketing, communications, and human development and achievement.

However, this is not a homebuying encyclopedia—nor does it pretend to be. All the real estate knowledge in the world is utterly useless unless you know how the game is played. My objective here is to help you win the "mind game" that is unavoidable when you buy a home—and in so doing, to make you richer. If these are your goals, *this is one book you can believe in.*

Something else this book is not is a compendium of real estate brokers' opinions and advice. Strangely, though, there are a number of "homebuyer protection" type books on the market that are exactly that. To me, that's like asking the fox to advise the geese on how to stay healthy. After all, brokers and agents work for the seller, not the buyer—don't they?

Furthermore, agents and brokers depend on a supply of willing and ready buyers to keep their commissions coming in. As I see it, this is a clear conflict of interest. How can brokers be expected to give objective advice to buyers, the party they *do not* represent? The party to whom they *do not* pledge their loyalty or confidentiality? The party for whom they *do not* work to get the best price or most favorable terms? Simply, they can't!

*Not One Dollar More!* does not rely on such convenient or questionable sources of *buyer expertise.* Brokers and agents have one primary responsibility—to the seller. The primary responsibility of this book is to the buyer. Not even in real estate can one serve two masters at the same time.

## The Power of Invisible Negotiation

Mostly, this is a book about *invisible negotiation.* I named it invisible negotiation for a number of reasons. First, it is not the negotiation you probably think of when you hear that word. Nor is it bartering or bargaining, as those terms are generally meant. Nor does it require you to talk tough, look intimidating, argue aggressively, act like an expert, pound the table, make threats, or issue ultimatums. And it certainly *isn't* haggling or bickering. No, you won't have to do or become any of these.

Most importantly, it does *not* lead to dispute or bad feelings between you and the real estate agent. Or, between you and anyone. So what is it? Well it's a way of getting what you want using courtesy and specific—but *uncommon*—know-how. No tedious learning. No heavy reading. And, for the most part, without anyone even suspecting that you are negotiating. And here's something you might find ironic—these skills are known and practiced by just a few. And they're seldom discussed.

One reason this kind of negotiation is not widely known is that it is quite difficult to write about. The bigger reason, however, is that those who know it have little or no incentive to share it.

Yet, it is a powerful tool and is easily learned. You will find yourself in tune with it almost instinctively—as you read and absorb what is in these pages. Then, all you have to do is use it when your money is on the line (any time you buy a home). I will show you how to do that, as practically and as simply as I can.

It's been some time since I first started thinking about how to embody these money-saving methods in a guide for the ordinary homebuyer—how I might help you escape the misfortunes and avoid the mistakes I have seen homebuyers make time after time; how I might keep it *simple, interesting* and, above all, *readable;* and, ultimately, how I might place in your hands the means to protect your own money when you are most vulnerable. Now—and I say this with relief—after three years of researching, writing, and revising, the task is completed.

## This Book and You: Making It Really Pay Off

Before you begin the search for your next home, keep in mind that you will be better prepared for negotiation by reading *Not One Dollar More!* a second time, then referring back to it as the need arises. Alternatively, you might find it beneficial to review frequently the particular sections that are most relevant to your situation.

But, you certainly do *not* need to read every chapter or become familiar with all sections to use this book profitably.

Any serious approach will help you to build powerful techniques and tactics into your thinking. Very quickly—almost automatically —they will become part of how you think, talk, and act. That's when you'll start feeling like a confident, capable negotiator, because that is what you'll have become. Then, from the moment you put this new knowledge into practice, you'll feel that you are in control—even when your practice is only a dry run in preparation for the real thing. And you'll begin finding plenty of non–real estate situations every day in which to apply what you've learned.

But what about instinct and intuition? I am often asked this question. Yes, pay heed to these always worthwhile qualities any time you negotiate. However, be cautious. Relying on these alone (as some buyers are inclined to do) is like trying to build a jigsaw puzzle blindfolded. You might get the job done, but the chances are remote and the cost is high. Just as you need sight to build the jigsaw puzzle, a basic strategy is needed to negotiate successfully (see it as a plan, if you prefer).

That strategy is built on the simple tactics you will read about in this book. Knowing and using these tactics will certainly help you get what you want—a better deal. But this knowledge is just as crucial—and valuable—as your first line of *defense.* With it, you will recognize when tactics, tricks, and deceptions are being used against you. And you'll know how to handle them.

Perhaps what will serve you best throughout the home buying process is the knowledge that, with rare exception, all prices are flexible and virtually everything is negotiable. That's how it has always been. Without question, the seller will always try to get more than the lowest acceptable price. But sellers demand more than they are willing, later in the negotiation, to accept. The critical point is this:

> *The seller's thinking, flexibility, and price expectation are affected and changed by you—to your advantage—when you use the skills of smart buying!*

It's important to remember, too, that traditionally the home-buyer has been the party *least* protected and most likely to become a victim in property transactions. Now, however, there is simply no need for that to continue. A negotiation involving a smart, capable buyer produces no victims and no rip-offs. When the agreement is signed—the one you shaped—the real estate agent and the seller *both* succeed in their individual goals. Don't, even for a moment, doubt this.

Despite all the hot air you might hear from people who sell real estate for a living, to protect yourself (your money and other interests) you will need to take deliberate steps to level the playing field. So, first, take sole responsibility for your own well-being. Keep it out of the hands of the agents and salespeople trying to get you to buy. Their trust, their confidentiality, their loyalty and their obligation, are all given to the seller. That's the law—period.

Nonetheless, important as this book may become to you, and particularly to your success in buying your next home, it is not the only book I suggest you read on real estate. (Such a book, if it existed, would be unbearably long and tedious.)

In the Appendix, you will find a list of carefully selected resources that show you simply and reliably how to do various things. From planning a move across country, to home building, investing in real estate, finding the best mortgage, economical renovation, and finding and buying a country hideaway—and lots more.

Also in the Appendix, the Resources section lists sources of advice and information—mostly free—and details of many useful professional services that stand ready to assist you.

I am certain that all homebuyers—experienced or not, big budget or small; just marrieds, baby boomers or retirees; country folk or city dwellers—stand to save time, hassle, and substantial hard cash with the know-how revealed and explained in *Not One Dollar More!*

## A Pawn in Somebody Else's Game?

This is a guide solely for buyers because, in the end, what is at greatest risk in every property purchase is the homebuyer's money. Almost always that means hard-earned cash. Often, it represents a lifetime's savings. The risks are much too great to ignore.

When you learn how to be a smart buyer, you'll experience a special thrill that comes from controlling the buying process rather than being just a pawn in somebody else's game. Rewarding as this feeling is, though, it's only the icing on the cake. Learning how to forge a good deal comes first. And the rewards last longer.

Let's face it. The fact that you are reading this book indicates at least one thing—that you want to win. It suggests, too, that you want to protect yourself from losing. But, if you are not going to lose, who is? The seller? No! Negotiating successfully doesn't mean taking advantage of anyone. The seller always retains the right to refuse your offer and to break off negotiation. By going for the best deal you can get you are doing nothing more and nothing less than what the seller and the real estate agent are doing to you.

The seller always has three options in responding to any offer you make: accept, reject, or send a counter offer back to you (which is another way of saying "let's talk about it"). Nothing you do in the course of negotiation will take any of these options from the seller. When buyer and seller reach a well-negotiated agreement, they both stand to gain. And, so too, does the real estate agent—a point we'll look at in more detail later.

## A Structure for Learning

One of the biggest challenges, as I see it, has been how to give the homebuyer essential self-defense buying skills. But a number of surveys suggest that a large percentage of book buyers don't read the books they buy. Many never get past the second or third chapter. To get over this obstacle and to ensure *Not One Dollar More!* speaks the language of the average homebuyer—not the language of the broker or the banker—I have omitted all avoidable jargon. In doing that, clarity has been enhanced. In fact, the entire book is written in the language I favor most, plain English.

Clear language alone, though, is never enough, especially when writing about a potentially confusing subject like real estate. In my later high school years in Dublin, I remember working somewhat randomly on teaching-related projects, and my father cautioning me repeatedly about how people learn. He emphasized time and again that to teach anything effectively I would, first, need to build an appropriate structure. The lesson sank in. That's what I have tried to do in this book—build a structure that makes it easy for you to read and learn.

If you are tempted to skip the earlier chapters and jump to the meatier parts, try to resist that temptation, at least on the first reading. Like all good how-to programs, this book has a deliberate foundation and a planned sequential order. The earlier chapters might seem basic but they provide a base that will serve you well later as you move logically through the book and build a solid understanding of how to save thousands of dollars.

Naturally, it is not the role of this book to tell you what you should buy, or where you should buy. It tells you how you may buy what you want, at the lowest possible price. In the process, I will show you how to protect yourself from the wealth-robbing pitfalls, bluffs, and tricks you are likely to encounter. I will also show you how to spot and grab opportunities that often are lost because they go unrecognized by homebuyers. In this case, *opportunities* translates into putting dollars in your pocket.

You'll find, too, many suggestions concerning your own behavior and actions, and the resulting disadvantages that are costly and always work against you. In most transactions, strange as it may seem at this point, it's your behavior that persuades and communicates more strongly than what you say. How you behave determines your personal power. And personal power is the single most important ingredient in producing positive results in just about everything we do.

The principles and insights explained in *Not One Dollar More!* apply anywhere in the world, to whatever type of property you plan to purchase. Whether your goal is a conventional suburban home, a mobile home, a townhouse, 50,000 acres of grazing land, or even a vacation home, the rules of smart buying don't change. One thing that does vary, though, is your spending budget. As it gets bigger, so does the amount you stand to save.

### The Key Ingredient—Action!

As you progress through this book, you'll discover that all you need to negotiate a money-saving deal is a basic understanding of what happens behind the scenes in real estate, a little common sense, and a few easily learned skills. Then, the real reward comes from the final ingredient, your willingness to put what you've learned into action. It is on this last part that some otherwise astute, well-informed buyers fall down. They gain the know-how but fail to use it when it comes time to act. Throughout this book I will help you avoid that problem. You can help yourself even more by remembering that knowledge by itself is *not* power. At best, knowledge is potential power. Until it is applied in an appropriate way—until it is used productively—it has no actual power.

When the time comes to apply one or more of the methods or tactics you learn from this book, stay focused on one point: whatever a real estate sales agent asks you to believe, accept, or agree to, the agent is not on *your* side and is not committed to protecting *your* money. A realty agent's overriding objective is to sell you the property you want to buy (and sometimes a property you might *not* want to buy) at the highest price he can convince you to pay. That's what he promised the seller he would do. As a result, it makes no sense to blindly accept the logic, the opinions, or the reasoning of someone who is out to get the highest price possible—out of you!

The responsibility for protecting your money falls on you and you alone. I wrote *Not One Dollar More!* with one purpose in mind— to show you how to buy the property you want at rock bottom price. Any time you succeed in doing that, you save money—and not loose change either. Typically, it's a substantial sum.

Hanging in the balance—up for grabs, in fact—are thousands of dollars. Sometimes tens of thousands of dollars. *Your* money. But no seller or agent is going to tip the balance in your favor and make you richer. They're not on *your* side.

*Not One Dollar More!* is! Let's get to work.

—*Joseph Éamon Cummins*

# PART ONE

# How Not to Lose: The First Steps

# CHAPTER ONE

# COME INTO MY PARLOR...

*Be wiser than other people if you can,*
*but do not tell them so.*
　　　　　　— G. K. CHESTERTON

Buying and selling real estate is a game, pure and simple. A game in which professionals and amateurs compete side by side. Nothing wrong with that, you might think, except for one thing. Typically, only the side that is selling is fully protected and represented from start to finish by a trained professional, the real estate agent or salesperson.

Alone, on the other side, stands you, the average homebuyer, professionally unrepresented, naively unprepared and uninformed (or misinformed) about the game rules, the smokescreens and the traps that exist only to separate you from your money—often in huge chunks. And often with swift and convincing efficiency.

The result is that you run a high risk of being outmaneuvered, outwitted, and outgunned. Ironically, although almost always completely unaware of the fact, the vast majority of homebuyers end up paying thousands of dollars more than is necessary for their homes.

Based on my own experience of buying and selling property, both privately and in a professional capacity, I believe that in about 95 percent of home purchases, a lack of basic negotiation skills causes the buyer to pay far more than what the seller would have accepted. I have no reason to believe the homebuyer fares any better when buying directly from a private seller (where no agent is involved in the transaction).

With just a handful of self-defense tactics you can avoid such disasters.

## Knowing What You Are Up Against

Now and again a novice buyer will forge a good deal almost inadvertently. Having a naturally assertive personality or, interestingly, an inability to make decisions, is often the cause. Both characteristics, when employed deliberately, can be very profitable in the negotiation process. More on that later.

Occasionally, a high degree of seller desperation can give rise to an unexpected price concession in favor of the homebuyer. Even so, the average homebuyer very seldom gets within a couple of thousand dollars of the seller's lowest acceptable price. Almost always buyers hand over substantially more than is necessary to make the purchase. Frequently, they miss the boat altogether and grossly overpay.

In a later chapter I'll explain in detail how I witnessed an unprepared and probably misinformed buyer pay *one hundred thousand dollars* more than the seller was willing to accept for his home. And, contrary to what might have just crossed your mind that very expensive mistake didn't happen on a $1 million or $2 million property. Nothing even close to that. The unfortunate buyer paid $280,000 when he could certainly have bought the same property, on the same day, at the same time for $180,000. Certainly this is an exceptional situation, but it illustrates clearly how terribly wrong things can go when buyers have neither the knowledge nor the power to protect their own interests, wealth, and standard of living—in short, when they lack the basic know-how to negotiate.

So far, I've assumed that you, like the majority of home seekers, plan to buy through a real estate broker or agent. Nonetheless, most of what I say applies in any property transaction in which you are expected to hand over money or to make a commitment to purchase. Later, you'll learn in detail how to handle and buy from a private seller.

Whether you intend buying privately or through an agent, this week or at some time in the future, I can offer you no better advice than to learn and use the basic skills and methods I've included in this book. They are not difficult.

One point to keep in mind is this: These skills and methods are not *anti* any organization. And, certainly, they're not anti the real estate profession. In fact, once you know what you are doing, a good agent or salesperson can be your most valuable helper, providing you with a gold mine of assistance you can use in buying at the lowest price.

Everything I've written here is simply and unashamedly pro buyer.

The quantity of real estate books you'll see in your local bookstore or library can be somewhat deceiving. Most have been written for professional investors, brokers, speculators, renovators, or salespeople. A handful provide good financial advice on mortgages, trust deeds, and the like. Others explain your legal rights, responsibilities and options, and in doing so many do serve to inform homebuyers.

But, so far, the layperson needing to know how best to protect his or her money by negotiating the lowest price has been left out in the cold—if you'll pardon the pun. By applying even a couple of the tactics and recommendations you'll learn from *Not One Dollar More!* you can redress that imbalance and, at the same time, reap the rewards they produce—usually in cold cash.

What this book won't do is eliminate the need for sound legal advice. I will assume you already appreciate the need to talk with your mortgage lender and your attorney before committing yourself to a purchase.

So, now that you are a little more aware of the task ahead of you, how do you discover and buy at the seller's lowest acceptable price? That's what we'll cover in detail as we move through the following chapters. But first, let's take a look at money from valid but often overlooked perspectives.

# CHAPTER TWO

# IT'S YOUR MONEY—
# BUT DO YOU KNOW
# WHAT IT'S REALLY WORTH?

*The obscure we see eventually,*
*the completely apparent takes longer.*
— EDWARD R. MURROW

To keep things as simple and as clear as possible, I'm going to standardize a couple of terms and make one or two assumptions. When I use the term *mortgage* I'm using it also to mean a trust deed. These are very similar and need no distinction for our purposes. When it comes to home loan interest rates, which vary continuously, I have chosen to use 10 percent as a typical rate in examples involving home loan repayments. (Don't worry, there are no mathematical equations or tables to struggle with.) However, a few simple facts of life about mortgages might surprise you—and help you appreciate the big savings that are possible. (See Part Seven: Finding the Money. Also see the Appendix for mortgage guides and kits.) Because large figures tend to confuse, making reading more difficult, I have opted in favor of the nearest round figure. Also, there are a number of tax advantages in owning property, but such matters are outside the focus of this book. And they are outside my areas of expertise. Your tax advisor may be able to help you save even more than the figures shown in the following examples.

Now, let's try to answer the question in the chapter title. Do you know what your money—specifically the price reduction you negotiate—is really worth?

Let's say you've followed the advice I've given you and you have managed to save $3,000 off the advertised price of a home you've just purchased. And let's assume, too, you pre-qualified for a 30-year mortgage. What's your next move? You have two options.

## When a Dollar Is Not Really a Dollar

Here's your first option: You decide to take a smaller loan. You simply inform your bank or mortgage company that you've negotiated a better deal and will need a smaller mortgage.

This looks straightforward enough. You have a small but well negotiated saving of $3,000, so you pat yourself on the back and tell everyone willing to listen the story of how well you performed and how $3,000 is not small change (and it certainly isn't). However, by exploring a little deeper you'll discover you did even better than you thought.

Hypothetical (but realistic) examples are generally the best way of illustrating points such as this, so we'll add a few more details.

*Example 1*

You had planned to borrow $100,000 but now, after negotiating a $3,000 reduction, you'll need only $97,000. Assuming you take a 30-year mortgage at a 10 percent interest rate and don't pay it off early, you'll pay back a total of approximately $306,000. (Remember, you borrowed only $97,000.)

Had you failed to negotiate the $3,000 price cut and instead were forced to take a $100,000 mortgage, your payback figure would have been approximately $316,000. Surprise! What looked like a saving of $3,000 is now a lot more. Let's see why:

Mortgage 1: $100,000 loan for 30 years at 10%. You pay back    $316,000
Mortgage 2: $97,000 loan for 30 years at 10%. You pay back     $306,000

What you've actually saved here is not $3,000 but $10,000 ($316,000 − $306,000). That's quite a big difference. But what if you managed to negotiate an even bigger price cut?

*Example 2*

Perhaps you got the seller to accept $10,000 less than the advertised price. So, you had to borrow only $90,000 instead of $100,000. What that means is that over the 30-year life of the mortgage, you'll now pay back almost $32,000 less than if you had borrowed $100,000.

Here's how:

Mortgage 1: $100,000 loan for 30 years at 10%. You pay back　$316,000
Mortgage 2: $90,000 loan for 30 years at 10%. You pay back　$284,000
Saving:　$32,000

Once again what originally looked like a $10,000 saving built up to become substantially more. In this example, almost $32,000.

The bigger the price reduction you negotiate, the better it keeps getting. What's more, higher interest rates result in even bigger savings for you.

If you do exceptionally well and hang in until the seller agrees to a $30,000 price reduction, you cut your payback figure by a whopping $95,000 over 30 years. That's the difference between taking a $70,000 loan and a $100,000 loan.

Here's an interesting point to keep in mind. Reducing the size of any mortgage by, say, $10,000 (it could be any amount) always produces the same total saving. Cutting your mortgage from $100,000 to $90,000, as we saw in the previous example, meant your payback figure was lowered by almost $32,000. Had you reduced, say, a $50,000 mortgage to $40,000, or a $200,000 to $190,000, the payback figure would have been reduced by the same amount, $32,000. Well, that's about it with the mathematics.

When you apply the methods revealed in the following chapters you can confidently expect to save large sums of money. And not just at the time of purchase, but over the life of the loan, no matter how long it runs.

In the first of the two options I referred to—taking a smaller mortgage—the essential point is this: The price cut you negotiate at the time of purchase keeps increasing in dollar value the longer you keep the mortgage on your home. Consequently, your successful negotiation puts money in your pocket in the form of lower loan repayments over the entire life of your loan. Even if you keep your home for only a couple of years, you reap the dual benefits of lower repayments and a smaller mortgage debt to pay off when you sell.

Now, here's your second option. Instead of going for a smaller loan, take your saving in hard cash. Naturally, by doing this you won't be reducing the size of your repayments, but it is, nonetheless, an attractive alternative.

Instead of cutting the size of your mortgage by the price cut you negotiated, cut the size of your down payment by that amount. Most likely you'll be putting down at least 10 percent. If you are trading up or down from your current home, you might be planning to hand over a sizable amount of cash as a down payment—perhaps 30 percent or more of the purchase price.

Let's assume that everything that was communicated to you from the outset by the agent and seller indicated that the house could not be bought for less than $150,000. Let's further assume you had envisioned making a down payment of $50,000 and that your lender had given you prior approval for a $100,000 mortgage.

Fortunately, at the eleventh hour (when, incidentally, most concessions are made) you managed to win a $10,000 reduction, making the new purchase price $140,000. Along with your $100,000 mortgage you now need to hand over only $40,000 in cash. Remember, you had $50,000 put aside for the down payment, which means you are now $10,000 richer than you anticipated.

What you do with that cash is your own business. You might use it to buy new furnishings or as a down payment, perhaps, on that new car you've been drooling over (which you would, of course, negotiate for!). Even better, you might escape to a tropical island for a long, romantic vacation; invest your $10,000 and watch it grow; or put it aside for your child's education.

You have an open choice, because you are holding what everybody wants—dollar bills! We'll explore the power of hard cash in later chapters and particularly its relevance in negotiating.

This option will work in most but not in all situations. When your down payment is extremely low it is difficult, and sometimes impossible, to reduce it any further.

For example, if you hope to purchase a $100,000 home with a 5 percent ($5,000) down payment you'll need a loan of $95,000. But your down payment is so low it might be impossible to reduce it any further. What if you succeeded in negotiating a $4,000 price cut making the new purchase price just $96,000? Let's see.

Assuming your lender has approved you for a $95,000 loan, the lender is very unlikely to give you that much on a home that costs only $96,000. In that case, your cash down payment would be just $1,000. More likely, the lender will offer you a smaller mortgage, probably around $91,000, making it necessary for you, still, to hand over your $5,000 for the down payment. Nonetheless, you'll have the benefits of lower loan repayments each month and a lower total payback figure. Still a winning situation.

In this example, your negotiated saving of $4,000, at a 10 percent interest rate over 30 years, is worth nearly $12,500 to you. Instead of paying back $300,000 as you would have done with the $95,000 mortgage loan, your total payback figure on the smaller $91,000 mortgage will be $287,500—$12,500 less. That averages out to a saving of more than $400 each year ($12,500/30 years = $417).

So, with either of the two options open to you, you win handsomely. And always by much more than it appears on the surface.

**What's in It for You?—Hard Cash and Peace of Mind!**

When I speak on negotiation I'm often asked the question, "As a nonprofessional negotiator, what kind of success can I expect?"

Let's apply that question to buying a typical suburban home. Although it looks like a single question, I believe there are usually two questions being asked here. They both need to be addressed:

1.  As a layperson can I *really* expect to negotiate successfully?

2.  How much can I save?

We'll look at both questions in this chapter.

*The Advantages of Being a Nonprofessional*

First and foremost, being a nonprofessional is a huge advantage. Don't, even for a moment, convince yourself otherwise. As you progress through the following chapters you'll come to realize how true it is. Professional negotiators certainly aren't famous for broadcasting the finer skills of their profession (understandably so, as it is, necessarily a low-profile occupation).

Perhaps the most important and best-kept secret is this: negotiation success very often depends on acting, looking, and sounding nonthreatening, genuine, ordinary, reasonable, nonexpert, detached and even somewhat indifferent. The slick, aggressive, high-power image is myth—the stuff of Hollywood and novels.

The keys to negotiation success are subtle and depend to a large degree on information, strategy, and persuasive communication.

When it is known that a professional negotiator is acting for one side in a discussion or transaction, the other side will frequently try to put complex counter strategies and barriers in place. The attitude often is, "You might be a hot-shot negotiator, but you're not going to get the better of us." As an amateur you won't engender such defensive reactions. Nor are you likely to face these types of professional obstacles.

Nonetheless, your ultimate success will rest squarely on your shoulders. Very few prices sellers place on their properties are cast in stone. Your best chance for success is to treat *everything* as negotiable, no matter what—or how convincingly—you are told by the seller or salesperson. After all, they are using strategies against you to get you to part with a bigger amount of money than you will probably have to—if you play your cards well.

But, before you jump in, you will need to motivate yourself for the face-to-face negotiation. That's more than just reading about it in the comfort of a fireside chair. It will come easier when you begin recognizing, as you will, the strategies that sellers and agents are using to keep the price up. Most of those strategies are covered in this book. It will also be easier if you keep a clear picture in your mind of the real value of the money you stand to save. Also remember that many price concessions are made when all hope for a further price reduction seems to have vanished.

### Who Will Take the Role of Negotiator?

I advise couples to decide early which of them will act as negotiator. It's usually best if the other partner adopts a low profile, acting more as a detached or even indifferent observer in face-to-face discussions. This is nothing more than a tactic on your part, of course, and works to blunt the effectiveness of the other side. What goes on behind the scenes between you and your partner may be a different matter entirely and is nobody's business but yours. Certainly, it's not for the agent or seller to know. In fact, the less they can read your true feelings, the better.

What's in it for you will be determined, too, by how well you do what all homebuyers *should* do—gather the necessary information before going into battle. You'll need to know about recent prices, details of properties already sold and those now for sale, neighborhood characteristics, the condition of the housing market, and so on. But here's where you differ from the typical homebuyer. Along with that information, you will also have in your arsenal the ability to use simple negotiation strategies and the ability to recognize and neutralize the strategies used against you. More precisely, you'll have the money-saving power these skills put in your hands.

The hard cash and peace of mind come from putting this power into action and also from keeping prominent in your thoughts that it's *your* wealth—*your* money—that's at stake. And it really is at stake, as you'll discover in coming chapters.

### What Can You Expect to Save?

Let's turn now to the second question of how much you, an astute homebuyer, can reasonably expect to save.

Although this question is asked all the time, there is always only one answer I can give: It will vary.

Initially, it depends on the price range of the homes you are considering. For instance, you might be happy to save $3,000 to $5,000 on a home priced at $100,000. But, on a $250,000 home your goal might be to save, perhaps $6,000 to $10,000. These savings, though, are deliberately conservative. Personally, I would aim to save more than $10,000 on a $250,000 home. Occasionally, I've been able to save as much as $30,000 and more in this price range. More commonly, a saving of $15,000 to $20,000 is attainable.

Let's be clear about one thing here. By *saving* I don't mean simply knocking off the padding sellers sometimes insist on adding to the price they believe the house is worth. "Room to negotiate" or "room to come down" is how many agents and some sellers refer to this padding.

I'm certain that if you follow the methods I've explained in *Not One Dollar More!*, you'll have almost as good a chance as any professional negotiator or buyer broker to save not only the padding but often substantially more. The case studies and detailed examples you'll read about shortly spell out clearly and simply how to gain the advantage and stay one step ahead in negotiating the biggest saving possible.

### Factors That Influence Your Success

Just about every time you buy a piece of real estate, both negative and positive factors come into play in determining the outcome. There simply doesn't exist a perfect negotiation climate—at least not in the real world. It's critical, therefore, that you allow nothing about a particular situation to dissuade you from negotiating. Only through actively negotiating will you discover what's there to be won.

The following are some of the more common factors that can affect the outcome of a negotiation:

1.  The economy locally and nationally—more specifically, how well or how badly real estate is selling in your selected area

2.  How anxious the owner is to sell. (The seller won't tell you, but you'll learn how to discover this in a later section.)

3.  The owner's *real* reason for selling

Although you have no direct control over such things as the economy or the owner's reason for selling, you can still learn to recognize, to create, and to maximize advantages in any buying situation. By that I mean there are always factors that are within your control. We'll explore and develop these as we proceed.

As any negotiator will testify, bargains don't drop out of the sky. They never did. But, if you listen long enough to non-negotiators, or to those whose allegiance is not to you (the agent, for example), you might begin to suspect there are no bargains to be had. That's just not true. For those with the know-how and inclination to go after them, there are always bargains. Often they are sitting under your nose. But who is going to tell you? The agent? The seller? Not likely. It is up to you to weed them out. Negotiation is the best tool for doing that.

In fact, successful negotiation incorporates the skill by which bargains are both discovered *and* created. Those who choose not to negotiate will find few, if any, genuine bargains. The logic behind this is simple and clear and shouldn't need further elaboration.

The biggest factor affecting your success will almost certainly be your own determination. In the 15 or more years since I started teaching in the area of human achievement, the search for answers has always fascinated me: What is it that enables people to set and achieve goals? My experience has taught me this: Regardless of how strong an individual's primary motive might be, if I can give that person additional reasons for taking the desired action, then the person is more likely to do it. And to reap the benefits. Let's talk about some of those reasons.

## Not Just Dollar Bills: The Alternative Values of Your Money

Every dollar sitting in your wallet or bank account has what you might call a *price tag* attached to it. To put it there you've had to give up something such as time, effort, or a possession. This point has special significance for homebuyers and can be more clearly understood by examining a few alternative yardsticks by which the value of money may be measured. The following examples describe important ways—often overlooked—to understand the benefits that come from getting the seller to accept a lower offer. These alternative values should also act as extra incentives to negotiate well.

*Labor Value*

Like most people, you or your spouse, or both of you, probably put in 40 hours of work each week at the office or factory. If you bring home, say, $400 each Friday, that hypothetical saving of $3,000 we looked at earlier takes on a new value. It now represents 7.5 weeks of your life at work ($400 × 7.5 = $3,000).

A $10,000 saving represents almost 6 months of toil at the same take-home salary ($400 × 25 weeks = $10,000).

But maybe you do better than most. Let's assume you take-home $667 after tax each week. That $3,000 saving is then equal to the take-home pay you'll accumulate for 4.5 weeks of work ($667 × 4.5 = $3,000 approximately).

On the same $667 take-home salary, a saving of $10,000 means you'd have to put in 15 weeks of work to equal your negotiation success ($667 × 15 = $10,000 approximately).

Sweat value (labor and time) is just one way of putting an alternative value on the price cut you negotiate. Here's another.

*Savings Capability Value*

How much are you able to save each month, or each year? You might already know the answer. If not, it's probably worth figuring out.

Let's assume that by cutting back on luxuries you manage to stash away $3,000 over a 12-month period. At that rate, the $3,000 price cut you negotiate is equal to one year of personal saving— without the time or effort or sacrifices such saving usually entails!

To match a price cut of $10,000 you'd have to save your $3,000 per year for 3 years and 4 months. So, when you succeed in negotiating a $10,000 price concession from the seller, you are, in effect, putting into your bank account almost 3 1/2 years of personal savings. And that's assuming you can usually save $3,000 per year. If you save less, or not at all, your negotiation success is worth even more.

*Purchasing Value*

A sum of $3,000 invested wisely for your child's education can make a world of difference. A sum of $10,000 might guarantee you a very comfortable retirement, depending on your current age and how you invest the money. On the other hand, you might consider it preferable to purchase a new wardrobe or to take an exotic vacation. Granted, neither of the latter has investment value, but they do make life a little sweeter. The money you save on your next home purchase is yours to use to buy whatever takes your fancy. It has purchasing value whether you choose to spend it today or to invest it securely for a later time.

These examples illustrate that money, when you earn it, save it, or spend it, can be viewed as something other than simply dollar bills. Cash in your hand is, essentially, a means of making life more fulfilling. And that is exactly what you stand to gain by being a smart buyer. The price concession you negotiate can be used to improve your life in many ways. It isn't just a numbers game.

All that may be so, I hear you say. But what if you are one of the lucky few who are independently wealthy? Then, does any of this make a difference? In my experience, based on a lot of personally conducted research, it's almost impossible for an individual to acquire and hold on to wealth without understanding the value of money, in all its shades. As anyone in the highest tax brackets will testify, one dollar saved is, almost always, worth more than two dollars earned.

As you begin to understand the subtle skills of negotiation, you might find a few surprises, things you wouldn't have imagined. There are many misconceptions about this subject and very few good resources to turn to. That may be because the best negotiators generally seem disinclined to write about their skill or to seek publicity. However, you can be certain the principles explained in *Not One Dollar More!* do work. They can add thousands of dollars to your personal wealth, whether your aim is to buy a modest timber home or a country estate.

For many years I've been applying these methods profitably. I've also taught them with considerable success to carpenters, cooks, professors, secretaries, clerks, lawyers, salespeople, and accountants—to ordinary people from all walks of life. You don't have to follow my advice slavishly or to speak the exact words I give you for dealing with agents and sellers. All you need do is understand, practice, and apply what you learn and add a sprinkling of common sense. Successful negotiation allows no opportunity to correct errors made in haste. And never any room to backtrack or delete what you have said or communicated.

By learning the strategies and methods I've outlined, you give yourself the power to protect and enhance your standard of living. When you apply them well, I'm certain you stand an excellent chance to recover the cost of this book hundreds, or maybe thousands, of times over.

In fact, *Not One Dollar More!* might easily bring you your biggest-ever return on an investment. But, for that to be so, you must first believe in your own ability to negotiate—and then DO IT!

# PART TWO

*Preparing to Win*

# CHAPTER THREE

# GOING INTO ACTION

*Always be on your guard because you are one
of all the people who can be fooled some of the time.*
—ANONYMOUS

OK, you've made your decision. You have a picture in your mind. You're going to search out and buy the kind of home you've been thinking about for too long. You may be planning to call it *home* or just live in it during summer months. Or perhaps you'll rent it out to a tenant and see it as an investment. None of that matters very much.

What does matter is what you do next. If you're like most people, you'll probably start by reading casually through the real estate section of your local newspaper and free property magazines. Before long, though, that seems tedious and a bit confusing. Instead, you decide to drive to a real estate office and talk to an agent, and perhaps bring along a note of one or two homes you read about. In the office, you look at color photos of properties for sale, pick out a couple that appear interesting, and ask relevant questions about things such as:

The condition and size of the home

The location and neighborhood

Local amenities and local authority plans for the area

Property taxes

Schools

Transportation

Maybe you'll inquire if the price represents good value for money. And, in between all this, you answer many questions about yourself, your needs, your money, and other vital—and usually confidential—matters.

Later, you come home, and after giving it some thought, you call the agent to talk about the homes you were shown. The agent suggests you reinspect the properties you favor most and mentions that there's another fine home you should see—one the agent believes will suit your needs perfectly. You make another appointment and hope it won't be too long before you find what you're looking for.

It's that simple. That easy. That's how it should be done, right? Wrong! In fact, if you want to give yourself the best chance to negotiate successfully, it's all wrong, from the first step. It's not the way of a smart buyer. It's not the way to get the best deal. It's not the way to save money. However, it certainly is the way to make yourself vulnerable and to pay more than you should for the home you buy.

It never ceases to amaze me that so many people approach home buying in the manner I've just described. Inevitably, these are the 95 percent of buyers who pay more for the homes they buy than is necessary; the buyers who take no steps to protect their most confidential business—or their money; who walk blindly into a host of potential traps and mistakes. The buyers who seldom, if ever, buy at the lowest price possible or get a true bargain.

If it sounds familiar, don't feel bad. These are not just the mistakes of amateurs. Many professionals with millions of dollars to spend on commercial and development properties make exactly the same mistakes. Here's an example of what I mean.

Recently, I conducted a two-day seminar for 110 business executives on the subject of negotiation strategy. The audience was made up mostly of senior financial officers and marketing directors. As soon as the seminar got underway, and without explaining what I was doing, I had each participant write down the answers to the following questions:

1. Do you own or have you owned a private home? Answer: 97 of the 110 said yes.

2. Have you owned two or more homes? Answer: 78 said yes.

3. Have you purchased three or more homes? Answer: 71 said yes.

Well, I'm sure you can guess my objective. That group of 110 executives had purchased a total of 330 homes. As I counted the results, an air of curiosity was sweeping the room. After all, this was a tutorial on business negotiation and had nothing to do with property.

Next, I asked them to take 5 minutes to write down precisely the sequence of actions they normally took in starting the search for a home.

Surprise, surprise! (I wasn't, but you might be). Of these 97 middle to senior management executives who each day made decisions involving very large sums of money, only 6 had ever used any deliberate strategy aimed at negotiating the lowest price. Only 6 had committed as much time to preparing for homebuying as the average person puts into purchasing a refrigerator.

So what?—you might think. It's still a fact that nobody sets out to pay more for a home than is necessary. That's certainly true. And if intention was all that was required, everything would be fine. But planned results are the product of *deliberate,* informed action. To put it more clearly, negotiation requires a plan—one based on know-how—and can never be left to chance.

I'm willing to bet that each of those 91 executives who had no plan (strategy, if you prefer) actually gave money away. The average was between three and four homes purchased per individual. A saving of even $5,000 on each transaction would have put $15,000 to $20,000 back into every one of their savings accounts on average. Had they employed the skills covered in this book, they might have doubled or tripled that saving—or even more.

It was clear from their answers that from the beginning they had all made similar mistakes, almost as if they had been conditioned to act in only one way. This *conditioning* cost them dearly. So, successful as these competent, professional people were, they had failed miserably to safeguard their personal wealth at a time when thousands of dollars were at risk.

Their first mistake was predictable, and typical of the average homebuyer. They went to talk with their friendly real estate agent much too early—and much too openly—for their own good.

### The First Commandment: Don't Rush In!

No challenge of any consequence should begin with face-to-face contact with a competitor.

Competitor? The real estate agent or salesperson? Absolutely! Metaphorically, it's like a gladiator jumping into an arena without a sword or armor. And the business of real estate is an arena your competitor knows intimately and rules powerfully. At this point, though, the problem is less a matter of place and more a matter of how you prepare, and then go about protecting your interests.

If the typical approach we saw is wrong, what alternative do you have? To answer that, let's consider a few situations in which you hand over money in exchange for products or services. Naturally, as the amount of money you spend increases, so too does the value you attach to what you purchase.

For example, you probably don't think very hard or long about spending $20 for a piece of clothing, especially if it's something you think you need. Once you find the item you want, the decision to buy is almost automatic. However, if your favorite pair of dress shoes are becoming increasingly shabby and worn, you're likely to give a little more time, thought, and effort before parting with $130 for a new pair. Still, your hesitation doesn't last very long. After all, you rationalize, you deserve to treat yourself and a pair of imported Italian slip-ons would look fabulous with your Irish tweed suit. It took a bit of thinking out but your decision seems right so you go ahead.

This time, though, you expect more. Along with attractiveness, you look for comfort and craftsmanship. And, overall, you expect a higher level of satisfaction than when you spent $20 on the piece of casual clothing. You ensure that the shoes really are as comfortable as they look. You'll hold them and feel the leather and maybe read what's printed on the inside. Next comes a try out around the store and a few admiring looks in the mirror before you make a commitment. Only then do you part with your money.

But just as things seem to be getting back to normal, you discover they aren't. The television your friend sold you 3 months ago has suddenly died. The TV repairer tells you it's not worth fixing, which puts you in a dilemma. You don't really have a lot of spare cash, but the championship playoffs are coming up in a few days and it would be a sacrilege to miss watching them. It takes no time at all for you to realize you have no choice. You'll buy a new television, but this time from a more reliable source.

You pore over the advertisements that came with yesterday's newspaper. You compare brands, features, styling, size and price, rejecting those that don't meet with your approval and creating a short list of models that do. Next, you call the store that looks like it's offering the best deals. Naturally, you ask the salesperson if the store can offer you a discount. The salesperson refuses, but you respond politely that you bought a number of expensive items, including your fridge and stereo system, at that store. The salesperson says that the store has the lowest prices of any retailer in town, but because you are a preferred customer, you can have a 5 percent discount, provided you pay cash.

So you drive to the store and request a full demonstration, making sure everything is just as it should be. You ask for confirmation of the store's "full refund if not satisfied" policy and the manufacturer's two-year warranty. Finally, you hand over your $600 and head for home with a new TV.

What has all this got to do with real estate? Everything. Let's investigate.

With each of these three purchases you behaved differently. As the price of the items increased, you took more time preparing, communicating, inspecting, and deciding. Another thing you did was look for progressively more assurances and guarantees. With the most expensive item you even persisted in asking for a discount, implying subtly that you might take your custom elsewhere if a discount was not forthcoming. And, best of all, it worked—for one reason. One very relevant and important reason. You recognized the *power* that was available to you in the situation.

Although you probably didn't consciously analyze it, you realized, undoubtedly, that the seller (the store) needed what you could provide—cash. In fact, the seller desired your cash more than you needed the television.

You knew and communicated one other very important point, too—that you had alternatives and options. You could bring your money to another store where you might have been offered a better price or a bigger discount. What is clear from your behavior is that you believed you were in the stronger position. And you communicated this convincingly.

Perhaps you would have made the purchase anyway, even without the discount, but the salesperson didn't know that. You were a customer with cash in hand. The salesperson perceived that the sale could be lost without the discount. *You* created these feelings and concerns. *You* put them into this person's thinking. *You* pulled the strings. *You* "manufactured" the nature of the exchange. And because you did, *you* had power.

We saw earlier that having options and alternatives (or the other side thinking you do) puts power at your disposal any time you negotiate. In fact, the power you acquire comes directly from the thoughts you place in the agent's or seller's mind, and is almost entirely unrelated to any "real" or "actual" advantages you may or may not be holding. What that means, simply, is this: if your competitor believes you have power and advantage—you do! Consequently, that's the message you should be sending from your first contact. When you recognize the significance of power in negotiation—real power and perceived power—you take a major step toward getting the outcome you are after, the seller's lowest possible price. Let's take a closer look at this phenomenon of power.

### Power and Predictability

Most of the considerations that go into buying a $600 television are similar to those that go into buying a $150,000 home. The difference is a matter of degree. There's a simple core reason behind this. In both cases, the seller wants, or needs, one vital commodity—the buyer's cash.

This person-to-person transaction is at the heart of negotiation and has been studied extensively. One thing we've learned is that human behavior is often surprisingly predictable in particular circumstances. We'll examine some interesting examples of this as we proceed through this book. Whether the individuals involved are real estate owners, store clerks, army generals, business executives, or high-ranking politicians, all are reasonably predictable in specific situations.

How can homebuyers use this knowledge to their advantage? First, by gathering relevant information. The more you learn about the sellers' wants and needs, the more predictable they become. This is true even if, in the end, you take no action—even if you act only as a passive observer. The information you know about sellers and their property always provides you with a distinct advantage—the power to influence a seller's thinking and, thereby, control the outcome. The better the information, the greater your potential power.

The essential point is that power and predictability are, together, built on information that is relevant to the task at hand. But information is a two-edged sword. It works for you when you have it. And it works just as powerfully against you when you don't have it. Here's what I mean. The more the agent or seller knows about the *intensity* of your wants, needs, and likes, the weaker your negotiating power becomes.

Because of that, you must learn to become something of a sponge, digging up and absorbing as much relevant detail and insight on your competitor as you can without being unethical. At the same time, you will disclose nothing about yourself or your situation that might be used to your disadvantage. Nothing that might be used to weaken the power you have been building methodically since you first made the decision to buy a home. You reveal only those details you have consciously and deliberately orchestrated, thereby reducing your vulnerability and putting maximum advantage on your side. Shortly, we'll answer the question of exactly what and how much you should reveal. Now, though, let's go to the next stage in your task of buying at the lowest price.

## Knowing What You Need and Knowing What You Want

Why do you want to buy a home? That's something only you can answer, but answer it you must, being very clear about your dominant motive—your most compelling reason.

Perhaps it will be your first home and you're really excited about the whole idea. It could be that your current accommodation is too small or too big. Or that you've had enough of your neighbors. Maybe you see real estate as a good long-term investment or a way to shelter some of your money from taxes. The reason I'm emphasizing this is critical. Once you're clear about your dominant motive, you'll be clearer about exactly what it is you need and want in the home you are seeking.

I'm a strong believer in writing things down. In fact, from the beginning, before you make any contact with an agent or inspect a home, it's advisable to buy a notebook with plenty of pages. You'll find many uses for it as your search goes on.

A good starting point is to write down a list of your basic *must-haves*, those things you consider indispensable. At this stage, it's necessary to include only the basics. For example, if you must have three bedrooms, that goes down. If a family room or study is essential, that, too, goes down. Maybe you need to be within walking distance of a convenience store or transportation. You get the idea. These aren't emotional criteria you'd *like* to have, but practical necessities. And here's the reason this exercise is so important. The pressure and emotions many buyers experience when searching out and inspecting prospective properties, coupled with life's routine challenges, can cause you to lose sight of what you really need.

At such times, your list of must-haves will keep you on track. Along the way, though, you are at liberty to change your thinking and make any modifications you choose—but only for the best of reasons. In other words, make only changes that are in your own interest and spring naturally from your search, not changes prompted by the agent for questionable reasons or produced by your own weariness or frustration. Make only changes you can live with because, in the end, that's what it will come to. Any deletion from your must-have list suggests that the item wasn't a must-have after all. Yet, you did write it down. So, write your list carefully and change it slowly, if at all. The danger in not writing down this information is that pressure, fatigue, anxiety, or someone else's opinion can affect your judgment and result in a bad decision.

Road traffic is a good example of this point. If you absolutely hate the idea of heavy traffic outside your door today, there's probably zero chance you'll grow accustomed to it over time, regardless of how attractive the home is. If the agent suggests that you'll soon automatically tune out the noise and become "deaf" to it, that's exactly what you should do to the agent's comments.

For reasons like this, I advise you to add to your list all factors that would definitely *eliminate* an otherwise suitable home from consideration. Later, in the heat of decision making, such a list will help prevent you from convincing yourself—or being convinced—that you can overlook one or more of these critical elimination factors. When it's written down, your resistance will be stronger and the chance of eventually getting exactly what you want—and need—will be considerably greater.

Your must-have list will also save you time, the wasted hours that go into inspecting homes that look good on paper but turn out later not to have one or more of your indispensable features or qualities.

All your *wants*—that is, your "would-likes"—can be left aside for the moment. They're probably too numerous to list anyway, and they're flexible. Many can be overridden by the "feel" of a suitable home. Still, you'll keep a general picture of your ideal home actively in mind at all stages in your search.

Now, your next consideration is money.

## How to Set Spending Limits and What to Reveal

Before your search proper begins, you need to know your spending limit. I believe the time to do that is *before* you start looking at homes, not when you have found the ideal property. Instead of putting all your hopes on one source of money, investigate two or more options for a suitable mortgage. Talk to mortgage representatives, loan officers, knowledgeable brokers, buyer brokers, and so on. Compare costs, fees, and what size loan is available to you. Who'll give you the best interest rate and, when all the attendant costs have been taken into consideration, the best annual percentage rate? (For sources of helpful information on mortgages, mortgage kits, guides, and how-to books, see the Resources section.)

When you find a lender that seems right, ask if you can get preliminary approval for a loan. Some lenders, such as a bank with which you have a good relationship, will provide this before requiring you to make a formal application. The amount to qualify for is the maximum you can get—not the amount you hope to spend. Knowing your borrowing limit saves hesitation and uncertainty later and provides the assurance that allows you to act when special opportunities arise.

Here's an example of what I mean. Say you've asked for preliminary approval of a $95,000 loan. Then, a few days later you find the home of your dreams—but you hesitate. No matter how successfully you negotiate, you know you will still need to borrow more than the $95,000 you've been approved for. Your thinking becomes clouded. Doubt and anxiety set in. You're not sure you can buy the home, so your negotiation lacks certainty, the energizing internal conviction that is vital to a good outcome. You've disadvantaged yourself by not having essential information. Now, there may be no way to start over again—no second chance for optimum results, even though you might eventually bring a deal together.

You see, although you asked your lender for $95,000, your *borrowing limit* might have been, say, $115,000. That's no good to you, though, if you don't know it or can't get an answer from your lender immediately. Now, I'm not suggesting you *take* the biggest loan you can convince your lender to give you. You might never even go close to such an amount. But it's helpful to know what it is. And it's even more helpful to have preliminary approval for that figure. This is a figure that is probably best kept in mind rather than written down with your other notes.

### How Much Do You Want to Spend?

Let's get back now to our core question: How much do you want to spend? This will be asked of you many times by agents and brokers. There are good reasons you should write this information in your notebook at the beginning of your search. But, it's my belief—and it goes against everything you'll be told—that you should *never* divulge this figure to a real estate agent or private seller. This is for you, and only you, to know.

What I'm about to advise now might seem to go against what I've just suggested. But, as we go on, you'll see the logic behind it. In your notebook, instead of writing down just one figure, make it two.

The first, your *comfortable spending limit* is the amount you are most comfortable spending to get the features and quality you desire in a home that meets all your requirements. In other words, the amount you want to spend.

The second figure is your personal *upper spending limit*. This is an amount you can afford, and are prepared to spend, but only for that truly special home that represents exceptional value for money.

The benefit of being clear about your upper spending limit is that it guides your decision making in potentially risky situations, like when a financially out-of-reach home grabs your heart. Everything inside you says, "I want it." But, when you consult your notebook, you are forced to accept that the figures just don't add up.

Let's look closer. It might be that you are comfortable spending, say, $110,000. However, although it is not part of your plan, you would be prepared to spend up to $125,000 for a once-in-a-lifetime opportunity. These are the two figures that go into your notebook. The third figure, your borrowing limit, is stored away in your brain, along with a mental note of how much cash you have available.

Here's how your situation might look (your actual figures might be very different):

*Notebook:*   What I want to spend (my comfortable spending limit), $110,000
What I can spend (my upper spending limit), $125,000

*Brain:*   My borrowing limit, $95,000
Cash I have available, $40,000

You'll notice that, so far, very little emotion has been part of this preparation. That is no accident. Successful negotiation does not rest on emotion, but plays to emotion. We'll see more of how this works, later. For the moment, remember that major financial commitments, such as buying a home, are far more likely to be successful when they are guided by pragmatic, rational thinking and solid preparation. "Heat-of-the-moment" decisions are much less reliable and should be avoided.

I feel too, that the *instinct* and *intuition* that many people believe they possess are poor and often dangerous substitutes for even basic knowledge and skill. They should never be relied on to the exclusion of good planning and solid preparation. Too much is at stake.

## Research: Finding Out What You Need to Know

Gathering information is an automatic activity in homebuying. It's inevitable, even for those buyers who don't work to a plan or who don't realize its value. In fact, it's possible to learn much of what you will need to know simply by listening to what real estate agents and salespeople have to say. The problem, though, is that a good deal of what you'll hear is haphazard and incomplete. Research of this kind seems almost incidental to the search rather than what it should be—the deliberate foundation from which the search moves constantly toward a successful conclusion.

The objective of research is relevant information. There are few short cuts and no substitutes. One of the recurrent challenges I face in teaching negotiation, even to corporate buyers, is to get the individuals concerned to make positive use of the information their research produces. That's often a problem, too, in society at large. Governments spend millions of dollars every year to gather statistics (information) on such things as the number of people living below the poverty line, or the level of illiteracy. But much too seldom—and often not at all—is positive rectifying action taken. Desired results are achieved only when someone decides to *act* on the information available. Bob Geldof made this point repeatedly to the media—and in action—when highlighting the plight of famine in Africa through Live Aid rock concerts in the 1980s.

Have no doubt that the corporate business world makes the same mistakes despite, in many cases, employing highly paid executives whose job it is to manage change. Many times those businesses that hire my services already possess the information they believe they need to acquire. Frequently, what they really need is to be shown how to use that information to bring about the desired change or to achieve a specific goal.

The point I'm emphasizing is this: Making use of the information you gather in your preparation and search is critical. And it has a definite effect on the amount of money you will eventually have to spend to get the home you want. Your brain is processing information continuously, every minute of every day you're alive. And most of our decisions, good and bad, are based on what we know at a particular time about the situation at hand.

However, a much more important consideration is how well we process that information. When our processing is accurate, we make better decisions. When our processing is inaccurate or absent, the opposite is true.

As a homebuyer, the amount of research you'll have to do is small. But the resulting information will need to be as accurate as possible. Where do you start? You already have! In fact, you're well on your way at this stage. That notebook containing critical details such as your must-haves, the list of critical factors that will eliminate any property, the maximum loan you have been pre-qualified for, your comfortable and upper spending limits and so on, will be with you from beginning to end in your search.

### Your New Surroundings

Now, your focus shifts to location. Which neighborhoods interest you and which fit into your budget on a preliminary look? Some areas that are affordable can usually be eliminated for one reason or another, thereby narrowing your focus. Or, you might already have selected a particular neighborhood. In either case, unpleasant surprises can be eliminated by further basic research.

The easiest way I know to get a feel for the affordability of a neighborhood is to check the real estate section of your newspaper or the common free *homes for sale* publications. These won't give you a full picture, though, especially if your plan is to buy a home that is less expensive than the average home in the area—often a sound strategy. Because you're in the preliminary research stage, it's still too early to discuss your situation seriously with an agent.

If you have friends or work associates who live in your selected area they may be able to give you details of recent sales, prices generally, taxes, how the area is developing, age breakdown, and other details that are important to your lifestyle. Then, when you've made your decision about where you want to live, you'll need to continue gathering and recording details of asking prices and actual selling prices of homes similar to the type you have in mind.

This activity continues for as long as your search does. Make a point, whenever possible, to note the difference between what the owner *asked* for and the price actually *achieved*. For example, the original list price might have been $150,000, later reduced to a new asking price of $145,000, but a well-prepared homebuyer might have bought it for $135,000. This is the type of information that is most helpful to know. You don't even have to remember what the price was called (list price, reduced price, asking price). Just record any figures you get for homes that seem appropriate. In some places, local newspapers publish the actual sale prices. You might have to check around to find the right publication. Failing that, most local real estate offices will have the details. When you call, let the person you speak to know that you're just "keeping an eye on the market at this point" and that you are not yet ready to buy. You can add that you may talk to the agent when the time is right. Keep in mind, too, that agents are essentially business people. With the prospect of a future client in the balance, you're likely to get all the assistance you need. Stress that you want accurate figures, but don't be drawn into a detailed conversation about your needs. The time for that will come later.

Note that everything you have done up to this point has been to ensure you are adequately prepared. If there is one secret to powerful negotiation, this is it. In fact, preparation is the key to all self-defense programs regardless of the activity involved or the goal sought. In our case, you might think of it as forging your armor in readiness for the fray. However, there is a little more armor to be forged before you are ready.

Your preparation, so far, has forced you to think hard and come up with early answers to very important questions. The significance and value of this will become apparent when you find yourself in the middle of a demanding negotiation; when you need room for clear thinking. But that's getting ahead of ourselves.

At this stage, you have a sharp, mental picture of the goal on which your search will concentrate. And you have gathered a good part of the information that will guide you when the negotiation begins. Altogether, this won't have taken you more than a few hours, yet your preparation proper is almost complete. Up to now, though, you have avoided any face-to-face discussion of your situation with a real estate agent or salesperson. And that's exactly as it should be.

Let's go over what should be in your notebook before we proceed:

- Your list of must-haves

- Your list of factors that will eliminate any home

- Names of your preferred neighborhoods or locations, ideally in order of preference

- General information on prices, taxes, schools, amenities, planned developments, dominant age groups, and so on, in your selected area

- Examples of list prices and actual selling prices—as recent as possible—and brief descriptions of the properties concerned (3-bdrm, Fam rm, kit, dining rm, garage, etc.)

- Your comfortable spending limit

- Your upper spending limit (in the event you discover an outstanding bargain that's too good to miss)

As you learn the secrets of negotiation, you might feel tempted to bypass this preparation work in a rush to absorb and apply the face-to-face tactics we're building up to. My advice is to resist that temptation. Your success in negotiating the lowest price possible will depend largely on the quality of the information gathered in the preparation stage.

Naturally, though, as you go through the negotiation proper you'll continue to gather relevant information whenever and from

wherever it comes. The more you accumulate, the better you'll protect your interests and your money. By the time you meet your competitor, you'll know how the seller thinks and how the real estate
game is played. And you will be ready and able to buy well. You'll
be an informed consumer able to hold your own in any negotiation
and against any tactic or strategy used against you.

# CHAPTER FOUR

# DEVELOPING A PROTECTIVE STRATEGY

*When you have to make a choice and don't make it,*
*that in itself is a choice.*

—MARK TWAIN

It's always surprised me that even the smartest of people, those you would normally think of as diligent, organized, and careful, are just as likely to approach buying a home in the same haphazard and naive manner as anyone else. It may be the case that these smarter types are less suspecting than people in general; less street-wise than they need to be in the game of real estate buying.

Despite all the invitations to do so, complete trust is something you *never* give to anyone anxious to sell you property. Caution is always called for. And trust, rather than being given, should be traded in minute quantities, if at all, and then only when you are certain it is justified. First impressions, no matter how much you fancy yourself as a judge of character, will never provide that certainty. The best advice I can give you is this: Reveal only the basic information that is necessary about your circumstances and verify, as often as you can, the "facts" told to you by a real estate salesperson or private seller.

That's the first step in developing a protective strategy—cautious skepticism.

Here's an example of where a fortune, literally, could have been lost—or saved.

## Case Study: Millions at Stake

Less than a year ago I was conducting a seminar in Australia on problem solving and human achievement. At the end of the third and final day, one of the participants (we'll call her Kathleen) presented me with a challenge I found impossible to turn down. What ensued is a good example of what can happen in the arena of real estate.

Kathleen, a business executive, had been negotiating for the purchase of a four-story building on the edge of the city on behalf of a corporate client. She asked if I would inspect the property with her and the agent. First, I examined the research that had already been gathered, then I acquired further details. Next, I inspected the building and spent one hour in a meeting with Kathleen and the sales agent.

Our discussion was cordial. The agent was clear and assertive. The property was for sale at a price of $10 million, which, he stressed, was below the market value. Weighing the proposition, along with what I had learned from the research and my own enquiries, I suggested to Kathleen that if her client was serious about buying the property he should hold off. Do absolutely nothing, I advised. My reading of the situation told me the eventual selling price might be closer to $5 million. She was willing to go along, so I outlined a strategy I felt would give her the best chance of buying at the lowest price possible. Timing and persistence, I warned, would both be critical.

Kathleen followed the strategy precisely, which included just two further brief contacts between her and the agent over the following 10 days.

Five weeks after I had first met the agent, he phoned Kathleen telling her he had just received an offer of $3.5 million and that the seller had rejected it. And, you guessed it, he then enquired if she would be interested in submitting an offer.

In the end, Kathleen's client decided against the property, but I'm sure the point is clear. The strategy used here can be just as effective in buying a residential home and is explained in detail later in the book.

For now, let's play a guessing game. Based on what you already know, how much do you think Kathleen's client could have bought the property for? Forget the $10 million. Forget $8 million or even $6 million. In my opinion, based on more information than I have given you here, I believe a figure of between $3.5 million and $5 million would have sealed the deal.

Your reaction—and a logical one too—might be that perhaps that's all the building was worth. Maybe it was grossly overvalued at $10 million, you say. Maybe. But that's not the most important point I'm making here. Think about this: What percentage of prospective buyers would have assumed a 50 percent reduction (or more) in the list price was possible? Very few, I would estimate, if any at all. Especially, since the line the agent was putting out from the beginning was that a sale looked imminent to another buyer who was showing a serious interest at $10 million. How many millions of dollars might such a mistake have cost an unwary buyer? It's almost too frightening to consider.

Yes, it is an exceptional case. But the irony is this. A less astute buyer might have paid, say, $10.5 million, and would *never have known* of his disastrous mistake. There's no way to tell how many buyers this has happened to. But however many it is, it's too many.

This case illustrates a number of relevant points. You might think that buyers operating at this level are always well prepared and that this is the kind of trap only the homebuyer is likely to fall into. Believe me, that is not the case.

As a nonprofessional homebuyer competing in a business dominated by professionals, you are, nonetheless, at greater risk. The record books are filled with tragic accounts of buyers acting on blind faith and impulse in every kind of market—real estate, stocks, commodities, stamps, coins, and many others.

When the time comes for you to buy, facing your own enthusiasm, time pressure, fear of loss, and your urge to negotiate, you must fight hard to remain in control.

### The Importance of Control

The first requirement here is to eliminate any potential misunderstanding about what I mean by *control*.

As a homebuyer, you can never dictate or control *all* the elements affecting any single transaction or negotiation. Nor do you need to. However, and this is the essence of what I'm emphasizing throughout this book, there are *always* actions, tactics, and elements over which you do have control. The more you focus on these factors the more you will take charge of the negotiation process.

Control comes down to having a plan—a strategy—and sticking to it even when confronted by a persuasive agent or seller. Control is not allowing yourself to be pushed, talked, or frightened into believing you will have to pay the seller's price. Control means knowing that "no" is very often just a reaction and seldom means "NO!" Control means being able to see through and see ahead. It means having the demeanor of a reasonable buyer but one who is definite while not appearing completely inflexible. Control means you pull your own strings and you know which, and when, to pull. Aggressiveness has no part in it. Nor does looking or sounding like an expert. Your negotiation skill hides behind your personality and below your opinions and desires. But all the time, you maintain a strong yet subtle control.

Let's make a few contrasts to emphasize the point. Control is subtle rather than obvious; definite rather than aggressive; understanding rather than arrogant; respectful rather than argumentative; genuine rather than domineering; resourceful rather than impulsive and persistent rather than accepting.

By maintaining control, you guard against two of the most insidious traps—being intimidated and being manipulated. Usually, they go hand-in-hand, a point we'll explore further as we look at specific examples of control in action.

To get a better understanding of control, you might need to challenge some of your current thinking. For example, if you believe you have a clear grasp of what *negotiation* means, it might be beneficial to put it aside, at least for the moment. By the time you finish this book, your perception of the process is likely to have changed permanently. By then, all the negotiation skills you'll need will be available to you, whenever you need them.

In applying well the principles of negotiation and the methods of taking and maintaining control, there are things, perhaps surprisingly, you do not need in order to achieve a successful outcome. Here are some of the most important.

## What You Don't Need to Pull Off a Good Deal

Contrary to what some people might try to get you to believe—particularly those with an interest in selling you real estate—you don't need a buyers' market, a weak dollar, high mortgage rates, low inflation, or a declining local population.

Successful deals depend, first and foremost, on you, the negotiator, and on the skills you bring to the situation.

If you're fearful about looking and sounding like a negotiator, you can stop worrying. That's not how it's going to be. You won't sound or look anything like that, whatever *that* looks like. You certainly won't stick out like a sore thumb or look conspicuous in any negative way. Nobody, except you and those sharing your aspirations, will know you are applying the principles you have learned from this book. You'll come across clearly as a genuine buyer but one who is not easily led, superficially influenced, or pushed into disclosing what is not in your best interest to disclose. Your skill as a negotiator, as I indicated earlier, is subtle and does not draw attention to itself. Not only will you not present yourself as a negotiator, you'll do everything you can to seem as natural as possible—courteous, respectful, and a serious buyer.

Behind those qualities lurk your conviction, your confidence, your knowledge of what goes on behind the scenes, and your certainty that this is one game you are not going to lose.

Now, as you prepare for handling the real estate agent, it's time to start forming a mental picture of yourself as a resourceful negotiator. If you look closely at your routine daily communication, you'll see that, in fact, is exactly what you are. To some extent you are negotiating all the time, only you don't call it that. You don't call it that because, up to now, you have had no need to analyze or categorize your interpersonal exchanges; no need to intellectualize what comes naturally to you; no need to stand back and examine objectively the fine skills you have developed for handling effectively the infinite variety of personalities with whom you continuously live, work, teach, talk, trade, and play. But you do, indeed, already possess many of the negotiator's best characteristics.

For this reason, some of the principles and tactics in the following sections may seem oddly familiar, like you've encountered them before. You have—at least some. It's true to say that you've probably been using many completely unconsciously throughout your life.

But that's not enough. Not for our purposes, not for buying real estate at the lowest possible price. Your task now, is to act *consciously*. To understand and apply the correct and most effective negotiation tactics at the right time—the time at which they are most likely to bring you maximum reward.

For most people, buying a home is an unnatural activity, which, consequently, causes feelings of being an amateur, uncertainty, insecurity, vulnerability, nervousness, and even fear. Regardless of the intensity of these feelings, they tend to close off, to some extent, many of the resourceful, natural qualities that guide us through our daily interpersonal encounters and exchanges. Let's change that.

### How Thick Is Your Armor?

We've already seen that the agent will be taking an overall impression of you from the moment of first contact. In fact, the agent assesses you against a list of criteria: your personality, how serious a buyer you are, your level of conviction and capability, how urgent your need is, how naive or aware you are, what impresses you, how much money you might be persuaded to part with (not the figure you state!), and so on.

It's in the agent's interest—and not at all in yours—to know as much about you as possible. In particular, the agent wants to be able to rate your susceptibility to influence—how impressionable you are to the kind of logic and emotion he uses to close sales.

Going back to the analogy I used earlier, the agent wants to know how thick is your armor. It's your responsibility to provide only the information that will assist your cause, and generally to disclose no exploitable weaknesses.

## The Agent Sells to Live and Lives to Sell

The skills of even the most congenial real estate salesperson are many and varied. These are professionals who live and eat only in relation to their ability to sell. Consequently, their skills are often subtle and very refined. The flashing smile and bright eyes can tempt you to lower your guard. If you do, you lose.

But the agents are simply doing their job. That job is to get the highest price for the seller. After all, they sell to live. And, if they're really sharp, they live to sell.

Does an agent seem like someone who might become your best friend? Someone to invite to your next family barbecue or Christmas party? A godparent, perhaps, for your new arrival? Hardly! What you're reacting to is a cultivated image designed first to disarm, then win the trust of buyers.

But agents are not wolves in sheeps' clothing. They're professional sellers; their success is measured by the number of sales they produce.

To make a successful sale on behalf of the seller, an agent sets out to learn as much about you as might be useful in influencing your decision to buy. Before the agent can do that, they (usually) have to sell you on their genuiness and credibility, directly or indirectly. The agent might mention, almost in passing, certain credentials and awards for expertise and professionalism. And, no doubt, you'll hear of other very satisfied buyers, just like you, who were helped, "just the other day."

To the real estate salesperson, ultimate success is a quick, no hassle sale at a price for which the seller will be ecstatic and refer business to the agent well into the future. And the buyer will be none the wiser about whose interests have really been served.

The more often agents achieve that, the higher the standing they enjoy in their profession. And the wealthier they become. Your aim, from this point on, is to make sure their reputation and success are not achieved at your expense.

### Four Traps and Phony Buyers

Here are the five most common—and most costly—mistakes I've seen made by ordinary homebuyers. In fact, the typical buyer is usually his or her own worst enemy. Not only do buyers fail to defend themselves against the misrepresentations, tricks, and deceptions that can be imposed on them, but frequently they put themselves at a disadvantage through what they do and say—voluntarily. It's almost as if buyers see the real estate salesperson as a confidant—a good friend, someone to whom their most personal thoughts and circumstances can be revealed.

The type of relationship that encourages this openness is often deliberately cultivated by agents, usually in the guise that buyer openness will make for better service. No doubt, there are good reasons for homebuyers to communicate clearly their needs. But there is no sense at all in disclosing anything that can later be used against them. Remember, the agent is professionally compelled to report to the seller all information—even "confidential" details about the buyer—that could affect the seller's ability to negotiate the highest price possible.

Here are four of the five traps that ensnare unwary buyers—and many buyers who naively believe they are capable and well prepared. These are the things you should never reveal to anyone hoping to sell you anything, especially real estate. The fifth trap, the Phony Buyer, follows:

1. *Anxiety.* A very common side effect of searching for and buying a home. It is typically caused by the leg work and challenge of finding the right property, getting financing, making the buy decision, fear of losing a desired home to another buyer, and so on.

2. *Urgency.* This type of stress is felt by the majority of buyers, who believe they are under time, money, or emotional pressure to act urgently. Even when this feeling of urgency is justified, it is never in your interest to reveal it to an agent or seller. Consequently, you'll have to disguise these feelings if you are to protect yourself adequately—and preserve your negotiation power.

3. *Budget.* Money, in all its complexity, is a very real and very common concern in homebuying. However, what you

reveal about your budget can walk you into the most costly of traps. If you follow my earlier advice on this point, you alone will know the maximum loan for which you qualify, a figure best kept in your head. In your notebook are two other figures: your upper spending limit and your comfortable spending limit. Which, if any, do you reveal to the agent? That's the question we'll answer in a moment.

4. *Emotional Attachment.* Here's a rule you should never break, no matter how strongly you feel inside. Never tell agents or salespeople that you have fallen in love with a home they are trying to sell you. Or, that a home is "just perfect" or "exactly what we were looking for." Never!

Let's take a closer look at each of these.

## Trap One: Anxiety

Regardless of what you are negotiating for, emotional anxiety is a liability—infinitely more so when it is obvious to the other side. First, it diminishes your ability to forge the best deal possible. And second, as your anxiety increases, the power and the options normally available to you tend to decrease. It's quite natural for you to feel somewhat excited and nervous going through the process of finding and buying the home you want. That can be controlled and disguised very easily. But the kind of anxiety that overtakes you despite your best efforts is sometimes nearly impossible to conceal from a sharp seller or agent. When the agent suspects there's an advantage to be gained—and there always is—he or she will be considerably tougher in any negotiation that follows.

A classic, non-real estate example of what I mean happened to me in New York City some years ago. I surrendered two of every negotiator's best weapons—power and options—through being overanxious to make a purchase.

I was in Manhattan on business with three very busy days and a lot to accomplish ahead of me. At the end of the third day, when my objectives had been accomplished, I decided to stay one extra day and to indulge my passion for photography. For more than a year I had wanted to buy a particular medium-format camera, and here was the perfect opportunity (New York has everything a camera buff could ever want—and good prices, too).

At 1 P.M. the clerk at the first discount store I visited confirmed he had in stock all four items I wanted. His *best* price, he said, was $1,800. I told him I'd check around and, if his price turned out to be the best, I'd purchase the equipment later in the day. After some hours I'd seen enough. The first store proved to be the cheapest by $68, so I returned, arriving at 4:45 P.M. The clerk's earlier dejection had now disappeared and was replaced with a mixture of glee and "I told you so." What the heck, I could live with that. At that stage all I wanted was my new Mamiya RB67 and to catch a cab back to my hotel. My flight was leaving at dawn next morning.

When the clerk placed the four items on the counter, we both checked the contents of the boxes and confirmed all was OK.

"That comes to $1,887," he said with a hint of arrogance.

"Hold on," I replied. "Four hours ago you said $1,800. You even wrote the prices on my list."

He hesitated, then blinked with disdain, parking his eyelids half open, half closed. His gaze passed right by me as if searching for something in the distance to focus on. At this stage I was sure integrity wasn't his strong point—I was right.

"That was four hours ago," he squeaked dismissively, "the best price I can do now is $1887." Then came the sting. "Take it or leave it. You won't get a better price."

I'd been taken for a ride. He knew it and I knew it. It was now after 5 P.M. and my options were limited. I could forget buying the camera, in which case my whole day would have been in vain, or I could hand over the extra $87 and chalk it up to experience. The clerk judged I was more likely to go along with his scheme. He knew I wanted what was sitting in front of me, and that I hadn't got sufficient time to get to another store before closing time. Although he didn't know it, my options were even more limited, as I was flying out at 6 A.M.

You guessed it. I paid the extra $87.

By way of analysis, let's try to answer a couple of questions about what happened here: Who had the advantages? And why?

Well, clearly, the seller had the advantages. I lost because I returned to his store, obviously very anxious to conclude the deal. You'll recall I said earlier that behavior communicates much more strongly than words. This is a good illustration of that. My behavior shouted messages like: 'You have what I want'—'Your price represents good value'—'It's almost 5 P.M. and I'm in a hurry'—'I'm tired searching around the city'—'I want to buy now'—'I have the money'—'I'm anxious.'

If that's not anxiety, I don't know what is. The same trap exists when you are buying a home—make no mistake about it. You need to ensure that your behavior does not communicate signals that damage your chance of a successful outcome. When you feel the urge to buy quickly or impetuously—perhaps because you are frustrated or weary—summon every ounce of control you can to hide those feelings from the agent.

Unless controlled, your anxiety will show itself through words, exclamations, actions, and facial expressions. Even the slightest sign of how you are feeling can be extremely revealing and easy to pick up by an experienced agent. The only safeguard that's of any practical value is to be forewarned and then to do everything in your power to remain cool and unexpressive, even if that means biting your tongue or swallowing the words that are screaming to get out. Later, in private, there are no holds barred. You can release your anxiety in any way that makes you feel good. But never in company with an agent or seller.

*Trap Two: Urgency*

Urgency, unlike anxiety, is not communicated by spontaneous expressions of delight or frustration. More often it is communicated directly through the details of your situation that you disclose unwittingly. Of course, the urgency you are feeling is reinforced and highlighted by how you act, especially when the pressure is on. In contrast to the individual who is naturally anxious, you might normally be a composed and confident person but when you know you must find a place to move into, for example, before the end of the month, all hell can break loose. When this happens, you lose control of the situation and you lose or weaken considerably your power to negotiate the lowest price.

The following illustrate some of the more common ways home-buyers reveal the urgency of their situations and hand over the advantage to the agent and, indirectly, to the seller.

1. You make it clear to the agent that the whole process of searching for and inspecting homes is one you detest, and you can't wait until all the hassle is over—if you don't go crazy before then.

2. The deadline by which you must vacate your current accommodation is hanging over you like a ton of bricks. As each week passes your stress level increases and, you caution the agent, you are becoming desperate.

3. You're getting married—or divorced—and need desperately to have a place of your own. Today, if possible, you explain, so that your life can proceed in a sane, private, and orderly manner.

These and other predicaments of homebuyer urgency, when revealed unwittingly or naively, are potentially very damaging to your financial health. Yet they happen all the time. It matters not which end of the market you are shopping in. This trap will catch the buyer with $10 million to spend just as surely as it will the buyer with $50,000. The only protection is to be aware of it and stay in control of what you reveal by following the suggestions I've given you.

It's ironic that homebuyers who typically handle many other types of buy and sell transactions with confidence and efficiency can be intimidated into dropping their natural defensive armor when facing a formally attired real estate agent who drives a comfortable sedan and sits in an executive office.

Even if you feel unnerved, out of your depth, or overpowered, there's nothing to be gained through passive compliance. In such circumstances your anxiety and urgency are contributing to your own spiralling insecurity. It's time to break away to assess the situation and how it might be improved. Revealing the urgency you feel can do nothing but add to your disadvantage and possibly cost you thousands of dollars.

*Trap Three: Budget*

Once you have completed your preliminary research, you'll have realistic upper and comfortable spending limits and know the type and quality of home you can afford. Now you'll have to prepare for one of the first questions the real estate agent will ask you—how much do you plan, to spend? What do you say? More importantly, what do you *not* say?

It goes without saying that you never divulge your upper spending limit. My advice is that you should not reveal your true comfortable spending limit either. At least not yet, if at all.

Before discussing money, you should first give a description of the type of home you want, making sure to be clear about the elimination factors you've recorded in your notebook. This will help the agent serve you better and will save you both a lot of time. Don't assume, though, that the agent will never try to convince you to buy something not quite right for you or encourage you to spend more money than you've indicated. When the right opportunity arises, the agent's likely to try both.

Directly related to how much you are going to spend is what you already know about prices and values in your selected area. Be sure to inform the agent that you have details of a number of homes that have recently sold, their selling prices and length of time they were on the market. If you are asked to identify the properties, deflect the question. Say you keep that information in another note-book, which you don't have with you.

It's very important not to make it obvious that this is part of a strategy. The comments I'm suggesting should be made matter-of-factly in the course of normal conversation. There's no need for eye-ball-to-eyeball emphasis: the agent will be taking in everything you say. It's not in your interest to identify and discuss particular homes that have sold in the neighborhood or their relevant details or mer-its. If the agent wants to talk about such homes, he'll have plenty on their own list to refer to and you can discuss them as much as you like—just not the homes from *your* list. Neither does the agent have to know if your information is accurate, sketchy, or just based on what you think you heard along the way. To you, they're reliable. That's all he needs to know.

What you are doing now is painting a picture in the agent's mind—a picture of an informed, logical, and intelligent buyer who won't be easily misled, convinced, intimidated, or persuaded.

Now, back to the question the agent wants you to answer—how much do you want to spend? You'll have to give some indication of the price range that interests you. My recommendation is that that figure should be 5 percent to 10 percent below your comfortable spending limit, adding that you might be able to increase the figure slightly for an exceptional home.

Let's take an example. If your comfortable spending limit is $120,000, you deduct 10 percent ($12,000), making a figure of $108,000. Your answer then can be turned into a range, say, $108,000 to $114,000, which you give the agent.

This approach provides an effective guide that will help the agent select appropriate homes. If you're in search of a more expen-sive home—let's say you've set $300,000 as your comfortable spend-ing limit—the range you'd suggest would be $270,000 to $285,000. Invariably you'll be directed or taken to homes with list prices in excess of your stated range.

In the first example, $108,000 to $114,000, very few agents would pass up an opportunity to introduce you to homes that meet your criteria in the $115,000 to $125,000 price range. Consider for a moment what would have happened had you revealed your true comfortable spending limit—$120,000. Very likely, you'd find your-self looking at homes priced between $115,000 and $135,000. At this point, the logic of declaring a lower budget should be clear.

However, if you find the quality of homes selected for your inspection are below the standard you expect, you'll have to revise upward your declared budget. *But only if you have similar experiences with two or more agents.* Remember, too, the list prices of essentially similar properties can, and do, vary from one agent to the next, and from one home to the next even within a company. In fact, in every area you'll find at least one real estate firm whose word-of-mouth reputation is based on the claim that they consistently get the highest home prices for their sellers. Naturally, they don't brag of this to buyers, the people they're getting those prices from. After dealing with two or three companies, you'll know if your declared budget is on target.

On the other hand, if you've been dealing with just one agent, and your budget seems to be coming up short, it could be that you were first introduced to a selection of hard-to-sell homes, or homes in which the agent had an extra incentive to sell (all real estate companies have them).

Another possible explanation is that you were shown the only appropriate homes the agent had permission to sell. In either case, you'll find out what you need to know with a single question—"Is that all you have in this neighborhood around my budget figure?"

One note of caution: It's always sad to see a buyer whose ego defeats him or her. Such buyers seek the approval not only of the agent, which is worthless anyway, but also the approval and admiration of their own spouses, partners, relatives, work associates, and others. The desire for approval is quite natural, but in homebuying, it's a major reason why some buyers frown on negotiating a lower price. Somehow, they see it as being beneath them, and consequently, they play into the hands of the agent and seller. Frequently, these non-negotiators exceed their budgets and pay the highest prices for the homes they buy.

Very often they commit themselves to mortgage payments too high for their incomes because there's no one to shout, "Stop!" Homebuyers must protect themselves.

When decisions are driven by ego instead of good sense, the result is almost inevitably a savings loss for the buyer. Conversely, it means a bigger payday for the agent and more money for the seller. The best prevention lies in your preparation—and in your notebook. The spending limits you've written there, along with your knowledge of the maximum loan for which you can qualify (but which you may have no intention of spending) offer no protection at all if you ignore them. Let your notebook guide your decision making and leave the ego-fuelled decisions to less astute buyers—a group among whom you will never wish to count yourself.

*Trap Four: Emotional Attachment*

Anyone who has ever sold real estate will have heard the sweetest words a homebuyer can speak—sweet, that is, to the agent and seller. What I am talking about are expressions like: "Oh, this is absolutely perfect", "I just love this", "I must have this", "This is for me—just what I've been looking for."

When you *must have* something that someone else is selling, and you communicate that feeling, you're almost certain to find yourself paying top price. That's giving money away—maybe many thousands of dollars. And all, not because you fell in love with the home, but because you let it be known that you did.

What your competitor knows, or perceives, is the key to how successfully you'll be able to negotiate. This is a fundamental principle of negotiation which we'll look into in a lot more detail, including case studies, later. For now keep in mind that there's no rule that says it's wrong to feel you *must have* a particular home. Or to experience that feeling in your stomach that tells you, "This is the one." But the moment those feelings are communicated to the agent or seller, you have thrown away your power to negotiate. And with it, probably a big chunk of money.

Here is the critical point to bear in mind, it's one of the great secrets of expert negotiators. That secret is this: it is not what is true or factual that helps you or hurts you—but what your competitor *believes* to be true or factual.

That's why it's OK to fall in love with a home, as long as the agent never gets to know about it. In essence, what it means is that you must hold back all information that weakens your power and offer only information that adds to your power. Your goal is to build these strengths gradually and convincingly throughout your contact with the agent and, in doing so, give yourself the best possible chance of affecting, then buying at, the seller's lowest price.

To emphasize this principle, let's do a role switch. Put yourself in the position of the agent. You have an older home on your book, one you badly want to sell. You've been advertising it heavily without any bites. In fact, nothing has been going well for you lately. Try as you might, you haven't sold anything for weeks. But, today, things are starting to look better. You've succeeded, over the past few days, in interesting not one, but two, couples in this older home, the Taylors and the Goldbergs.

When you call each couple to invite them back separately to view the home a second time, the following reactions are communicated to you:

Buyer 1:    Mr. Taylor: *"We'd love to. I told my wife many times that if we kept on looking we'd eventually find a house that we both feel is just right. Now, it looks like our search is over. Could you tell me what price the owner would accept? And could we move in in sixty days?"*

Buyer 2:    Mrs. Goldberg: *"Well, that house is almost identical to two others we are now looking at with another agent. We might be interested, but not at the price the owner is asking."*

Remember, in this scenario, you are the agent. Now try to answer the following questions:

1.  From which couple are you likely to get the higher price?

2.  With which couple are you likely to adopt a tougher, less compromising stand on price?

3.  With which couple are you likely to wrap up the deal quicker?

4.  Which couple are sitting ducks?

Don't award yourself any medals. At this stage, the answers should be obvious. There isn't a snowball's chance in hell of the Taylors getting the home at the seller's lowest acceptable price. Why? Because of the information they gave you about their feelings—unnecessarily and unwittingly. Call it surrender. Call it innocence. Call it whatever you like. It happens all the time. I call it losing. It's costly. And it's avoidable!

The Taylors didn't just break the rules of smart buying. They destroyed them. Their reactions demonstrated anxiety, urgency, and strong emotional attachment. Ironically, this type of mistake is seldom recognized by buyers even after it has cost them dearly.

Let's continue with the Taylors and Goldbergs and introduce a shock development. Remember, you're still playing the real estate agent. To your horror, the Taylors have just called to tell you the money they were planning to use to buy the home is not now available. You have only the Goldbergs left. On them rest all your hopes. So you go to work to save the sale. Does it now seem likely that you'll have to work harder to create a deal and earn a commission? Bet every last penny on it!

Will you be in as powerful a position as you were with the Taylors? Not a chance! Will you be as stubborn or as uncompromising in your negotiation as you would have been with the Taylors? Certainly not.

We could go on, but there's hardly any point. The Goldbergs, if they continue to negotiate as well as they began, might be able to take an ocean cruise with what they'll save on this home. But there's still one key question worth asking: Who wanted the home more, the Taylors or the Goldbergs? On the surface that seems like an easy question. But is it? If you answered, the Taylors, you are not allowing for the possibility that the Goldbergs are smart buyers. In fact, you have no way of knowing the answer to that question. And neither did the agent. The Goldbergs might possibly have wanted the home even *more* than the Taylors. But they didn't communicate that.

On the other hand, the anxiety, urgency, and emotional attachment of the Taylors was patently evident while the Goldbergs remained detached and discriminating. Make no mistake about it, these are the impressions agents note and record. Impressions that enter their thinking and create their perceptions.

This is the foundation from which the tone and direction of the negotiation proceeds and on which the seller's lowest acceptable price will be achieved or lost.

As we saw earlier, perception *is* power. But it's just as true that power can be retained or given away. In our example, the Taylors gave away power. The Goldbergs retained and used power. They stayed in control of what they communicated and created the impression of being genuinely interested. But, they could take it or leave it. No anxiety. No urgency. No emotional attachment. And, consequently, no gift-giving to the agent and seller. No surrendering of hard-earned money.

Well, they're the four traps, the mistakes that are always expensive no matter what price range you're in. Being aware of these traps will help you negotiate wisely, confidently, and profitably.

## The Phony Buyer

Staying aware of the four traps we've just looked at will certainly help you negotiate better than 9 out of 10 homebuyers—and reap the rewards that come with that. However, before you get involved with an agent or salesperson you need to learn how to deal with the phony buyer tactic.

In the hypothetical example we just constructed, we saw two buyers interested in a particular home at the same time. But that isn't very realistic. In fact, it's rare for an agent or a seller to be so fortunate. Most of the time the agent is delighted to have a single interest in any of his properties. Had the Goldbergs been the only interested party from the beginning, their position would have been just as strong, or stronger.

The point here is that it is more realistic to expect that you won't have competition from another buyer when you set your sights on the home you want to buy. Something else you can expect, though, is that the agent might go to great lengths to convince you the opposite is true, that if you don't act quickly with a full price offer (or close to it) you'll lose the home to the "other buyer." That the home will be snatched out of your grasp, leaving you no second chance. Most such claims are nothing less than outright deceptions—deliberate fabrications designed to get you to part quickly with your money, and to put you under pressure to sign on the dotted line.

On the infrequent occasions when such an other buyer claim is true, your personal judgment of the agent's behavior will probably give you some clues. For example, the agent might react to your reluctance to accept the *other buyer* story by suggesting you make an offer "of any kind," or words to that effect. If you suspect the other buyer might be real, start asking specific relevant questions—as specific as you can make them.

For example, when did the other buyer first inspect the home? (Remember, if there is another interested buyer, that buyer may 'belong' to another agent.) How many times have they seen the home? Is it a family or a couple? How many kids are there? Is there an offer in writing at this point? If not, why not? And so on.

Your objective is to see if you get specific answers or vague replies. If the other buyer is real, it shouldn't be too difficult for the agent to provide at least some factual details, even if the buyer is not using that agent. On the other hand, if it's a case of *phony buyer*, it won't sound so convincing. The signs to watch for are universal: fumbling, vague generalities, stalling, avoiding answering, too many uncertainties, a willingness to supply an abundance of trivial details. If this is what you hear, the chances are you have a phony buyer for a competitor.

Here's a nice twist and a little piece of poetic justice. When seen through, the phony buyer tactic tends to backfire on the agent and work strongly in your favor.

One way of gaining the advantage is with a statement like this:

Buyer:   *Well, I am interested in the home, but I'm not interested in competing against another buyer. Let me know if the sale doesn't go through for any reason. If I haven't bought one of the other properties I'm looking at, I might consider making an offer. But if it sells, don't worry about contacting me.*

That's called turning the tables on the agent. Not only have you not fallen for the ploy, you've made the agent believe there's a risk of losing you altogether as a buyer!

Such a move on your part is likely to put you in control or to strengthen whatever control you already had. The picture you have just painted in the agent's mind is of commission dollars slipping away. And that, dear reader, is the last thing an agent wants to let happen.

He or she might not do an about turn on the spot, but expect a phone call shortly after to let you know the good news—the other buyer dropped out. And expect, too, an invitation to inspect the home again or even to consider making an offer—this time without competition!

Control. You've grasped it, put it to work, and gained a distinct benefit that can be measured in dollars. Now you proceed to negotiate confidently and carefully for the lowest price. No triumphalism on your part. And at no stage do you let your guard down. On the outside, continue as before, with no change of attitude and no sign that you realize you have just laid the phony buyer to rest.

Your task is not yet accomplished.

## Fine Tuning Your Basic Strategy

Now that you're in the final stages of preparation before entering the agent's arena, let's review briefly the protection you've built and acquired.

1. You have researched your selected area, including prices.

2. You have a clear picture of your needs and wants; your must-haves; and the factors that will eliminate any home from consideration.

3. You understand that anxiety and urgency must never be communicated to the agent. Nor must any emotional attachment you might develop for a property regardless of how ideal it seems.

4. Your budget figures are written down—your comfortable spending limit and your upper limit. You also know that the figure you give to the agent should be approximately 5 to 10% below your comfortable spending limit but that you are free to increase this figure if need be (if the homes shown to you by two or more agents are below the standard you desire). Also, you know the maximum loan for which you can qualify.

In essence what you now have is what negotiators refer to as a *basic strategy*. It's not yet complete, but it's taking shape. Let's add a few more simple but valuable tactics before you stride confidently into the arena that your competitor typically dominates. The following tactics are concerned with one of the most important principles of negotiation—building the right kind of relationship with the other side (that is, the kind that is conducive to your success).

Although they don't work for you, real estate salespeople assist you, even if only for their own interests. Despite being your competitor, agents nonetheless still merit your courtesy, respect, and an appreciation for their position and concerns. In giving these qualities, you in no way weaken your power. I'm certain, in fact, that the opposite is true, that your advantage is increased.

How does a courteous attitude assist you? Well, in my view, as humans, we all prefer to deal with people who make us—or allow us—to feel good about ourselves. These are the people for whom we'll go that extra mile. When courtesy is absent, we won't normally go out of our way to be helpful unless there's a very compelling profit motive involved.

For all this, though, it's also true that when you give out good feelings they won't always be returned. Does that mean that your efforts in such cases are wasted? Certainly not. Your goal, ultimately, is to save as much money as you can. And it's on that you should stay focused. Courtesy is always your ally in negotiation.

How else might you prepare for meeting and dealing with the agent on his own turf?

### Information is a Double-Edged Sword

Your greatest assets are the information you gather and the insights and skills you learn from this book—in other words, information and know-how. But, be warned, this combination will work for anybody. And that includes those with an interest in selling you your next home. Agents already have some degree of know-how—that's why they're selling for a living. But what they don't have is the information about *you* they vitally need to get you to pay the highest price—unless you provide it, that is. Expect an agent to try continually to pry that information out of you, either directly or subtly. Almost never is it to your advantage to accede to these requests or indirect inquiries, at least not with 100 percent honesty. Why? you might wonder. Doesn't an agent need this information to help you? Well, that's a line you'll hear from just about every agent or salesperson you'll come across. *But it isn't true.* And generally, neither is it genuine.

The more an agent knows about you, the easier it is to predict how you will act and react. The more predictable you are, the more vulnerable you become. The logic is basic. Military leaders have known it for eons. The more predictable the enemy, the more likely the victory. Think of the millions, maybe billions of dollars, that are spent every year to eavesdrop on other nations, satellite observation, spies masquerading as diplomats, electronic data systems interception, the selling of official secrets, and so on. All, for one purpose—to learn how the other side is thinking. Usually, it's dressed up and given a fancy name such as *reconnaissance* or *intelligence* or some other such label. But what it is, is information gathering. It's so vital that it's normal policy for governments to "leak" erroneous information to the other side. This, they refer to as *disinformation* (in layman's language, lies).

The objective of these lies is to make enemies think they have acquired classified facts when all they have acquired is deliberately constructed fiction. As long as an enemy *perceives* it has factual information, the advantage rests with the other side. It's a treacherous game when it involves hostile nations. However, it's a good illustration of the power of information and how it must be guarded.

Naturally, when buying a home, your goal will not be to withhold all information about your situation. The agent will need to know certain things to be able to help you. Guidelines for what you can safely reveal are covered in this and other chapters. You'll base your answers on your needs, preferences, and other specific details from your notebook and on what you discovered when conducting your research.

One agent question, however, merits further comment. All agents will inquire how you plan to finance your purchase, and whether you already have loan approval. Most of the time, I believe it is in your interest to have this approval *before* you start your search. (See Part Seven: Finding the Money, for tips on getting the best mortgage.) Alternatively, do some checking and make certain you can qualify even if you don't make a formal application. If you have done either of these things, you can answer with a general statement such as: "The money situation won't cause us any problems. We're in a position to buy when we find a home we like."

Notice that your answer provides only minimum information, no details, no bank or finance company name, no figures. Still, you have assured the agent that you are a *qualified buyer*. That means you aren't just looking at homes for pleasure, amusement, or planning for 12 months down the road. You are ready, capable, and willing to make a purchase. These are things the agent is trained to determine directly and indirectly before investing time and effort in working with you. As we've just seen, you can satisfy this need without revealing anything that can be used against you.

It is not necessary to follow these suggested responses precisely—just as long as you obey the principle enshrined in them: Avoid being spontaneously informative or unnecessarily specific. And reveal only that which is in your interest to reveal. No more.

## What You Must Never Forget About the Agent

As you prepare to put into practice what we have covered so far, you'll greatly increase your chances of making money by keeping in mind the following points.

Whether the title is broker, realtor, consultant, associate, or salesperson, any individual whose job it is to sell real estate is a professional. Typically, they come across as courteous, respectful, warm, friendly and nonthreatening. That's professional. But one thing they are not is your friend! Neither should you see real estate agents as people in whom you can openly confide. Nonetheless, I'm not suggesting, either, that you view them as your enemy, at least not in the usual meaning of that word. They are clearly your competition because, quite simply, the agents' financial duty and allegiance are to the sellers. Their goals, their loyalty, and confidentiality are not yours.

If you fear that an agent's charm and manner might be deluding you into thinking otherwise, even momentarily, you can snap your thinking back to reality by answering a few critical questions: Who is the agent working for? Who's paying the agent? Is the agent committed to getting the top price for the seller, or is it the goal to sell you the home at the lowest price possible?

Clear enough? I hope so.

You can be quite sure that the agent won't have come up against more than a handful of buyers as well prepared for the task of buying as you will be. Even at this point, by virtue of what you have learned so far, you are miles ahead of the typical homebuyer. In the following chapters, as you acquire more insights and specific know-how, you'll find it easier to protect your money and save thousands of dollars more than you probably ever imagined.

When you've accomplished your task, the agent will certainly remember you. Perhaps you'll be remembered as being stubborn and opinionated. Or perhaps even a pain in the neck (fairly unlikely). But note this point well—all that is completely insignificant and irrelevant to your task to buy at the lowest price possible!

When you achieve your goal, the agent still makes money, though not as much as if you had paid a higher price. But the agent will get over it very quickly. It's one more sale to their credit, and as the saying goes in the real estate profession, *any* sale is a good sale.

For you, the price you pay is a fact you'll have to live with indefinitely. You won't easily or quickly get over the out-of-pocket costs of a bad deal, even if you *never* discover you could have bought for less. As a homebuyer, you'll always have much more at stake than any agent or salesperson. You'll always have more to lose and, consequently, more need to protect your well-being—financial and emotional.

Just in case you need it, here's one final consolation you might like to think about. Real estate people harbor a grudging respect for smart buyers—even admiration—irrelevant as such things are.

The singular goal you must never lose sight of, despite deliberate and spontaneous distractions, is to buy the home you want for the fewest dollars possible. All your efforts and thinking must be guided by this goal from the beginning of the buying process to the end.

# CHAPTER FIVE

# THE INITIAL ENCOUNTER: HOW TO HANDLE THE AGENT

*All the professions are conspiracies
against the laity.*
    —GEORGE BERNARD SHAW

Your preparation has gone well; you've acquired the basic know-how, insights, and negotiation skills and are alert and aware of how the game of selling real estate is played. Now, you can confidently arrange the initial face-to-face encounter with the agent.

What's the best way to go about this? Simple. Select one real estate office that seems to have the type of homes you want, in the neighborhood you prefer. Then, call the agent, but make sure you don't get trapped into a long, detailed conversation. Simply, say that you would like to drop by to have a general talk, as you *might* consider buying a home locally.

Maybe something like this:

Buyer:   *Hi. My name is Joseph Cummins. I'm considering buying a
         home in your area, maybe within the next three—possibly
         six months. Could I drop by and talk with you on Wednes-
         day around 5 p.m.?*

Here's the most likely response you'll get. And how you might proceed:

Agent:   *Certainly, Mr. Cummins. Can you tell me something about
         what kind of home you have in mind, and approximately
         how much you'd like to spend?*

Buyer:    *Well, like I said, I'd just like to have a general talk at this stage. I haven't made any hard decisions yet. But we can go over some details when I see you.*

The agent will probably persist, if only just a little, explaining that by knowing your needs and budget they will be in a position to select specific homes and to gather the information you need to know. That way, the agent can have details and even photos ready to show you when you get there. Sounds good, but it's not really what you want, yet.

This might require from you a pleasantly assertive response stating that you'd prefer to leave that aside for the moment.

Remember, from this initial contact forward, *you are painting a picture in the agent's mind.* The process continues with every contact, right through to the conclusion of your business.

Should the situation arise where your initial contact is with the office sales manager who then refers you to one of the salespeople, you can count on the manager also passing on their impressions of you. As a smart homebuyer, it's always your responsibility to establish consciously that impression. An image or impression that will assist you throughout the process and especially when the negotiation proper begins.

The best way of doing this is by staying in control of what you reveal and the demeanor you project. From the earliest point, the agent will be rating you—assessing you as a person and, more relevantly, as a prospective buyer.

As we go on, we'll explore what the agent will try to find out on both counts, and we'll look at some of the methods the agent might use.

For the moment, let's proceed with the initial encounter. As it turns out, you find the agent much as you expected—warm, courteous, friendly. You go along with the pleasantries. Behind that, though, you are marching to a different drummer. You provide a basic description of the type of home you are looking for and your preferred neighborhood or area. You describe the elimination factors and your budget. Your notebook should contain this information. If it does, it will show the budget figure you'll give to the agent and how you calculated it—by subtracting 5 to 10% from your comfortable spending limit. If you prefer, you can present your budget as a range. Something like: *"I'm prepared to spend approximately $108,000 to $114,000 for a suitable property."*

## Two Keys: Staying Calm and Alert

Behind your tactical defenses, you may feel more nervous than is obvious to anyone besides yourself. That's perfectly OK. The cause may be the normal pressures connected with homebuying or maybe work, time, or personal situation pressures. None of this should be evident to the agent—at least, not to a degree that marks you as an anxious, vulnerable buyer.

In your initial discussion, and at least once later, remind the agent that you are a serious buyer and are prepared to buy as soon as the home and the price are both right. This keeps the picture of a sale—and the income it represents—in the agent's mind. As long as that goal seems achievable you will be served well. By reminding of your seriousness, you keep feeding the goal. But be careful, because you can overdo it.

After your initial getting-to-know-you encounter, another good time for this reminder is when you have rejected a number of properties. At that point, the agent's enthusiasm might have dropped just a little and their interest in you might benefit from a jolt. Let the agent know how much you appreciate their assistance. Then use a conferred expectation. Tell the agent how nice you find it to deal with a knowledgeable professional, one so helpful and one who really cares.

If handling the agent in this sometimes patronizing way doesn't sit easily with your personality, consider giving the task to your spouse or partner. Negotiation is business and it requires flexibility if you are to adopt the tactics that contribute to your ultimate goal. It might help you to see it as a kind of stage play in which you have the leading role. When the show is over, you can revert happily back to your normal demeanor. With thousands of dollars—your dollars—at stake, it will pay you to understand how the game is played and to plan accordingly. The way you'll read it here is how the game is played almost everywhere in the modern world. To my knowledge, what is in these pages has never before been revealed in a detailed educational program for the benefit of the average, nonprofessional homebuyer.

In praising, and even patronizing, the agent, don't lose sight of the fact that the agent is, at all times, your opponent. This is a time to remain clearheaded and to realize that the agent is playing a game too. Courteous, friendly, and even charming as you are treated, their pledge is to get the best terms and the best price for the seller. The agent knows how to make it work because it's their game. And they plays it well.

Your best and most profitable defense demands tactics and a strategy. After many years of research and study in the psychology of human communication and negotiation, I know of no better protection than that which I have spelled out in this book. It pleases me when, from time to time, I hear from business executives I've trained about deals in which they achieved profitable results using my methods. But the best satisfaction I get is hearing from ordinary, nonprofessional individuals about how they saved personal rather than company dollars.

## Taking the Inquisitive Agent in Your Stride

By now you have a grasp of how to respond to the agent asking the most likely and most probing questions. When unanticipated questions arise, you have in place a strategy that can be applied across the board. The principle that protects you best is to weigh up what you say before you say it, whether the question is asked in a formal discussion or in an apparently spontaneous or casual manner. A particularly vulnerable time is when you are driving with the agent to inspect your first property. Being so physically close will tend to cause you to relax your defenses in favor of a more open communication. Beware!

When the agent is talkative and overinquisitive regarding m ters you don't wish to discuss, there are options you might consider. The one I like best will enhance the amicable relationship you are trying to develop. Instead of avoiding or deflecting his inquisitiveness, simply switch roles—you become the questioner. You'll recall in an earlier chapter we noted that people like best to talk about themselves. Now is your opportunity to put it to good use. Ask:

How long have you been in real estate?

What's good and bad about it?

Do you live locally?

What changes have you seen in the neighborhood?

What problems should buyers new to the area watch out for?

What are the most common reasons owners are selling?

What plans are in the works for the area?

Why did you choose your present home location?

How has the cultural or ethnic make-up of the neighborhood developed?

Where are the best shopping and schools locally?

How about transportation?

What are the most popular amenities?

Because the agent knows you see them as a credible and knowledgeable professional, they won't want to let you down now or make you feel your confidence was misplaced. So what will the agent do? They'll sing! The agent will do everything possible to live up to your conferred expectation. The agent will answer all your questions, giving you as much accurate and positive information as possible.

It's also true, though, that you're unlikely to learn anything from the agent that will deter you from buying in her area. Nor will you learn confidential details about a seller or a specific property. Still, the strangest things can happen when you handle the agent with skill. So stay alert for information that might help you later but, while doing that, be skeptical about stories and statements for which no proof is available, especially those that are obviously intended to influence you in one way or another.

Encouraging this kind of conversation isn't something you should adopt just to avoid having to find answers to the agent's probing questions. It's an excellent way of adding to your research, data you'll have at your disposal when you deal with the next agent. There, you'll do the same, then carry even more "insider" information to your meeting with the third agent. By using these subtle skills and quiet power, you'll help build the amicable relationship that moves you closer to a successful negotiation.

It's a good idea, too, to let it be known that you are looking forward to seeing homes with a number of agents. If the agent questions the benefit of this, hold your ground and say that you believe it's in your best interest to do so. Then add a little encouragement such as: *"But I do hope we'll be able to do business with you. We appreciate good, helpful service."*

If you believe, even for a moment, that in making this kind of statement you are being insincere or manipulative, remember these three facts:

1.  You're on your own.

2.  You are doing nothing more than protecting your money.

3.  You're up against a trained professional seller whose job it is to get the best terms and maximum price out of you.

So stay focused. And make a comment about how you value honesty when an appropriate opportunity arises. Later, this might dissuade an agent, to some extent, from using heavy pressure when it's time to make your offer. You've provided an image of honesty and genuineness to live up to and they'll hesitate to tarnish it.

On the other hand, your aim is not to make an agent feel so comfortable that they believe they have a captive buyer. Keep the agent on their toes by mentioning other homes you've seen and other agents you have talked to or plan to talk to. You'll keep the agent sensitive to your needs and willing to serve when you cause them to believe that they just might lose you to a competitor. That's when you're most likely to receive the best service. It's the age-old dilemma of when to use the carrot and when to use the stick. Here, the secret lies in the balance you adopt and how convincing you are. With the help of this book, you'll be well prepared to deal with these matters.

## Why and How You Should Stay Unpredictable

You can be certain that the foundation you establish in the first and second meetings with the agent will prove very significant later, when you find a home you want to buy. You'll discover the significance of this in more detail shortly.

One of the wisest teachers I ever had constantly preached this central point: when we give up the ability to surprise, we become predictable. Predictability robs us of a distinct advantage. It usually diminishes or eliminates our control of a negotiation situation. Your aim, therefore, is to avoid being taken for granted by the agent— remain unpredictable.

By following what we've covered in this section, you'll deter or deflect most attempts to manipulate your thinking. A gullible, anxious, unknowledgeable, impressionable buyer you now certainly— and obviously—are not. Nobody will pull your strings unless they are reasonably sure what will pop out.

To understand better the importance of predictability in today's world, consider what happens when you go for a bank loan, a new credit card or, say, apply to become a police officer. The institutions involved go to extremes to gather the information that will enable them to assess how financially, behaviorally, and otherwise predictable you are. Only when they can rate how you are likely to behave will they look favorably on your application. If an adequate amount of information is not available you'll be turned down, despite the fact that you might have all the necessary qualities.

In these circumstances the need to establish predictability is generally positive. In negotiation the opposite is true. Predictability is as dangerous as it is in poker. Your defense lies in the rule we've already highlighted: You reveal, imply, say, show, and express only things that will enhance your chance of winning your objective—to buy at the lowest price possible. Nothing else.

Of course, as humans, we're all quite predictable to some extent. Without this, the whole structure of our society would collapse. Consequently, most people don't give it a passing thought. It would seem strange to be any other way than the way we "are." But we must adopt the quality of unpredictability if we are to achieve our goals in negotiation. As soon as you begin, you'll find it intriguing because you already have all the skills you need. You're already an old hand at it—unconsciously.

Here's a brief but telling account of a recent spontaneous incident in which the effectiveness of unpredictability was cogently— and amusingly—illustrated.

### A Toast to Unpredictability

I had been engaged to negotiate a number of very expensive media production contracts. On behalf of my client, I screened the interested production companies and selected one that seemed most suitable. My next step was to achieve understanding and agreement on deadlines, technical standards, content, and so on (and, ultimately, to negotiate a budget that was realistic but as competitive as possible). Although I could call on my background in media, I did not know, and was not familiar with, the principals with whom I would be negotiating. After many ups and downs and hours of discussion and problem solving, we ironed out a deal that was good for the production company, and particularly good for my client.

A celebratory dinner was organized for the evening the contracts were signed. And, as is common in such situations, a number of light-hearted toasts were offered to everyone and everything in sight (and to some things that were not yet in sight, such as the programs). Without warning, just as the meal was about to be served, the managing director of the production company, now slightly intoxicated, struggled a little unsteadily to her feet and wobbled dangerously for a second or two. She summarily dismissed the waiter and demanded silence. The lady had something more urgent on her mind than mere food. With fingers gripping her martini glass like it was a beer bottle, she thrust a high, toasting gesture in my direction. A little too strenuously, it turned out. The cocktail splashed over her hand, over her watch, and ran down her sleeve. She paused momentarily, but only to stare curiously at the damp patch spreading on the linen table-cloth. Long enough to collect her thoughts, though.

Then, with an undeterred air, she lowered her chin, locked it abruptly, and fixed a sniper's stare in my direction. What she said sounded like broken English or a speech being made under water.

*"I give this toast," she said, "to Mr. Cummins. Every
time I thought we had him figured out, he said something
that proved we hadn't got him ... we hadn't got him figured out at all. Or he did something ... something ...
what was it now?..."*

An embarrassed *"sshhh"* came from her partners,
nervous at what she might blurt out. *"...he did something we didn't expect. And I'll say this; each time ...
every time we met, the only thing that was predictable
was that he'd be as unpredictable as the last time. I'm
happy about the deal. It's good for us both. But I'm also
glad it's over, and that I'm not married to him!"*

With that she sat down to hearty laughter and applause.

What's interesting about this from our point of view is that,
although totally unaware of the fact, she identified one of the key
strategies used by all top negotiators. That is never to help your
competitor predict accurately how you will respond in a potentially
decisive set of circumstances. That's critically important, as we'll see
shortly, when it comes time to talk dollars.

## Using Your Quiet Power

Here's a piece of advice I can't emphasize too strongly. Don't come on
with the agent like you know it all. Earlier, I stressed that negotiation
is a subtle skill, and now is the time to practice that subtlety. The
power you have at this stage is *quiet power*. It isn't something you beat
people with. Nor should you use it to intimidate or alienate the other
side. All such negative actions will only work against you.

Your objective is to build the kind of professional relationship
that will motivate the agent to assist you in any way possible. Usually, that means many ways.

Homebuyers who parade themselves in an aloof manner or as
experts certainly do not receive the same quality of service. Their
mistake lies in ignoring or overlooking the fact that agents are a rich
source of information and can be very beneficial to the buyer's
objectives.

Take advantage of it. Use their inside experience and their specialized knowledge. Encourage it with inquiry and attention. The
strategy is to bring all possible advantages onto your side, and
building a good relationship facilitates that.

## Conferred Expectation

Here's another piece of advice you might consider unlikely. Ask for
help! It makes good sense for a number of interesting reasons. When

we ask for a person's help we place that person in an elevated position. That opens the door for positive reactions. Yet an elevated position doesn't simply confer feelings of higher status or value. Particularly in one-to-one situations, the person elevated usually feels a greater *responsibility* to the other person. And most of the time it happens unconsciously.

Conferring status or value establishes an expectation and a standard to be lived up to. It's a perfectly human desire to try not to disappoint those who, we believe, have placed their confidence in us. These are the feelings you must try to engender in the agent or salesperson if you want to maximize his potential to be of benefit to you.

It's what I refer to as *conferred expectation,* and it's a universal phenomenon. Parents use it with children daily: *"I know you are going to be very good while daddy watches the game on TV."* Or, perhaps: *"Daddy and I love you and we know you mean it when you promise you won't ever again push your three sisters down the stairs when we're not at home."*

Teenagers are the group that probably hear it most often: *"We'll allow you more freedom because we trust you and because we know you wouldn't do anything that would hurt us."* Or, *"This grade D in English is not really you. I know you are capable of getting a C or better next time."*

In the military, this phenomenon of conferred expectation is practiced universally by putting people in uniforms and giving them behavior codes, ranks, and weapons.

And, of course, lovers do it, too: *"Even though I'll be far away, I trust you. I know you'll be faithful to me."* Or even: *"You're so wonderfully passionate and romantic I know our first evening alone together will be unforgettable."*

Asking for assistance, though, can be much more direct and still deliver the advantages inherent in conferred expectation.

For example: *"Using your expertise, could you help us figure the total monthly repayment on this home?"* Or: *"I can see your agency is very resourceful. Do you think you could find out...?"*

At seminars I'm sometimes asked, especially by salespeople, what is the best way to get past the secretary when the objective is to talk to the boss. I always answer the same way: Ask for help. This acknowledges the secretary's authority, which tends to reduce defensiveness, and it shows that you respect the importance of his or her position.

Real estate agents and salespeople are no different in this regard. They react to appreciation and acknowledgment as naturally and as positively as you or I do.

One final thought before we move on. In asking for the agent's help and complimenting his expertise, you are simply using a conscious tactic to extract maximum benefit from your association with the agent. This does not mean you should accept or put automatic trust in any recommendations, suggestions, or advice. Nor does it mean you should reveal anything but the minimum of personal information or drop your guard in any way.

Of course, asking questions is not your prerogative alone. The agent has a few that you should know how to handle.

### "Why are You Buying?" A Question You Should Know How to Answer

Why are you buying? Most real estate salespeople have listened to their trainers and sales managers repeat ad nauseam that they must discover each buyer's *dominant buying motive.*

Consequently, you'll hear, as I have so many times, variations such as these:

1. *Do you mind if I inquire, Mr. Cummins, what is your reason for buying at this time?*

2. *Why have you decided on a three-bedroom home in this area, Mr. Cummins, if I may ask?*

Sometimes the inquiry is less well disguised. Occasionally, it's even quite blatant, which should set off alarm bells in your brain. For example:

3. *The more I know about your situation, Mr. Cummins, the better I can help you. What is your chief reason for buying right now?*

Other variations exist, but mostly the form of the question will resemble one of these and will be easily recognized for what it is.

How should you answer? Let's look at each of the variations separately.

Question 1:  *Do you mind if I inquire Mr. Cummins, what is your reason for buying at this time?*

Well, no, you don't mind. But only because you are prepared for it and you expect it. Therefore, you won't be caught off guard. Will you?

Here's the answer I recommend (or something similar):

> Buyer:    *Well, we really hadn't been planning to buy until next year*
> *(or three months, six months, etc.). But, we like the neigh-*
> *borhood. If we can find a home that's suitable—one that rep-*
> *resents really good value, to us, we'll bring our plans for-*
> *ward.*

Just a few simple sentences. Or maybe they're not as simple as they appear. What have we communicated? Lots! First, we said loud and clear—*no anxiety, no urgency, no desperation.* Second, we put conditions on our decision to buy. What we said, in effect, was that we would buy *only* if the right home is available, at the right price.

Make no mistake, these messages penetrated. The agent filed them away, which is exactly what we intended, isn't it?

> Question 2:    *Why have you decided on a three-bedroom home in this*
> *area, if I may ask?*

A similar answer will do here, but perhaps one with a minor variation:

> Buyer:    *We had been planning to buy a three-bedroom home for*
> *more space but not until next year. However, we like the*
> *neighborhood and if we can find ... (as above)*

Once again, the crucial point is *no anxiety, no urgency, no despera-tion.* We'll buy *only* if the home and the price are right.

> Question 3:    *The more I know about your situation, Mr. Cummins,*
> *the better I can help you. What is your chief reason for*
> *buying now?*

This is the kind of reasonable sounding question that can catch you napping, particularly when it is asked in an assertive manner— as it often is. The tone of the agent can be disarming, but you can never allow your ultimate goal to stray out of your thinking. By staying concentrated on that goal, you'll find it easier to stay in con-trol. Your answer might be something like this:

> Buyer:    *"Up to now, our plan has been to buy next year, but if we*
> *find a suitable home that represents good value for money,*
> *to us, it shouldn't be too difficult to bring our plans for-*
> *ward."*

Your answers in all three cases are clear and to the point. But you haven't divulged anything that can be used to pressure you later. Neither have you revealed confidential details the agent might feel obliged or inclined to pass on to the seller, consequently weakening your position in the negotiation.

If an agent probes further into your reason for buying, especially if the agent becomes even mildly aggressive or confrontational, try giving the same answer again. At that point, the agent will almost certainly get the message and back down. If not, there's no shortage of congenial salespeople anxious to sell you property.

# PART THREE

---

# *Winning: Keeping the Odds in Your Favor*

# Chapter Six

# Viewing Properties: Your Chance to Move Ahead

*The power of accurate observation*
*is commonly called cynicism by those who have not got it.*
—George Bernard Shaw

Up to this point, I have focused largely on preparation and on the things you should avoid saying and doing in your association with the real estate agent. Let's look now at those things you might best be doing and saying as you inspect homes together.

Some real estate companies prefer to have their agents drive you to the selected properties, while others like to arrange to meet you at the various locations. Now, despite the fact that this book is designed to teach you how to buy and, as I stated earlier, not where to buy or what to buy, there is something I must say on this subject of location. However you arrive at a home for sale and however attractive it might appear, you cannot even begin to give it serious consideration until you have familiarized yourself with the immediate surroundings. That takes in much more than just the route by which you drove, or were driven, to the home. What's behind it? Two blocks down the road? Three streets away? A mile to the east and west? What's the character of the closest neighborhoods? Are there problems only locals will know? And so on.

The old Latin phrase reminds us: *caveat emptor*—let the buyer beware. In other words, you buy at your own risk, so stay alert and check things out as thoroughly as you need to.

When you arrange together to view a list of selected homes, your relationship with the agent moves into a different phase, even a different mood. This is when the agent's eagerness to sell can rub you the wrong way. You will probably need to be definite or even firm at times, but be careful not to appear to be offended with or personally critical of the agent.

After all, you've worked hard to establish a collaborative relationship, one in which you both stand to gain. And although the agent is indeed your competitor, an openly competitive or combative approach will not aid your goal of buying at the lowest price but will linger throughout the home viewing stage, benefiting nobody.

According to various surveys, most homebuyers look at between 6 and 12 homes before selecting one to buy. However, if your average is higher than 12 (and mine certainly is), that's fine, too. The fact that you have purchased this book and read this far undoubtedly establishes that you are anything but average when it comes to learning how to protect your money through smart buying.

## Five Questions You Should Always Ask

When you find a property that is of real interest to you, you will generally ask a lot of questions. That's exactly as it should be. But, here's the problem: That intense spate of questioning signals very strongly that you are very keen to buy, or possibly even hooked on the home. So, what's the solution?

Well, there's no way you can avoid asking the all-important questions. Nor do you want to hide completely your interest in the home. What you need is a little disguise and a bit of camouflage. Here's what I mean.

The problem starts when you've just seen a number of homes, all of which you have dismissed quickly and without questions of any significance. Then, as you view the next home, you might manage to stay calm and unexpressive, but you look for detailed answers to *dozens* of questions. What have you done? Well, your obvious change in behavior has probably told the agent loudly and clearly that he has the right home and a hot prospect. That's not in your favor.

The agent, instinctively, will have picked up your high level of interest. Yet, from your point of view, it seems like a catch-22 situation. You need answers to your questions, but you are anxious not to reveal your excitement about the home. How do you achieve both?

Here's the best solution I know. Don't dismiss *any* property, even those in which you have zero interest, without asking a set of serious and relevant questions. You don't have to engage the agent in long-winded conversations about these no-hopers, but don't show disinterest, either, and don't ignore the responses. That way, when you find a home that does interest you, your interest and curiosity will seem part of your normal inquisitive personality and will be far less revealing.

What initial questions should you ask? The following list of questions will generally elicit important, specific information you will need on any home you might consider buying. The same set of questions can be used with properties in which you have no interest. The answers then, of course, will be irrelevant. However, as we've just seen, the exercise is not.

*Question 1:*
*What price is this listed at?*

Or, a good alternative. *'What is the asking price on this one?'* Take note that the way in which the question is worded implies that you see the price only as an *asking* price. On another level, it implies that no one, including you, pays such a price. Just like an ad for a used car that reads, "*BMW 1990 325E. Exc Cond, Asking $9500.*" There are hard prices and soft prices, but you can be pretty sure this $9500 is a soft price. You might have to pay $8250 or even $9000, but you know you won't have to pay the *asking* price. Unfortunately, many homebuyers fail to discover the *degree* of flexibility in list prices, asking prices, and even "reduced" and "discounted" prices.

Although residential homes are seldom promoted with an 'asking' price (except in a depressed housing market), the price tag on virtually every property is, in fact, exactly that, an asking price.

*Question 2:*
*Why is the home being sold?*

Think about it. Homeowners don't sell without good reasons. Usually strong, even compelling, reasons. Here's one of the most important points I'll make in this book: *Most sellers need to sell more than most buyers need to buy!*

What sellers need is your cash, for any number of different reasons. The saying that "cash is king" really is true in this context, more so than in most other areas of investment. By knowing the owner's reason for selling—the true reason—you'll be able to determine how strongly motivated the seller is. For example, sellers are very strongly motivated if they have already purchased another property and need a sale to close the deal. Similarly, people who are moving out of town are more eager to sell.

More often than buyers or agents know, the underlying reason for selling is debt—to pay off creditors and bill collectors. This is usually difficult to discover. Typically, a more respectable reason is fabricated by the seller and told to the buyer. But telltale signs of the true reason for selling are often evident, if you look for them.

Keep in mind that real estate salespeople are trained, and generally expected, to discover the seller's *dominant selling motive,* just as they are to discover the buyer's *dominant buying motive.* If an agent sidesteps your question regarding the reason for the sale, or offers a vague response, you have one course of action—pin him down. Anytime you ask a specific question demand a specific answer. If one is not forthcoming, be suspicious. Start digging for clues and be cautious about less-than-convincing explanations you are offered.

*Question 3:*
*How soon does the seller wish to close?*

What you are asking here is, essentially, how quickly the seller needs your cash. If the agent responds, as the agent is likely to, *'Well, what suits you best?'* the agent may not be saying what you think they are.

Your first impression might be that the seller is flexible and is in a secure position. But that might not be the case at all. What if the agent is aware the seller—their client, remember!—absolutely must close within 60 days and is anxious to listen to any reasonable offer from a buyer who can agree to that? Then, when you answer the agent's question spontaneously: *"Sixty days is what we need, or sooner,"* you've put your foot in it.

Why? Well, is the agent now likely to say, *'That's absolutely wonderful because the seller, too, needs to close within 60 days?'* I don't think so. More likely the agent will grasp the opportunity to play a little game. Perhaps they'll respond, *"Unfortunately, I don't believe 60 days will suit the owner. But I'll tell you what I'll do. If everything else is all right, I'll see if I can get him to meet your need for 60 days. I can't guarantee it, but I'll do my best."*

That's the game. And you just surrendered a huge advantage. Where did you go wrong? Lots of places!

First, when you asked the specific question, *"How soon does the seller need to close?"* you failed to insist on a direct, specific answer. In fact, you fell for one of the oldest tricks in the book. You allowed the agent to answer your question with a question. From their perspective, that was a very sharp move. For you, it did no good at all. It just led you down a dark alley where you lost a major negotiating point. Here's the warning again: *Insist on specific answers to your questions!*

Second, you revealed vital information, which was then used against you, when you said, *"Sixty days is what we need, or sooner."* At any stage, when you are asked when it would suit you to close or move in, you have two good responses to choose from:

1.   We haven't determined that yet.

2.   How soon does the owner wish to close?

You might also combine both responses in a single answer. Whatever you decide, you have at your disposal that same trick we've just seen—answering a question with a question. This time, though, it's you who are in control.

When the question about moving in is put to you simply to find out the time frame you have in mind (when no particular property is being given your serious consideration), your best response is usually, *"No urgency. Let's see what happens."*

*Question 4:*
*How long have the owners been living here?*

Sometimes, as with a vacant or rented home, it might be more relevant to ask, *"How long has the home been vacant?"* Or, *"How long has the seller owned the home?"* It's easy to underestimate the importance of this question. What if the seller bought the property just six months ago? Would you be curious? Even suspicious? Why would someone buy a home and then sell it just six months later? Or even three years later? You'd better find out. And particularly when the owner is living in the home. If the agent's response is not specific or convincing (assuming you are interested in the home) try knocking on a few neighbors' doors. There's a good chance that will be all the local research you will need to do to fill in the missing pieces.

This question is just as relevant, though, when the seller has owned the home for many years. In that case, the seller is probably sitting on substantial equity (potential profit) due to the rise in home prices since the home was bought. Any reasonable offer will probably look good to the seller compared with the price that was paid. Knowing this might signal a good opportunity for you to negotiate strongly and be a little more stubborn on price. Here again, an hour of friendly research among the closest neighbors can often be more informative than reams of details the seller's agent provides. Most importantly, it is very often the only way to get believable answers to key questions. At the same time, it gives you a perfect opportunity to weigh the kind of neighbors you might soon have.

*Question 5:*
*What repairs or upgrading have been carried out by the current owner on plumbing, electrical wiring, heating/cooling system, roof, and so on?*

The agent won't have ready answers to all these questions. Generally, the agent will respond in one of four ways:

1.  Tell what they know.

2.  Tell you they don't know.

3.  Tell you they will ask the owner.

4.  Give their opinion (which is not what you want).

If work has been done in any of the areas you listed, it may well have been because a problem existed. The seller's answers will probably point to those problems and include assurances that they have been remedied. Still, you've established that problems did occur. And that gives you a perceived advantage.

According to the way most people think, something that has been repaired seems to have decreased in value. In fact, the opposite may often be true, especially with a home. Nonetheless, there are seeds of advantage for you in the list of repairs that have been carried out.

For example, a car that has had extensive bodywork repair would hardly be seen as having the same value as an otherwise similar model that has never needed repair. This is how most of us think in relation to all kinds of goods. Ironically, though, a house that has had, for example, a new roof put on would almost certainly be worth more than before the work was done. And it would be worth more than a home of similar age and design that still has its original roof (assuming that it was age, and not damage, that led to the repair).

Nonetheless, repairs generally mean problems. With a home of any age the need for major repairs might suggest poor construction, ground problems, deterioration, damage, poor design, and so on. Such repairs give rise to buyer reservations. By communicating those reservations, you alert the agent to the fact that you'll have to be convinced of the soundness of the property before you buy it.

It may be the case that the repairs don't cause you any real concern. But that is something for only you to know. As you negotiate for the lowest price it is *perceptions* that count. If the agent perceives you have reservations because of the repairs (or any other point) they'll start thinking of ways to make the purchase more attractive to you, incentives to get you to buy. Typically, that means a price concession, sooner or later.

To make it crystal clear, you might say, *"The home seems fairly OK. If it wasn't for the repaired brickwork and smallish kitchen I might be tempted to make an offer."* What you are really saying, and what the agent is hearing, is: "I can take it or leave it. I'd be interested only if the price was right." Only *you* know it's a tactic.

Behind all that, you might consider it an ideal home, one that suits your needs in almost every way. In fact, you might have fallen head over heels in love with it. But the agent should *never, never, never* hear such sweet words. I hope that makes it clear enough. I'll expand on this later. Let's now delve a little deeper into the thinking of the agent.

## Knowing How Your Competitor Thinks

Along with the five we've just discussed, there are many other questions you can ask, whether you are interested or not. For example:

What's the quality and extent of the insulation?

Has it ever been extended?

When was the electrical wiring last checked? (Chances are it wasn't—a point for you.)

Why is the water discolored?

Why is the water pressure so low?

When was the plumbing last checked?

How come there are so few electrical sockets?

What faults has the owner made you aware of?

What faults have you noticed yourself?

Notice that totally absent from your comments is any kind of compliment or praise. You are trying hard never to sound very enthusiastic, especially when you find a home that appeals to you. That's why you've been asking questions about each of the homes you've inspected, even those in which you had no interest whatsoever.

In response to your questions, you can expect that the agent will lavish praise and point out special features in each home. You'll hear comments like: 'Notice the 10-foot ceilings giving a sense of space and style. And the fine timber doors.' While you might love high ceilings and have a passion for fine timber, your reaction, nonetheless, should be contrary. Something like this:

Buyer:    *I'm sure many people like high ceilings but it's really not a feature that's important to me. The doors are nice but, personally, I feel flush doors would have been more appropriate in this style of house.*

The agent is likely to have a comeback line that takes you in another direction (remember, a professional seller isn't dissuaded easily). Here's an example: *"I see your point about the doors but look at this. When have you seen such huge gardens—front and rear?"* Now, you might feel ecstatic about the big gardens, but that's not how you respond. Here's a much safer reaction:

> Buyer:   *Yes, I noticed them, and kept in good condition, too (this really isn't a compliment, as you'll see). The problem is the enormous amount of time that's needed. I always seem to have the problem of just not having enough time for garden work—much as I would like to.*

The agent's enthusiasm might diminish somewhat, but he'll keep plodding along. When there are no more features to compliment, the agent might add forlornly: *"I believe you are making a very good decision concentrating on this neighborhood. It's very go-ahead and a great place for kids. And also as an investment area."* By now you can almost guess the response. Perhaps:

> Buyer:   *Yeah, the area is nice. But we have seen (or will see) a couple of homes in an area we like even better, about 10 minutes south of here. There are some really attractively priced homes there, and the environment is terrific.*

You get the idea. But, be careful. Don't go overboard. If you dismiss everything, the agent will soon lose interest in you. Judgment is the key.

Should you decide for any reason that you cannot respond in a way that diminishes the features highlighted by the agent, you cannot afford to be less than neutral about them. For example, a neutral, *"Yes, I noticed that,"* or, *"Yes, the ceilings are high,"* won't give away your true interest. It's most important, though, never to let slip any clues to the excitement you might be feeling inside.

When you pull off a successful purchase, you can throw a house party, dance a jig in celebration and generally let your hair down. But when you're in company with the agent you're a *negotiator*—every moment! Privately, of course, very little has changed. The two sides of you are distinct and separate and should not overlap. The agent must never be made aware that you were prepared to pay a higher price.

It should be clear to you now that the negotiation process is a continuous one, beginning *before* the first contact with the agent and ending only when your business is concluded. In this process, as in life, you are *always* communicating, whether you like it or not;

whether you mean to or not. The silent (nonverbal) and spoken (verbal) messages you send out enable others to form perceptions of what type of person you are. We are all in this together. We categorize and classify people according to the messages we pick up, even over the telephone. And, as we saw earlier, this information is the basis on which we predict others' behavior, and how others predict ours. Buying real estate provides one of the best examples of this. Now that you are aware of it, you'll find many other examples in everyday living.

In any endeavor, when predictability threatens to disadvantage us, we have only two options, generally, for overcoming the problem. Total isolation or selective control of the messages we transmit. For those who can leave society behind, the first option might be the preferred solution. But for the rest of us, staying in control of the impressions we give off, and the perceptions we create by so doing, is the more practical answer. Especially for you, the homebuyer, whose dual goal is to protect your wealth while acquiring the home you want at the lowest price possible. And always with an air of courtesy.

## What Are the Agent's Real Needs?

Now, let's take the real estate agent's strategy of getting to know as much about you as possible, and turn it about face. Let's focus on their strongest needs and wants and those things that usually make them tick.

### Need One: To Sell Homes

First and foremost, real estate agents need to sell properties—to survive. Their job is a stressful one. Consequently, they're likely to be suffering a degree of anxiety and, almost always, urgency. At times even desperation. Sound familiar?

### Need Two: A Supply of Willing Buyers

They can never have enough buyers on their books. Almost invariably, the opposite is true; they're short of serious, qualified buyers. Often, in fact, they may have no more than one or two. That's contrary to the notion spread by agents that there are buyers around every corner waiting to pounce if you procrastinate.

### Need Three: A Monthly Quota

They probably have monthly sales quotas to meet. And at least 50 percent of the time they're likely to be behind quota. Yet even when they're ahead they're equally anxious to have the best month possible and pocket the extra income, which, mentally, might already be spent, or earmarked for a pending expense. Another sale might even put an agent in the running for salesperson of the month, or retire a debt. Agents need commission dollars *incessantly*.

### Need Four: Fresh Properties

Time is money to every agent. To devote energy to fresh properties, agents need to sell stock (homes) consistently. Stale properties—those that have been for sale longer than normal—become harder to sell and drain enthusiasm. This can lead agents into a rut, a kind of vicious circle—no enthusiasm, no sale; no sale, no enthusiasm. To be successful, agents must remain motivated, psyched up. Fresh properties, sales, and serious buyers do that for them.

### Need Five: To Get Sellers to Be Flexible

Despite their commitment and responsibility to the seller's interests, which the majority of agents take very seriously, their primary goal is to achieve a sale. For that reason, they will use their persuasion skills, when necessary, on the seller to get an offer accepted. They consider such action necessary when they fear losing a serious buyer and the sale (and, of course, the commission). Your aim should be to channel an agent's thinking in that direction. This is critical to your success, and something we'll explore in more detail shortly.

### Need Six: To Achieve a Reward

When agents have made an investment of time, energy, and effort in a homebuyer, they feel a compelling incentive to earn some reward. Up to a point, this need increases as the investment increases. Consequently, as time passes in discussion, negotiation, pondering, offer making and presentation on a particular home, your power increases; your position becomes stronger; and your chance of getting a better deal improves. In the vast majority of property negotiations this time investment is in your favor and can be very advantageous, provided the agent sees some likelihood of a sale. Some light at the end of the tunnel is needed to keep an agent motivated.

## Why the Agent—and the Seller—Need You More Than You Need Them

As we've just seen, the seller and the agent both have many compelling needs for making the sale. Typically, the seller's and the agent's need for money and income is more urgent than the buyer's need to purchase any particular home.

Has anyone selling real estate ever told you this? Not likely. It violates the rules under which agents work and is certainly not to their benefit. Yet, these are facts. And they put power in your hands.

Having this knowledge places a different complexion on things for an astute buyer. No longer are you the low man on the totem pole. From this point forward you are no longer simply hoping that the agent and seller will deem your offer worthy. Instead, you see your role as the problem solver, the person who is providing much-needed cash to the agent and seller; cash that will answer *their* financial needs and solve *their* other problems. In short: *They need you more than you need them.*

If you are beginning to sense a feeling of power, then count yourself among the elite and potentially most successful of home-buyers. And keep in mind, too, that the principle holds true in many other situations quite apart from homebuying. When you are exchanging money for assets or goods of any kind, you will generally be in the stronger position, despite what others might try to make you believe. As a buyer, you have the choice of spending your money in any number of ways—or not spending it at all. You have what financial people call *liquidity*. You have options because you have cash. The fact that the cash is being provided by your lender doesn't change a thing.

On the other hand, an owner with a home to sell usually has restricted flexibility and few options—until the asset is turned into cash. When the home proves hard to sell or sits on the market for a while or is rejected by a serious buyer because of condition, location, or price, the seller's perception of value lowers and the seller's power diminishes. The home doesn't have the same degree of desirability that was imagined. Consequently, price expectations drop.

Quite simply, value and price depend, ultimately, on you, the homebuyer. The factors we've discussed here put more control in your hands and guarantee you a stronger negotiating position.

Time to move on. Let's assume that all has gone well so far. You've inspected a selection of homes and have asked a series of questions about each but have divulged no potentially damaging clues about what has really impressed you. However, known only to you, you're very excited about one property. It grabbed your interest the minute you walked through the door. What do you do? How do you take the next critical step along the road to buying this home at the seller's lowest price? That's the subject of the next section.

## KEY POINTS TO REMEMBER

Now that we are into the negotiation proper, you will find a reminder list of key points, like this, at the ends of selected chapters. This feature will help you to recall and retain some of the most important points covered in the chapter and will make it easier for you to assimilate them into your thinking.

- Ask at least five similar key questions about every home you inspect.

- Stay in control of the verbal and nonverbal messages you transmit to the agent or seller.

- Even if you are very excited about a home, do not openly praise the property. Keep your enthusiasm to yourself while in the company of the agent or seller.

- Remember that agents have their own weekly and monthly agenda of personal and professional needs that they must strive constantly to satisfy. Their first need is to make sales.

- Remember, too, that agents and sellers in virtually every case, need you more than you need them. They need your money and they need the sale wrapped up, usually as quickly as possible. Until they get these things, they get nothing. You are in the strongest position of the three parties—but not until you realize it!

# CHAPTER SEVEN

# WHEN YOU FIND
# THE RIGHT HOME

*It takes two to make a bargain,*
*but only one gets it.*
            —ANONYMOUS

After showing you through a selection of homes, an agent will generally try to get you to talk about your likes and dislikes. The agent will want to know which home appeals to you most so that he or she can encourage your interest. But, for now, it's time to bid farewell—not a word about the home that, inside, is exciting you so much. An appropriate parting comment might be: *"Thank you for your help. There are other homes I plan to look at. If anything you've shown me feels like it's worth a second look, I'll give you a call."*

If you haven't already done so, your next step is to drive around the area in which the home you like is located and make sure you're happy with the immediate environment. It might soon become your home, so be certain it has the things that are important to you. Check the standard and condition of surrounding properties. Note the roads that carry heavy traffic. And locate amenities and schools if such things are relevant to your wants and needs.

If everything is to your satisfaction, let a day—maybe two— pass, then recontact the agent. Tell the agent, matter of factly, that you'd like a second look, making sure, again, to keep your enthusiasm in check. Here's an example: *"I don't remember some things about that house on Martello Court. I wonder if I could take another brief look?"*

It's inevitable, of course, that the agent will recognize this as an indication of interest. What the agent won't ever know—unless you say so, which you won't—is just *how* interested you are.

Don't let too much time pass between your first and second inspections. A minimum, though, would be 24 hours. Anything less could give away your true feelings.

As you go through the home again, you'll notice a lot more than you did the first time. I recommend that you make notes, now, of features, color schemes, and anything that grabs your attention (as we'll see later, these notes could give you a distinct advantage during negotiation). Mention to the agent that your notes help you in comparing homes that might interest you. Make it sound like something you do routinely.

This is also the time to ask again the questions you asked on your first inspection, perhaps phrasing them a little differently or asking to have your memory refreshed.

What is the asking price?

What is the owner's reason for selling?

How long has the seller owned the property?

How soon does the seller wish (or need) to close?

What repairs or upgrading have been carried out?

What about electric wiring condition? plumbing? roof? foundation? heating/cooling systems? insulation?

What problems or faults has the owner made you aware of?

How long have the tenants been living there (if home is rented)?

Add as many more questions as seem relevant, making sure you get specific answers each time.

The question: *"What faults has the owner made you aware of?"* puts pressure on the agent to reveal what they know, yet it's the one question most homebuyers *never* ask. Every home has faults—without exception. The agent will feel an obligation to tell you what faults the seller divulged. If the agent says they are aware of no faults, the agent will probably sound uninformed. This can create suspicion and apprehension in a buyer. Either way, it means points for you. But be careful to phrase the question as it appears here as, in this form, it is most effective.

When you ask the agent a question to which you anticipate a less-than-ideal response, stay alert for the unexpected. For example, you inquire when the electrical wiring was last inspected or renewed, anticipating that such work hasn't been done. But the agent surprises you with: *"That's an excellent question,"* (only because the agent has a good answer, of course). *"There are receipts showing that the wiring was completely replaced just six months ago."* Now it's time to bite your tongue and subdue any expression of pleasant surprise. As I see it, though, you still have two choices in responding.

A disinterested OK is appropriate but doesn't capture any advantage. "What advantage is there to capture?" you might wonder. Well, how about coming back with this: *"I guess the old wiring must have been causing problems. Has any damage been done internally to the walls or the insulation? Was there a fire? Do you know?"*

That's a very strong response, just when the agent was gloating. But see how the tables are turning? What the agent saw as a positive point has just evaporated. Now the agent is likely to have fewer definite answers at the ready. Just opinions, *which don't come with receipts—or guarantees.* The agent can't give assurances about what conditions exist in the walls of the home. Does the agent know there definitely hasn't been a fire? Probably not. Therefore, *"Not that I am aware of"* might be the strongest answer available, at least until the owner can be called.

The same tactic can be used for almost any repair that has been carried out. Even a repaired or replaced roof could be construed as work that became necessary not simply to stop water getting in, but to halt spreading damp and prevent further damage to internal timbers. In other words, how much damage was done before the repair was carried out? These are not easy questions for the agent to answer and can turn a point to your advantage, which, originally, looked like a point for the agent.

### Always Pleasant—Never Naive!

This is the perfect place to stress again the importance of having developed an amicable, personal relationship with the agent. If you haven't done this, your comments might be taken as mildly contentious by agents having touchy personalities. However, in the context of an amicable relationship, your concerns will be viewed as legitimate and understandable.

That is one reason you've built a collaborative relationship with the agent from the outset (one in which you are both seeking a mutually beneficial outcome) rather than a combative relationship (win or lose, head-to-head opponents). Behind all this, the negotiator inside you knows well that the agent is indeed your opponent, by virtue of two simple facts. First, the agent is pledged to the seller to get the highest price possible. And second, the more the agent gets *you* to pay, the more dollars the agent keeps.

But remember, too, that what you *know* and what you *do* are not the same. You know the agent's objective is the highest price and that yours is the opposite. Your strategy, though, for getting the home at the lowest price, is based on you ensuring you do not *treat* the agent like an opponent. In short, you take steps to avoid building an opponent relationship.

By allowing the relationship to develop along the lines I suggest, you are practicing the principles of good negotiation. Your skills are sharp; you're alert and your armor is in place. But it's always subtle. You do nothing to make the agent and seller aware that they are dealing with a skillful negotiator. That is the environment that will give you the best chance of success.

Remember, one of the foundations of winning negotiation is being able to control the perceptions of the other side. When you follow these suggestions, the agent will be unaware that you are negotiating with a powerful strategy. Most likely, the agent will think of you as a naturally careful, discriminating buyer. That makes your task easier.

When the excitement of finding the home you want to buy threatens to lower your defenses, you might find it helpful to keep in mind this motto: Always pleasant—never naive!

### Time—Making It Work for You

At some point on your second or third inspection you'll decide that you are definitely interested in owning the home, or that it's not quite right for you. In the first case, your thoughts will start focusing on how much you might offer and what price you might eventually be able to buy it for. But your best move now is to slow up. Then, when you decide to make an offer, keep two points in mind, both concerning time:

1. Allow at least one hour for the inspection as you stroll from room to room. Look at things twice or three times, then go back and look again if you need to. If this is going to be your home, you want to know what you're getting.

2. If you decide to make an offer on the home, wait until you have left the property before telling the agent.

Let's look at what's behind these tactics. As a negotiator, you gain a definite advantage when you get the other side to invest substantial time. The more time invested, the greater your advantage. The agent's time is valuable but is generally given willingly to a serious, qualified buyer, which, of course, you are.

The longer the agent spends showing you the property, finding answers to your questions, getting their own questions answered, and generally working to bring about a sale, the more the agent stands to lose should you decide not to buy the home. Naturally, as an astute homebuyer, you dropped a few comments about one or two *other* very attractive homes you've seen, and how they compare. As we saw earlier, the agent must *never* be allowed to know that any one home is the only one that interests you. At the same time, don't kill the agent's enthusiasm by making it seem there is little if any chance of making the sale. Again, balance is required. And a little baiting.

If you mention twice that you are looking seriously at a few options, that should be sufficient. The agent isn't likely to forget.

As you meander around the interior and exterior of the home, the agent might become anxious or even a little impatient. That's fine. In fact, it plays right into your hands. The anxiety comes from smelling a probable sale (chances are the commission has been calculated already). If the agent seems impatient, it may be due to another appointment or some other commitment. None of that is particularly relevant to you. Your aim is to control time to the point that it serves your interest best.

If the agent has "a pressing engagement" and cannot give you any more time for your inspection, suggest the agent call in and have a colleague stand in for them. If that's not feasible, say you'd like to come back again to complete your assessment. At that point, the agent's most likely response will be to ask what is causing your indecision. You reply that there are a couple of things you are unsure about (list a few items that you have questioned, such as wiring, plumbing, noise, lack of brightness, small kitchen) and that there's another home that compares closely and that you find attractive, but that will sell at a lower price. In other words, there's competition for your money. But you are, nonetheless, interested.

The anticipation and uncertainty this puts into the agent's mind benefits you all the way through the negotiation proper. The agent believes there's still a good chance to make the sale, but only by working hard to remove the obstacles. This message will be carried to the seller, along with your offer.

Throughout this stage, stay focused on the fact that the agent is very anxious—even desperate—for a sale, a point we covered earlier, and that the seller is probably just as anxious, if not more so. Most of the options are in your hands. The agent is in the middle and earns not a dime for the time invested in you—until you buy. The seller wants to unload the home. Meanwhile, time is going by for both, which is negative. Conversely, you are making time work for you, which is positive.

However the agent deals with the time you demand for a second, third, or fourth inspection, there comes a point when you *must* communicate your interest in making an offer. But, it's a good idea to let *the agent* initiate the idea and do the work. Here's what I mean.

## Crawl and Stall Before Making an Offer

As your interest becomes obvious, anticipation will prompt the agent, sooner or later, to encourage you to make an offer. That's how it should be—rather than *you* suggesting it. A little reluctance on your part will make an offer—any offer—more valuable when you are "convinced" to make one. The agent's "accomplishment" takes some of the emphasis off the size of the offer and puts it on the fact that he or she actually succeeded in getting you to make an offer.

After you've deflected earlier indirect suggestions, the agent is likely to come straight out and ask you to make an offer. For example: *"It's a beautiful home and definitely won't last. I'd strongly suggest you make an offer today."* Or, *"I'll be speaking with the owner tonight. What kind of offer had you in mind?"* In either case, you respond the same: *"I'm really not sure what I'll do. The decision is very hard. I'll think about it and let you know."*

At this stage, having left the house, you'll have to tolerate the agent recounting all the fine features of the home and how it represents excellent value. You simply listen, showing little emotion, agreement, or concern. Eventually, they'll get to the pressure—not heavy-handed, just subtle pressure. You'll be cautioned that if you procrastinate you risk losing the home to another buyer. It could be gone tomorrow. Maybe you'll be told that if you don't act immediately, one of the other buyers who has shown an interest is likely to snatch it away.

Of course, there's always some risk, when you procrastinate like this, but it's rarely worth worrying about, except in a very hot real estate market when there's a buying frenzy.

You'll recall what I said about this agent tactic. The *other* interested buyers are almost always phony. They're created to scare you into making decisions quicker than is in your best interest. Unfortunately, this tactic sometimes pressures unwitting buyers not only into making *quick* decisions, but into making *wrong* decisions. Our psychological and emotional nature means we are all potentially vulnerable in such situations. We desire a thing more when someone else is trying to beat us to it or take it from us. Much of today's advertising is based on this phenomenon.

Here's another example of how the agent might apply the *don't lose it* tactic:

> Agent:   *If you've got a genuine interest in this home, I feel bound to let you know there is another serious buyer who might decide to put an offer on it today.*

A variation is this:

> Agent:   *Look folks, I'd hate to see you lose out on this home. I have to tell you there's a couple who is really keen on it and is checking on finances before making an offer. To be safe, I'd advise you to make an offer now.*

These signals should cause you no panic. Instead, they should make you smile inwardly, as they indicate an agent who is hungry and likely to be just as resourceful in getting the seller to agree to a lower-than-expected price.

Here's how I recommend you respond to this agent tactic:

> Buyer:   *I appreciate you letting us know. But we're the kind of people who make decisions carefully and slowly. If someone else buys this home, I say good luck to them. We have a couple of other homes we like also.*

Or, an alternative:

> Buyer:   *Well, if someone beats us to this one, it'll sure make our decision easier.*

How can the agent respond to statements like these? Except, perhaps, by asking if a lower price, or some other concession, would make your decision easier. Or, perhaps by suggesting you make an offer lower than the asking price (which, of course, is the only kind of offer a smart buyer would make). The agent might go on to assure you that they could possibly get the owner to consider an offer, say, $3,000 below the asking price. If any such concessions are suggested by the agent, your crawling and stalling have worked just fine.

If the agent makes no such suggestions, don't fret. You haven't yet played any of your trump cards. All you've done, so far, is dealt yourself a superior hand, which you have yet to play. And, because of the control you've exercised, the agent has no way of being sure of what's in that hand. Or in your mind.

## How to Make an Offer

Let's assume you've found the home you want to buy. It has all the qualities and features you desire and is listed for sale at $178,500. (When I use *offer* here, I am referring to what is often called, more correctly, a *purchase offer*.)

To illustrate a number of relevant principles, I'll give you a brief but exact account of a purchase I handled for my local bank manager. Whether your budget is higher or lower than this figure is insignificant. The principles do not change. As we examine what happened, I'll add comments that will make things clearer. Then, later, to illustrate different points, we'll look at other case studies. You might find it beneficial to read the examples a couple of times before proceeding, giving special attention to the explanatory comments.

First, here's an introduction to the banker's situation. He and his wife (let's call them Mr. and Mrs. Mellon) had inspected the house just once, two days before seeking my assistance. They informed me that this home was one they'd admired for some time, and they were ready to move because their home was too big since their family had grown and left.

My first question to them was: *"Is this a home you MUST have?"* In other words, did they *need* this house—period? Or only if the price was right and represented the best value available? (They also had some interest, I discovered, in at least one other home they had seen.) Had this been a must-have situation, my power as a negotiator would have been diminished. Any time you must have something so strongly that you cannot accept the possibility of not having it, you are not in a position to negotiate most powerfully.

Luckily, the Mellons said they would be very excited about owning the home, but it wasn't a must-have. That gave me the green light.

By the way, a word of caution: A property that seems like a must-have in the beginning can turn out to be something less on a second or third inspection. In the excitement of discovery, the alternatives, which are always there, are often not obvious. New properties come on the market every day. Often, when you miss one, you find another that is *more* appealing. Consequently, my advice on must-haves is to be certain that's what it really is.

If you are absolutely convinced you cannot live without a particular home and are prepared to pay whatever it takes—don't!

Slow down. You can still negotiate using the principles in this book. You'll just have to tread a little more cautiously and be prepared to compromise earlier than you might otherwise do. You might not be in a position to hold out for the seller's lowest price, but that doesn't mean you can't save money, even a substantial amount. Just be certain the agent and seller don't get even a whiff of how excited you are inside.

Now, let's get back to the Mellons and see what happened. Watch for a number of tactics we covered earlier. Remember, this is an actual, though condensed, account.

### Case Study: Making Money for a Banker

Before inspecting the home, I checked with a few local real estate sources and read catalogs, newspapers, and brochures for an understanding of values in the area. Armed with that information, I called three local agents and gathered more details. Eventually I had a good picture of real estate in the neighborhood in question. Next, I went into a branch of a bank not far from the home and asked to speak with the manager about buying real estate locally. Within two minutes I was in her office. I explained that I was acting on behalf of a friend who was planning to invest in local property and asked her to give me accurate details of the neighborhood housing over the past few years—values, prices, sales, and anything else she could provide. It was very much in the bank's interest to assist me, as my client represented prospective business. Naturally, I pointed this out (and later recommended the bank to my client). The manager gave me all the help I needed and even some I didn't expect.

I discovered that prices were static; they had hardly moved at all in the previous 12 months. Surrounding neighborhoods had experienced slight decreases in prices in the same period and the number of sales was lower all around. Properties were taking longer to sell because people were buying in less expensive neighborhoods or not at all. In short, it wasn't hard to figure out that local real estate salespeople weren't exactly having a party.

As I drove to the property, I contemplated the advantages that would serve me well when the negotiation got under way. When we met, I instructed Mr. and Mrs. Mellon, in private, not to communicate anything, verbal or otherwise, that would alert the agent to their feelings. The agent began by pointing out the features and providing other relevant details, then left us to wander about from room to room while he kept a polite distance.

The house was about 25 years old and had undergone repairs and alterations. I asked six or seven questions concerning the work that had been done and, as expected, the agent did his best to answer, assuring me that he believed everything had been done to professional standards. I informed the agent we'd keep the house in mind, along with two others we'd seen; that we had a few yet to look at; and that we'd give the whole matter consideration over the next few days. Then, without any lead up, I asked: *"What's the reason for the sale?"* He hesitated momentarily as I stood silently staring at him. The couple, Mr. and Mrs. Smith, had lived in the home for eight years, he told me, and Mrs. Smith had accepted a promotion to her company's head office in another state, where they had *already* purchased a new home.

That was more information than I expected, more than he had to provide. Incidentally, had I suspected he had been less than completely truthful in his answer, my next move would have been to talk with a few of the sellers' neighbors. After a few short, friendly discussions about the street and immediate neighborhood, I'd have learned as much as I needed to know about why the Smiths were selling.

Next, I asked the agent: *"How soon do they wish to close?"* This time he was more guarded *"What would suit you best?"* he responded, answering my question with a question. (Remember, when you ask a specific question, insist on getting specific answers, not generalizations or rebounding questions.) No ingenuity was needed to figure that the sellers would be anxious for a quick close, seeing how they had already bought another home. A definite sale would take a lot of weight off their shoulders and allow their plans to progress unhindered.

My response to the agent's question was: *"We're not certain at this stage. How long has the home been for sale?"* Again, the agent hesitated, then gave me a less than satisfactory reply: *"Um ... I think about three months."* I was sure that was an understatement, but it made little difference. Even after three months, any sellers would be anxious, particularly those on the verge of a long-distance move.

As we prepared to leave, I mentioned again that we were potentially interested in a couple of homes, including the Smith's, and that we'd be in touch.

The agent then employed a tactic to close the sale: *'Folks,'* he said, *"there are always good homes on the market but I think you'll agree, this one is unique. It certainly won't remain on the market much longer. In fact, I know one of our offices is taking a second inspection on it this afternoon. I know you'll have noticed that there's absolutely no work to do. You could just move straight in and enjoy it."*

Then came a bolt out of the blue. Mr. Mellon, the prospective buyer, had been a good student and a keen observer. Without the slightest giveaway, he said: *"Well, what you say is right. It's just that my wife would prefer to create our own decor. We'd have to change all the carpeting here and a lot of the more masculine decor, to suit our furniture. Apart from that we like it."*

The agent didn't respond immediately to Mr. Mellon's points, so I interrupted his thoughts with another question: *"What, did you say, is the asking price on this?"* He responded: *"It's for sale at $178,500. But I think the owners would consider an offer close to that."*

We then concluded our business for that day.

When the agent left, we reassessed the situation. The Mellons now wanted the home even more than before. The seller, we had learned, needed a definite sale, as soon as possible. The agent, in desperation, had even suggested a lower offer and was very keen to make the sale. We had shown no anxiety, urgency, or emotional attachment. Things were looking good.

Two days later we made a third inspection, at which time the agent didn't seem as enthusiastic, probably because his expectation of a sale had been dampened by our previous contact. That's exactly what our strategy had been designed to achieve. Also, his investment of time was growing. On this occasion he made no mention of any other buyers interested in the home (I'm sure you know why). After about 30 minutes, we decided it was time to start the negotiation process proper and to talk serious figures, and maybe even close the deal.

Here is what transpired. I've kept the accounts as short and as readable as possible, though still accurate in important details.

After the third inspection, with the agent still inside the home, the Mellons and I stood close to our car in the driveway. This was deliberate on my part, an 'exiting' tactic similar to standing up, putting on your coat and walking toward the door. That's the point at which concessions and deals are very frequently made. In this case, the agent approached us and the following exchange took place.

Buyer:  *In the next day or two we'll buy one of three homes that offer us what we want. We have no finance problems. If we made an offer on this home, how soon would you present it to the owner?*

Agent:  *Right away, this evening. What offer do you have in mind?*

Remember, he's not expecting full price. He already suggested a lower offer during our second inspection.

Buyer:    *We'll need an answer by tonight. We'll write up an offer for $153,500.*

Agent:    *Thank you for the offer but I know the owners would not accept that figure.*

Buyer:    *What offers have the owners had since the home went on the market?*

Agent:    *I don't believe there have been any offers. None they could accept. But that's common. It doesn't reflect negatively on the home. It's a top quality property, I'm sure you'll agree.*

Naturally, I wasn't about to add to his praises of the home at this point.

Buyer:    *In my estimation, the home is in reasonable condition. But, compared with other homes we're considering, it's not worth what they are asking for it. If it was, it would have sold by now.*

By referring to the price "they" (the owners) are asking, you help the agent to distance them from the price. It's not referred to as "their" price; therefore they feel less compelled to defend it in the same way or to the same extent as they would if it was "theirs."

Agent:    *Would you be prepared to make an offer around $170,000? I feel I might have a chance of getting that through for you.*

I deduced from this that the agent was reasonably sure the owners would accept that figure of $170,000. But, was it likely to be their lowest acceptable price? I certainly didn't think so, though we were making good progress.

Buyer:    *We're not prepared to pay more than we believe the home is worth. I'd like you to present our offer of $153,500. If they say no, that's fine; we'll consider our other options. By the way, the owners need have no fear. We're genuine buyers with a cash deposit we can put down straight away.*

The agent agreed, somewhat reluctantly, to write up the purchase offer at $153,500. We would close in 120 days, we told him, knowing that this *wasn't* what the owners preferred. My clients, the

Mellons, were willing to close much sooner and were in a position to do so without any inconvenience. My tactic, though, in looking for this 120 day close was to gain an advantage I could concede later. You'll see how this unfolded.

Another tactic I used was to have the agent insert a written expiry clause in the offer. The clause read simply: This offer is made at eleven A.M. on September 15, 1993. If the sellers' response is not communicated to the undersigned by midnight on September 15, 1993, it will be automatically withdrawn and become void at that time.

This compelled the agent to move quickly. Of course, it also encouraged the owners not to sit around for days thinking it over. Notice, too, that it didn't say the owners had to accept the offer, just that they had to respond in one way or another before the deadline, if negotiation was to continue.

A deadline for a seller's response is usually a good idea. But this one was unusually tight, just thirteen hours. Possibly too tight for many sellers—24 hours is more reasonable. Occasionally, even longer is justified, especially when one of the sellers is not local (for example, where a divorced couple are joint sellers or where an inherited home is being sold by the beneficiaries).

At 7:30 p.m. the agent called asking if he could come around to talk to us. The sellers, he told us, had sent back a counter offer. (A *counter offer* means that the seller is saying no to the price or terms offered, or both, but is keen to keep discussions going and, consequently, is suggesting a compromise.) When he arrived, he lapsed immediately into an impassioned monologue about the super-human effort he had used to convince the sellers to be as reasonable as they could possibly be. He went on to assure us that the figure they had sent back to us was considerably lower than their hereto-fore bottom price. (He was a wonderful guy.)

Their counter offer was this: They would accept $167,500, an $11,000 reduction from their original $178,500. On the purchase offer, our figure of $153,500 had been crossed out and in its place, for our acceptance, was $167,500. Also, they had changed our 120 days closing time to 45 days. After speaking privately with the Mellons, I informed the agent that *neither* change was acceptable to us and that we'd have to conclude our business there and then. Unless, that was, there was a way *he* knew to bring the deal together. We restated our view that the property, in our opinion, was overpriced and that was the reason it had sat on the market so long. And, at $167,500, we felt it was still overpriced compared with the alternatives we had. Here's how the dialogue continued:

Agent:   *What do you believe is a fair price, bearing in mind everything this home offers and its excellent condition?*

Buyer:   *Based on what we've seen in today's market—not six
months or a year ago, probably $156,000 to $157,000. Anyway, it's too costly for us to settle in 45 days. It means a
loss of interest income on term deposits that would have to
be cashed in, meaning we'd be paying an even higher price.*

Agent:   *Folks, as you know well, all the best agreements are based
on compromise. The owners have been very generous. What
do you say we re-submit the offer halfway between your figure and the owner's figure of $167,500? That's $162,500. I
have no way of knowing if the owners would accept that
low a figure but I'm willing to try. It's worth a try, don't
you agree?*

With a show of reluctance and finality, I agreed to increase the
offer to $159,500—a much bigger jump than I would normally rec-
ommend, but I was guided in this decision by my client's judgment.
However, we declined to accept the owner's 45 days closing and left
our 120 days unchanged. The agent left, promising to contact us
within an hour.

At 9 p.m., he called once again, asking if he could come back
over. We agreed. At this point, he was genuinely looking haggard.
His investment of time and effort was growing with each hour that
passed. But, he was a professional. And he smelled a deal in the air,
as, I suspected, did the sellers.

We still had an ace up our sleeves, though, so we weren't anywhere near the end of our negotiating power. We knew with certainty now that a closing earlier than the 120 days we'd offered was
something the owners badly wanted. Perhaps it was even vital to
their plans. The Mellons were flexible concerning the closing, so we
still had something we could concede. However, at this stage, they
were getting nervous we'd lose the deal altogether. I didn't think
that was likely, but I understood their concern.

The agent laid out the new counter offer. Our figure of $159,500
had been rejected and in its place was $165,000 (the owners had
dropped another $2,500, from $167,500). Our 120 days had been
crossed out again and back came 45 days.

I wasn't surprised by anything that had happened so far.
Although much of my later negotiation work has been with higher-
priced residences and increasingly with non–real estate corporate
contracts, there are always common factors involved; always signs

and signals that can be recognized. And almost always there are feelings that are complex and don't lend themselves to easy descriptions. All these together provide a means for assessing how much to push, when to ease up, when to make a concession, and how likely an agreement is. This is knowledge we acquire automatically—knowledge we call on every day in many different activities and tasks. But we seldom stop to think about it. Negotiation is no different in that way.

Despite the late hour, I felt we were close to an agreement in this case. The sellers were clearly anxious, and everyone's anticipation was heightened. My experience warned me that a deal would have to be struck *now*, in this atmosphere. If I let things cool down, or gave the owners too much time, they could easily think themselves out of any offer we left them with to consider. There could be no sleeping on it. That was certain.

I took the offer document from the agent, stared at it silently for a full two minutes, then handed it back to him. I said nothing. His face dropped. His eyes begged for an acceptance. Or, at least, another offer. The silence seemed endless. Even Mr. Mellon was bemused, despite the warning I had given him about how I might react. I let the silence linger for a few more barely tolerable seconds. Here's how the deal concluded:

> Buyer:    *We'd like to write a new purchase offer. This is the final offer we'll make. It'll be valid only until 10:30 p.m. We won't accept a counter offer. Either it's accepted as we write it or our business is over. We'll make a new offer of $161,000—not one dollar more. However, we'll agree to the owners' 45 day closing.*

I wasn't sure from the agent's expression what he was thinking. I emphasized again that it was our final offer—we wouldn't make another one. Dare I say it, it was now "take it or leave it." That's what I wanted to communicate to the sellers.

Did I mean it? Well, this game of negotiation is based, as we saw in earlier chapters, on perception. I created the perception that I meant what I said. That was enough. That's the answer.

By 10:15 p.m., the Mellons had bought the home at $161,000 with a closing in 45 days. They saved $17,500, and were thrilled with the outcome. Did we achieve the sellers' lowest acceptable price? No doubt we did well, but I feel we might have done better, though not that much better.

Let's look at another case study with different factors involved.

### Case Study: Saving $30,000 on a $210,000 Home

Negotiating on behalf of a buyer for the purchase of a private residence has special rewards regardless of the amount of money involved. Usually, a home purchase consumes some or all of a buyer's life savings. This case study is just such a case.

A couple I had met previously, Eli and Ben Robinson, asked me to assist with their goal to buy a particularly attractive Victorian house that had recently been renovated completely by the owner. They had arranged to meet a local real estate agent at the property, which was for sale at $210,000. I agreed to accompany them, after explaining how I would approach the matter. Then, I spent 20 minutes with them, before we met with the agent, and went over some of the basic principles of what to do and not to do during the inspection. And, generally, how to play it cool. I told them I knew the neighborhood very well and was familiar with local real estate prices.

The Robinsons had a maximum budget of $180,000 and, from the beginning, were very pessimistic about their chances for getting the home. Nonetheless, they liked it so much they felt almost anything was worth a try.

According to the agent's data sheet, the home, on the fringe of the city, was standing on a small block measuring 42 feet by 100 feet, making a total lot area of 4200 square feet. We found the entire house to be in excellent condition and were very impressed. Not a hint of our excitement, of course, ever reached the agent, who was a very experienced lady and very proud of the home. She stated she saw no problem in achieving a price at, or very close to, the asking price, though there had been no offers so far.

But that wasn't quite the way I saw it. My research with regard to nearby sales had been very productive. I was able to compile a list of homes, some very comparable, that had sold in the previous two to three months. Everything indicated to me that the owner was asking $15,000 to $20,000 above the fair market value, which, in my estimation, was between $190,000 and $195,000; certainly not the $210,000 list price.

A neighbor told me the home had been for sale for between three and four months, despite the fact that properties were selling quite well throughout the area. That gave me an insight into how the owner must have been feeling. We let a couple of days pass before arranging a second inspection. In that time, Eli and Ben found another home that interested them in an adjoining neighborhood but it would remain a definite second choice. There was no question that they still wanted the Victorian-style home, but only if they could get it for not one dollar more than $180,000, which, as I indicated earlier, was every cent they had to spend.

From the beginning, the agent had pushed us to make an offer. She even suggested a figure of between $200,000 and $210,000, stating that "$205,000 might just buy it." She'd do her best, she assured us, to get the owner to accept that price, but couldn't guarantee that he would.

Here's how it continued:

Buyer:   *I have a list of homes that have sold in the area during the past three months, along with descriptions and selling prices. These details and my own knowledge of the area suggest that the owner of this home has overpriced his property.*

Notice here again that the agent isn't made to look responsible for the price on the home. We don't want to provoke a defensive reaction, as that would only create division and a bigger obstacle. The way my statement was presented, her competence wasn't questioned.

Agent:   *It might well be a little high. The owner will look at an offer, though. He has purchased a home in the country. Still, it's hard to find a home to compare with this; I'm sure you'll agree. A couple of similar homes sold for around $200,000 not so long ago.*

Buyer:   *I understand what you are saying—the property is unusual. But a 70-year old renovated home wouldn't interest the majority of homebuyers. We're looking at another property this afternoon. It's very impressive and has a lower price than this. And there's also a third home not far from here. Whatever we decide, we'll buy within the week.*

Agent:   *Why don't you make an offer on this and I'll see if I can get it through for you. Maybe the owner would accept $200,000. Would you buy it if you could get it for $200,000?*

Buyer:   *We won't make an offer above what we believe the home is worth. If we decide to make a written offer today, can you guarantee you'll take it to the owner today and get an answer right away?*

Agent:   *Certainly, I'll present it to the owner myself this evening. What offer do you have in mind?*

Buyer:   *I believe the home is worth $168,500. I'm prepared to offer that.*

Agent:   *The owner would never consider selling for that. I'm sorry; it's way too low.*

Buyer:   *But you are prepared to present it to him, as you said. Aren't you?*

When a home has been for sale for three or four months, especially in an active market, and has attracted no offers, the agent who listed the home will usually try to get the owner to drop the price. The objective is to prevent the home from sitting on the market and becoming stale, (which makes it harder to sell). The best evidence an agent can use in persuading an owner to reduce the price of his home is legitimate offers from qualified buyers. The agent can then advise the owner that "this is what the market is saying. We should listen." The alternative, the agent argues, is to stick with the original price, in which case the property languishes on the market and starts to look suspect when others are selling.

This logic is usually valid. The more realistically priced a property, the sooner it sells and the sooner the agent pockets a commission. In our case study, I figured the agent was contemplating such a move, which was one reason I picked such a low first offer of $168,500. I had no expectation of it being accepted. But, as you know by now, that's all part of negotiating.

Before we return to our case study, here's a critical point, one you should do whatever is necessary to remember. *Whenever you are negotiating to buy a home, the first figure you offer will generally determine the price you will eventually pay.* The same is true for anything for which you typically negotiate. For example, let's say you are negotiating for a car that has a price tag of $10,650 and you make a first offer of $10,000. What have you really done? Instantly, you have eliminated any chance of buying the car below that figure. It's possible the seller would have accepted $9,200. Or $8,900. But you'll never know, because you made too high a first offer. Now, you are locked in to paying at least $10,000, probably more.

You influence and arrive at a seller's lowest acceptable price *by working UP to it!* Keep this principle indelibly in your thinking. You can never go down from your first offer. Only up. So, start low. And increase your offer by small amounts, each time with a show of reluctance. Remember, also, that the seller and the agent both realize the opposite is true for them. They can never go up—only down—

from the asking price. That's why it is often set higher than is justified in the first place.

Let's return to our case study now and see how the deal developed. Remember, the asking price was $210,000 and my first offer was $168,500. You'll recall also that my estimate of the home's value was $190,000 to $195,000.

The agent's response later that day was pretty much as expected:

Agent:    *I'm sorry; I couldn't get the owner to send back a counter offer. Your offer is just far too low. He did say, though, that if you make a reasonable offer he'll give it consideration.*

This wasn't as complete a rejection as it might at first seem. There was no counter offer but here was a slight sign of hope. What had the owner in mind when he said he'd consider a 'reasonable' offer? Now we had to find out.

Buyer:    *I consider $168,500 a fair and genuine offer based on what has sold in the area. I'm not sure we'll make another offer for this property but we'll think it over and call you.*

Agent:    *Would you be prepared to offer $198,000, or even $196,000? I think there's a chance he might consider that kind of figure. The home is well worth that.*

Now, I was sure the agent had tried to get the seller to reduce his price. From what the agent said, I concluded the owner had probably indicated he would accept $200,000. I had no way of being sure of that, but I was sure of two other things. I had become even more convinced that my own estimate of value ($190,000 to $195,000) was, if anything, the maximum the house was worth. And I knew, also, that the Robinsons had not one dollar more than $180,000. After consulting with the couple, I continued the negotiation.

Buyer:    *OK, we're prepared to make one more offer. If it's not accepted, we'll just let it go. And, once again, I'd like it written out and presented immediately. We don't want any delay that might cause us to lose out on another home we're interested in.*

I made my second offer at $171,500, an increase of just $3,000, despite the fact that the seller and I were—on paper, at least— $41,500 apart ($210,000 less $168,500).

The agent phoned later to tell us that the owner had rejected our offer. But, this time, had sent back a counter offer at $190,000. The agent insisted there was no more flexibility in the price. This was his bottom price. The way the negotiation had gone had built up some anticipation of a sale in both the agent and the seller. But it was time for a new tactic.

Incidentally, note the seller's first concession on price—$20,000 (from $210,000 to $190,000)—a bad move strategically for him. It signalled very clearly that he knew his asking price was way over the top. Or, that he believed he would not now achieve that figure. I also read from that move that he was becoming motivated to sell.

The new tactic we adopted was a powerful one—time. We did absolutely nothing for four or five days. During that time, the agent, who had worked very hard for the sale, phoned three times to ask if we planned to respond to the owner's counter offer of $190,000. Each time, our answer was the same: We were considering putting an offer on another home. In a desperate valiant attempt, she "pressured" us to make one final offer. That is exactly what we wanted her to do. Eventually, we did. Here's what transpired:

Buyer: *We're willing to give it one last try. If this fails we'll walk away from the property. As I said before, we won't pay more than we believe the home is worth. Our final offer is $173,500 and we'll agree to any close that suits the seller, once it's over 30 days. That's it. We'd like an answer today. If we don't hear from you by 4 p.m., consider the offer withdrawn. Our deadline for the other home is that tight.*

Some hours later, the answer came back—another rejection. This time it was a counter offer from the seller at $186,500. He had conceded another $3,500 and I felt there was more to go.

Despite our earlier threat to walk away, we "allowed" the agent to talk us into making a fourth offer. But, this time, we assured her we would definitely buy the "other" home the following day. I gave the agent full details of the second home the Robinsons liked, which she could verify, if she wished (something I rarely do, but in this case the interest was genuine). At this point, our chances of buying the house for $180,000 or less didn't appear very good. Still, we could only guess what was going on in the seller's mind. We were making progress and had one or two tactics yet to play.

Our fourth offer was $176,000, an increase of $2,500. We emphasized to the agent that we were now losing interest and weren't even certain we were being wise making this fourth offer. One way or the other, we stressed, it's our final try. Take it or leave it—not one dollar more. We inserted a conditional clause on this newly written offer stating that it would expire at noon the following day, at which time it would be automatically withdrawn.

The agent knew well she had to work extremely hard to save the sale. If she failed, all her work would have been in vain. Everything now had reached a true climax, and we were all aware of the fact. So too, we suspected, was the seller.

At 11 a.m. the following day the agent called me and had this to say:

Agent:    *I have a very good—exceptionally good—deal to offer you. I spent two hours convincing the owner to give it one more try. The owner will accept $180,000. He's being more than reasonable. It's a fantastic price. Bear in mind, he's come down $30,000. You can't ask for more than that, etc., etc.*

We signed the papers at $180,000 and bought the property—a full $30,000 below the asking price. As you can imagine, the Robinsons were thrilled. Had I been negotiating on my own behalf, I would have seriously considered sending back another offer, probably around $177,000 or $178,000. My assumption would have been that a seller who was prepared to accept $180,000 would be unlikely to turn away a definite sale for one or two thousand dollars. That's a small sum, but in my view, still worth negotiating for. However, the couple made the decision and they got a great deal on a beautiful home.

Let's return to the principle of making a low first offer and increasing it very gradually. And let's examine why it worked so well for the Robinsons.

### The Importance of Making Your First Offer a Low One

Here's a question you might like to ponder. What if our first offer in this case had been, say, $175,000? How would you have rated our chances of buying at $180,000? Not very good, I'm sure you'll agree. And here's why: *The seller's thinking is always conditioned by the size of the first offer made by the buyer.* As is the agent's.

The process of making a low offer and increasing in small increments takes up the agent's and the seller's time and shapes their expectations. Consequently, their focus moves from how "much" they might get for the property and goes to what they might have to accept. The seller begins distinguishing between lower *actual* figures (reality) and higher *imaginary* figures (unreality). The longer this continues, the greater the degree of compromise they are likely to make.

A low first offer from an obviously genuine buyer tells the seller something else very clearly, that the seller is going to have to compromise to make the sale. Before this point, many sellers have inflated, and often unrealistic, expectations. And while it's true that the seller always has the option of rejecting an offer and breaking off negotiation, in practice it's seldom that simple. Sellers need to sell. Usually, more than buyers need to buy. Letting a genuine, qualified buyer slip away is a mistake a seller can often regret later, regardless of how low the buyer's first offer might have been.

As far as sellers and agents are concerned, there are never enough homebuyers. It is also true to say that because buyers hold what sellers and agents both need (cash), the buyer is usually in the strongest position of the three parties. The problem, and it can be a costly one, is that the typical homebuyer seldom realizes this fact.

However, it's not enough simply to make your first offer lower than you believe the seller will accept. (By the way, it can't be so low as to be totally unreasonable. There's nothing to be gained by, say, offering $85,000 on a home priced at $140,000.) Be sure, too, to *state your justification* for your low offer (the price of comparable homes, for example, your estimate of the home's value based on other factors, or the limit of your budget). And, when you do agree to increase your offer, do so with a show of reluctance. Better yet, let the agent "talk you into" a higher offer. Never agree without requiring some convincing. And don't ever make it known that you planned to make a second higher offer anyway. Such an admission would defeat your credibility and possibly irreparably damage your chance of buying at the seller's lowest price.

Remember, increasing your offer substantially in one move works against your interests. In fact, it's dangerous. It signals that you are simply trying your luck and suggests that further rejections by the seller will prompt you to make even larger offers. Along with that, it defeats any argument you might have used to justify your lower offer and, therefore, damages your credibility.

Although this saving of $30,000 on a $210,000 home is achievable, it isn't likely to happen as frequently as homebuyers would wish. Nonetheless, it illustrates the principle of creeping up with your offers, and the benefits to be gained from the tactic. You'll recall that my first offer was $168,500, a full $41,500 below the asking price of $210,000. My second offer closed that gap only slightly, an increase of just $3,000. Had I increased my first offer by, say, $10,000 or more, I would clearly have thrown away the advantage gained from creeping.

There are a couple of good lessons behind this point. A $10,000 increase would have set a size precedent for any further increases I might have made. The negotiation would very likely have broken down had I followed that $10,000 with, say, a $1,000 or $2,000 increase.

Another drawback has to do with your budget. A big increase communicates to the other side that you are nowhere near your spending limit—that you have a lot more spending power in reserve. This weakens, and sometimes destroys, the effectiveness of the No More Money tactic, which can be very useful in the later stages of a negotiation.

More than any other mistake, though, when you increase your offer by a large amount you present yourself as an unknowledgeable buyer, which leaves you vulnerable and can prove very costly.

Let's put what we've covered here into two short rules:

1.  When you increase an offer, show reluctance, procrastinate, and hint at the fact that you might just forget the whole idea. The mood you communicate should be one of seriousness and uncertainty.

2.  Regardless of how far apart you and the seller are, increase your offers by small amounts. And try to make your increases progressively smaller. It's better not to do in one jump what can be done in three or more smaller jumps.

## Protect Yourself Legally

In the beginning of this book, I stressed that my objective was not to provide you with legal advice. It always makes sense to consult an attorney before entering into any contract to purchase real estate. If you don't have one (or, perhaps, even if you do), shop around. Ask at your bank for referrals, talk to friends, or call a buyer broker or a real estate company (not the one you are dealing with). If all else fails, look through your local yellow pages. What you want is an attorney who welcomes real estate business and who is prepared to have a *no-cost preliminary meeting* with you. It may take no more than one call to find an attorney with whom you are comfortable. On the other hand, you may have to search longer for the right one—one that has expertise in property transactions.

The important thing is that this is done *before* you are ready to make an offer. For maximum protection, I suggest you consider making your offers on an 'Offer and Acceptance' form. This form has blank spaces for the details of your agreement and states that you and the seller intend to enter into a full Purchase and Sale Agreement later.

Don't, however, rely on your agent or broker to provide you with such a document. Broker's forms are generally weighted in favor of the broker and seller. Some do *not* guarantee return of your deposit if you should pull out of the deal. Others bind you to using the broker's Standard Real Estate Agreement if your offer is accepted by the seller.

A contract drawn up, or one approved, by a competent real estate attorney working on *your* behalf gives you maximum protection. Make a point of asking the attorney you select to provide you with a couple of Offer and Acceptance forms or an equivalent. Then, carry them around with you, and when the time comes to make an offer you won't need the broker's form. These Offer and Acceptance forms are standard documents in many real estate attorneys' offices and shouldn't cost you anything. Just don't let the agent know until the appropriate time that you'll make the offer on your attorney's Offer and Acceptance form. If your attorney doesn't routinely supply these forms (in some parts of the country they are not common) seek the attorney's advice on alternative ways to protect yourself in the situation.

## Using Escape Clauses For Protection

If you feel less than certain that you will be able to go through with the purchase for any reason, you can—and should—go one step further. Insist on adding an *escape clause* to your offer. This allows you to back out of the agreement without incurring any penalty or disadvantage. This clause should already be in the Offer and Acceptance form supplied by your attorney. If it isn't, ask how to add it.

Such a clause might state that you will go through with the deal, but only if certain other things happen. For example, you'll complete the purchase provided your partner or mortgage lender or attorney approves it. Remember, this offer document is not the full Purchase and Sale Agreement. That will be drawn up (or approved) later by your attorney if your offer is accepted. And, it will spell out in detail the conditions attaching to the purchase.

The escape clause (often called a *contingency* or *contingency clause*) in the Offer and Acceptance document serves only one purpose, to allow you the right to withdraw without any cost or further obligation to you. This is a matter you should cover in your preliminary talk with your attorney. At the same time, seek advice on how to go about putting a deposit on the home you select. And keep in mind that an offer to purchase can be withdrawn at any time prior to acceptance, with or without an escape clause.

When it comes to handing over money, my own approach is one of caution. Even when protected by an escape clause, I believe it's wise to give the agent the smallest possible deposit (sometimes called an *earnest money deposit* or a *good faith deposit*). This is the money the agent looks for before submitting your offer. If you decide later to pull out of the deal, a properly worded contingency clause can guarantee you will get your money back. Without such a clause, you could forfeit your entire deposit.

### Placing Other Conditions on Your Offer

As a negotiator, another of the most important reasons for placing conditions of one kind or another on your offer is to have something to bargain with later. *Leverage* is how it's commonly referred to. When you have conditions, you have the power to make concessions. Another benefit is that making concessions shows you to be a reasonable person willing to compromise. Shortly, we'll consider specific conditions of this kind and how they benefit and protect you.

First, though, keep in mind that a condition should never be conceded lightly. Better to hold out until it is necessary or until it is strategically most beneficial. Better still, "allow" the other side to extract the concession. Make it appear that you haven't *given* it up but that they have *won* it or prized it from you. In negotiation, such a small victory for the other side can bring you much greater advantage in the end. Let's see why.

When you make a concession easily, without hesitation and struggle, more will be expected from you. On the other hand, when your opponent has to fight hard to win a concession, he believes he has won a bigger victory. The satisfaction this produces tends to dull his appetite for continued battle. In one way, this is a deflection tactic by you. It diminishes the other side's need to achieve ultimate victory which, to a seller, usually means getting the highest price and the best terms he can get.

Having concessions to give away enables you, also, to control the momentum of the exchange. And, of course, the perceptions of the agent and seller. The conditions you've imposed on your offer may be insignificant to you, but only *you* know that. Remember our earlier case study with the banker and his wife, Mr. and Mrs. Mellon? We held on to our condition that settlement would be in 120 days, knowing that this was less than desirable for the seller. Then, when it was most beneficial to us, we conceded and closed the deal.

The logic behind this tactic is often misunderstood. It might, on the surface, seem reasonable to assume that the side that wins a small victory, such as getting the buyer to make a concession, will push for bigger gains. In my experience, that is very rarely the case, once the buyer hesitates and protests before conceding. Perhaps the explanation of this phenomenon has to do with a kind of battle fatigue—victory dissipates energy, produces satisfaction, and relieves aggression. Or, perhaps it's just that the winning of a small victory moves the victorious side, consciously or unconsciously, toward a position of balance.

Whatever the explanation, this tactic works. Having made one or two minor concessions, you're likely to be seen by the seller and agent as a still somewhat difficult, but not altogether unreasonable, buyer. That makes for a continuation of the negotiation and keeps the prospect of a good deal—for you—alive.

Before we look at specific conditions (contingencies), keep two points in mind. First, there are two types of conditions, dispensable and indispensable. The latter you can never concede. But, you can usually afford to bargain with dispensable conditions in return for the seller being flexible on price, terms, or some other point. Be clear, before you rush to test this strategy, exactly what is dispensable and what is not, making sure your partner sees it the same way. Second, bear in mind that if you're in doubt about any legal matter affecting your rights or protection as a homebuyer, an appropriate "third party" condition enables you to seek the advice of your attorney or some other expert or authority before committing yourself. A phone call is often all that is necessary to get the answers you need.

Now, what are some of the more beneficial conditions you can use, both tactically and for protection? A general answer would be anything that improves or enhances or guarantees the value of the purchase—to you. And not just financial value, as we'll see.

Here are some examples of commonly used conditions:

*Time:* You already know that buyers and sellers generally work within typical time frames when transferring ownership of a home. As a buyer, you'll usually get to specify, first, the length of time you would like to elapse from your offer being accepted until you become the legal owner—the settlement period. If you can afford to be flexible with your settlement date, you might decide to make a change simply to suit the seller's needs in return for, perhaps, a price reduction or some other concession. A specific, designated settlement date might be one condition you place on your offer.

*Property Related:*    Let's assume the home you want to buy has an old timber shed in the back yard. It looks dilapidated and you have no use for it. Along with that, it's an eyesore and detracts from the home. The answer, you decide, is to make your offer conditional upon the seller agreeing to have the shed and any residual debris removed before the settlement date. Or, your condition might state that you will accept the property with the shed in place, provided the owner agrees to compensate you for the cost of having it removed. When the owner accepts this condition on your offer you can feel contented that the problem will be solved, one way or the other.

*Home Repair Related:*    You suspect that the home you are interested in has a leaky roof, but you are not sure. To delay until a roofing professional inspects the home might not be to your advantage, as somebody else might buy the home in the meantime. However, it would also be a mistake to engage a professional and pay for a roof inspection too early. Should you later fail to reach agreement on price with the seller, the cost of the roof inspection is an expense you will probably have to accept. The best solution in such circumstances is to negotiate as you normally would but to place a condition on your offer that stipulates either of the following: (a) that you will go through with the purchase only if the roof is inspected by a professional and found to be in sound condition or, (b) that you will go through with the purchase only if the owner agrees to pay for any repairs that might be found necessary by the roofing professional. (Of course, this might be only one of the conditions written into your offer.)

As your negotiation progresses, you can decide to drop this type of condition in return for the seller making an appropriate price concession. Be sure, though, that you have a reasonably accurate idea of how much a needed repair is likely to cost.

You can adopt the same approach with electrical wiring, plumbing, heating/cooling, landscaping or any other feature that causes you concern.

(For more information on home inspection services, see the Appendix.)

*New Homes:*    Although builders and their representatives will seldom tell you this, you can often negotiate "extras" when you buy a new home. Things like better quality or more extensive landscaping can often be acquired at no extra charge. So, too, can better carpeting, additional interior painting, fencing, extra power points, security system, and other such items.

Consider making your offer subject to these concessions being granted. In other words, insert the extras you wish as conditions on your offer and continue to negotiate strongly on price. You might eventually have to give up one or two, but you're likely to come away with a better deal than if you sought no extras and, therefore, had nothing to concede. This is especially beneficial when the builder is trying to sell several vacant properties. The only way you'll find out is by asking around. Naturally, the builder or the agent won't tell the full story.

The list of possible conditions available to a homebuyer is endless. There is no sacred code that limits the number you can use or that prohibits you from seeking exactly what you desire. Neither is there any reason not to ask (at least) for those things that will make you feel better, wealthier, more comfortable or more fortunate in your new home.

Nonetheless, if your demands are highly unreasonable or impossible to meet, you stand to kill the interest of the agent and seller. Ultimately, it's up to the seller to say yes or no. So ask away, but frame your "asking" as conditions on your offer, particularly with critical matters.

I strongly believe that protective conditions are not used nearly enough by homebuyers. But, as I emphasized before, there are very few out there teaching or helping the average homebuyer to buy safely and intelligently.

Talk with your attorney for more information about how to place conditions on your offers. Do this in your preliminary meeting—which should be free—when you are discussing the use of Offer and Acceptance forms.

### Should You Send Other Information to the Seller along with Your Offer?

This is a worthwhile tactic and one you might favor. Some negotiators, including buyer brokers, use it routinely.

All you do is attach details of local homes that sold recently at prices that support your offer. This information can include a list of addresses, home descriptions (number of bedrooms, etc.), asking prices and selling prices, all relating to homes that are largely comparable to the one on which you are making the offer. Of course, you'll include only homes that make your offer look fair and reasonable.

A percentage of sellers can probably be sufficiently influenced by this approach to agree to a price concession. However, others are more influenced by the development of the negotiation process: the discussion, the specific problems and expenses the new buyer will incur, the price justifications, the passage of time, the home inspection findings, offer and counter offer, and so on. Attaching home sale details to the initial offer can also play a part in this process. So, if the idea interests you, fire away. But don't rely on it alone.

Here's a final note of caution before we leave this section. When you have negotiated a price and terms that are acceptable to the seller, make sure you and the seller sign the agreement immediately. This holds true whether you are using an Offer and Acceptance form or a full Purchase and Sale Agreement. Your attorney will have ensured that there are no "sudden death" clauses in the agreement as this, in some cases, would allow the seller the right to take another offer after accepting yours. This is another reason for having your attorney draw up or approve any agreement you plan to use.

Alternatively, you can insert a condition that makes a *standard* purchase offer form subject to your attorney's approval or alteration. Or, even subject to the agreement being re-drawn later on your attorney's forms. Either way affords you necessary protection.

When done correctly, signing this agreement takes the home off the market and locks the seller into honoring what has been agreed. You'll also be protected by other conditions about which your attorney will advise you. One of these could be that the agreement can be terminated by you without penalty if the home inspection report turns out to be unsatisfactory. This, of course, is when you make an offer prior to the home being professionally inspected.

Making the purchase agreement subject to the approval of a third party (such as your attorney, husband, lender, etc.), is often referred to as a *weasel clause.* Don't let that stop you from making good use of it. All it does is put more protection on the buyer's side. And that is exactly where the greater protection is needed.

### KEY POINTS TO REMEMBER

- Keep in mind when you buy a home that you are also buying the surrounding neighborhood. So take a long, slow tour of the area and make sure it has the features you want and need.

- In your notebook, make notes of significant features or any positive or negative aspects that grab your attention as you inspect a home. They may prove useful, even valuable, later.

- Ask the agent specific questions about every home that might have even remote interest for you—particularly the tough, relevant questions the agent will have to work hard to answer. Then insist on getting definite answers.

- Time is your ally. Learn how to make it work for you, especially when you find a home that captures your interest.

- Crawl, stall and procrastinate before making an offer. Then, let yourself "get talked into" it by the agent. And when it is necessary to increase your offer or make a concession, do so with a show of doubt and reluctance. Let the other side work hard to "win" the offer from you. That way, they'll value it more and will not be too keen to go through the 'extraction' process again.

- When talking to the agent, refer to the price of the home as the price "they" are asking. Don't make it sound like it is the agent's price. If you make it "theirs," the agent will feel compelled to support and defend it.

- Place a deadline on your purchase offer—a time by which the seller must respond or your offer will automatically be withdrawn and will become void.

- On your offer, try to hold on to at least one condition that you are willing to concede. But don't concede it until late in the negotiation. Then, in return for your conceding, look for a corresponding concession or for final agreement. This is sometimes referred to as the Red Herring tactic.

- Any time you are negotiating to buy a home, the first figure you offer will determine the price you will eventually have to pay. Choose it well.

- The best way to influence—and eventually arrive at—the price a seller agrees to accept is by inching up to it from your first offer.

- Shop around for an attorney who is competent with real estate (many are not) and consult with him or her before you begin your search. Preliminary consultations of this kind are usually free.

# CHAPTER EIGHT

# DEAL TIME: CREDIBILITY, CONCESSIONS AND TACTICS

*The pure and simple truth is
rarely pure and never simple.*
—OSCAR WILDE

By way of introduction to this chapter, let's restate a principle of negotiation we mentioned in an earlier section.

Any time you increase your offer, the increase should be based entirely on the last figure you offered. It should not be dictated by or based on what the seller expects. Or, by how far away you are from the seller's position.

Here's an example we'll use throughout this section to illustrate the importance of this and other points. We'll assume I want to sell you my home. Through the real estate agent, I tell you it's worth $143,000. You offer me $125,000, which I reject. However, I tell you I will accept $139,000. That positions us, right now, $14,000 apart ($139,000 minus $125,000).

You insist you can buy a better home for less money a couple of streets away and you act like you are ready to cancel your interest in my home. Then, the agent comes up with a stroke of genius. The agent suggests what the agent says is a fair compromise—that you meet me halfway. That we should 'split the difference.'

Should you go ahead? No! Let's see why. And how you might proceed in this hypothetical situation.

## Why You Should Almost Never Agree to 'Split the Difference'—And Other Buyer Mistakes

By agreeing to meet me halfway, you allow me, the seller, to dictate the size of your new offer. My figure of $139,000, wherever I got it from, becomes the benchmark. It now dictates where the price will go from here. It now determines what you will eventually pay. Any figures you had in mind, such as your estimate of the value of my home or what you felt you might be able to get me to accept, lose their significance at this point.

Consider also, that I may be employing a tactic to get you to pay a higher price. For all you know, I might deliberately have hiked up my asking price to well in excess of what my home is worth. In fact, maybe I did that with just this kind of 'compromise' in mind. (Even if the home had been appraised close to the asking price, that is still no guarantee of value. Appraisals on the same property often differ widely, for a number of reasons.)

For now, let's assume you decide to meet me halfway. That means you will come up another $7,000 (from $125,000) and I will drop down by the same amount (from $139,000). Your new offer then becomes $132,000, the offer the agent brings to me. But now, I start thinking, particularly about your willingness to add $7,000 to your first offer. I wonder:

> Is your willingness to pay $132,000 based on the value you see in my home?
>
> If so, what does this tell me about your first offer of $125,000?
>
> Am I to assume your $125,000 offer did not reflect the real value you saw in my home? That you were simply bargain hunting?

You see, now I know you believe my home is worth $132,000— at least. I figure you believed this all along; that your $125,000 was just a feeble try at bargaining. Then I start wondering how far you might go. You're clearly no negotiator. Maybe I'll push a bit harder and see what I can get.

Do you see what is happening between us? Your credibility has just evaporated. And with it, your power to influence my price. Perhaps you'll pay $135,000. Or even $137,000. Or more. After all, I got you up a huge $7,000 very easily and quickly. In one jump, in fact. I figure you'll go for another few thousand, at least. Clearly, I, the seller, am controlling what you'll pay—not you.

What's more, is there any obligation on me to accept your new offer? None whatsoever! I might instruct my real estate agent (after all, the agent is working for me) to tell you that I am not now prepared to sell for $132,000; that after thinking about it I realize it's just too low. My home is worth $137,000 and that's what I want. And, anyway, another buyer is showing keen interest and is on the verge of submitting an offer.

You see, I figure you are very keen on my home. Maybe you've even fallen in love with it and want it at any cost. I'm smug and confident, also, because my agent has told me how much you have to spend and how perfect my house is for you. And lots of other things you told the agent—but shouldn't have.

Who is in the stronger position now? You might protest at my rejection of your halfway offer. You might even accuse the agent of misleading you. In response, the agent pleads innocence, telling you they acted in good faith and did their best to get you the home you want. Then, the agent adds that in their professional opinion, $132,000 would be like giving the home away. And he reminds you that you can still buy my home if you act quickly, before the other buyer. The agent would be prepared to present a new offer for you, immediately. Pay $137,000, before someone else steals the home. (Agents play angels all the time.)

Obviously, you've now lost control. What can you do? You scratch your head hard. You know you have been outmaneuvered. Your expectations were falsely raised, but you are now so committed emotionally to the home, it's disheartening, to say the least, to pull out. For a while, you thought the home was yours. You even visualized how your furniture would look and which rooms the family members would occupy. Unlocking yourself is probably impossible.

However, you're still $5,000 away from my price ($137,000 versus $132,000). So you begin rationalizing the situation. You tell yourself it's only $5,000, and, after all, the original price was $143,000. And $5,000 mortgaged over a number of years won't increase your monthly payments by that much. Inside, it gnaws at you. But going ahead sure beats starting the search all over again tomorrow. It would be foolish to lose it for $5,000 (so, too, says the agent, with a cultivated look of conviction). And on and on the thoughts roll. Until, eventually, you think yourself into paying my price. I win. How about you? Do you win, too?

In the end, only I know I would have accepted a lower price. I might even have gone as low as $130,000, if I had to. And there really wasn't any other keen buyer. But you'll never know these things. You failed to discover, or to influence, my lowest acceptable price. What were your biggest mistakes? Let's do a quick check.

Your mistakes in this make-believe transaction were those to which most homebuyers are vulnerable. Here is a list of your most serious—and most costly—errors:

1.  You were too quick to accept my price as a basis to work from.

2.  You were too extravagant with your second offer (an increase of $7,000).

3.  You were too quick to compromise.

4.  You were too willing to believe you risked losing the home to another buyer.

5.  You were too quick and too extravagant with your third and final offer ($137,000).

Your ability to negotiate successfully was weakened further by two things. You saw yourself owning the home too early in the negotiation and you did not verify the agent's authority when they implied that meeting me halfway would buy the home.

All these problems are dealt with throughout *Not One Dollar More!* because they include the mistakes I've seen buyers make most frequently. Shortly, we'll explore and illustrate a small number of simple tactics, extremely effective money-saving techniques you can use in almost any situation. Right now, though, let's look at some basic self-defense you could have used in this situation to get a better deal.

### A Few Self-Defense Basics

First, to negotiate successfully you must be seen to be a genuine and believable buyer. You accomplish this by letting the agent and seller know the foundation or 'logic' your offer is based on. *Only two* foundations are acceptable, and you must be able to justify and defend them. Make it clear that you are basing your offer on one or both of these:

1.  Your estimate of the value of the property (what you feel the home is worth)

2.  Your spending limit (your inability to pay a higher price)

Both, of course, will often be tactical positions. They won't necessarily reflect your actual thinking or your true position. The first, stating that your offer represents what you believe the home is worth, is the stronger of the two arguments. And, it can sometimes be effectively combined with the claim that your budget just can't stretch any further (more on both, later).

For this and other reasons, any offer to split the difference should never be entertained in the early stages of the negotiation. Never before a stalemate seems likely. Nine times out of ten, as I see it, it results in the buyer paying a higher price. The single exception is in the final stages of a negotiation, when only a small amount separates the buyer and seller.

Splitting the difference or meeting halfway can be justified, for example, where you have offered, say, $130,000 and the seller is stuck stubbornly at $133,000. Such a compromise could be the making of a good deal. Even here, though, procrastinate. Act like you are reluctant and hesitant (don't say that, though, just *show* it). Make it seem that you are wavering and on the verge of pulling out.

In our example, major problems started when you agreed to meet me halfway. If you were prepared to make a second offer for my home, you should have done it with a show of reluctance. Then, it should have been a small increase. Perhaps only $2,500 or $3,000. Your third and fourth offers, if you had to make them, could have added anything from $1,000 to $2,500 to the previous figure.

Incidentally, it's a good idea to make increases progressively smaller, whenever possible. By that, I mean a $3,000 increase should be followed by a further increase of, say, $2,500 or less. It is *most important* not to make a small increase and follow it with a larger one. For example, an increase of $3,000 should not be followed by an increase of $5,000 or $7,000. Only in very rare cases, can this rule be broken. One instance is when it is *certain* to close a deal. Progressively smaller increases have the added advantage of signaling to the seller and agent that your budget is running out.

Another basic error is in assuming that what the seller or agent says, is credible. Or fair. The only opinion of what is *fair* or what is *good value* that is worth anything, is your own. Certainly not the agent's or seller's. That's too much to expect, seeing how they're on the opposite side to you.

Listen as well and as long as you choose. But try to read between the lines, question relevantly and specifically, challenge what you are told, look for evidence, verify, get hard facts. Do whatever you have to do but rely on your *own* intuition and knowledge, act on your *own* logic, seek your *own* counsel, apply your *own* tactics, dictate your *own* pace. Base your actions on your *own* feelings and impressions, on your *own* needs and objectives. Stay in control!

When making a first offer to an agent, whether it's verbal or written, communicate clearly and emphatically that your offer represents the fair value of the home *to you!* Additionally, you might then state that it is the limit of your budget—all you can afford to spend. It is totally irrelevant what evidence the agent or seller offers to dispute your opinion of the home's value. Your offer represents what the home is worth *to you.* You might explain that it is based on the prices of other homes you've seen and, in particular, on one in which you are definitely interested. Don't be persuaded out of making the first offer you have in mind, even though it's below what you might later agree to pay (only you know that, of course) as the negotiation process gets moving. Crawl slowly and be patient. In negotiation it's the tortoise, not the hare, that wins in the end.

In trying to buy my house at the lowest possible price, had you emphasized that your first offer of $125,000 was what you believed the property was worth and that you'd have no interest at a higher price, the agent would have worked much harder to get me to accept that figure or something close to it. As it was, you jumped $7,000 with your second offer, indicating that you believed all along that the home was really worth more than you first offered—at least $7,000 more. (If not, why would you make that second offer?) That move made it easy for me and my agent and to figure you out as a buyer and, eventually, to outmaneuver you. Consequently, you paid a lot more for my home than an astute buyer would have paid.

You also failed to control the momentum of the negotiation. Instead of stalling and showing signs that you just might buy another home at a better price, you increased the momentum. You should have been trying to slow it down. You jumped at splitting the difference when you should have made an apparently reluctant, slightly increased offer and stretched things out in preparation for a possible third offer.

What you said, in effect, was: 'The home is worth $125,000.' Then: 'Yes, I'm prepared to pay $132,000.' That communicated something to the agent which was costly and disadvantageous to you. Your actions contradicted your words. And, naturally, your actions spoke louder, as actions always do. The solution is to ensure that your image, your words, and your actions are in sync, that they support each other and reinforce the impression you need to make. Then, you are in a position to negotiate strongly and to concede gradually, and reluctantly, when you have to. You dictate the momentum. You have credibility. You stay in control.

### Introduction to Tactics

In the next section, on buying from a private seller, you'll find examples, case studies and detailed explanations of a selection of the most powerful negotiation tactics for the homebuyer. These will give you a big advantage in most of the situations you're likely to encounter, and they can be used with equal success whether you are negotiating privately with a seller or through a real estate agent or salesperson.

Even better, you won't have to study for hours to understand the tactics I'll give you. They're surprisingly simple, and easy to memorize and learn. And, the more familiar you become with them the better prepared you will be to defend your money and to win bigger price concessions from the seller. But there's another valuable benefit, too. You're likely to find yourself applying what you learn, not just in homebuying, but in countless other areas of interpersonal communications. In fact, in just about all areas of your day-to-day living.

However, tactics on their own are relatively ineffective. To work well, they need the disciplined approach this book teaches you, coupled with your natural enthusiasm to succeed. Tactics—think of them as jewels in a crown; high points in a performance. They aren't the crown itself, nor are they the performance. But when the demeanor you develop is one of confidence, definiteness, and control, tactics become potentially most powerful. Then, you have a strategy.

One caution: You must be careful not to overplay any tactic. State it (or apply it) once or twice strongly and clearly and repeat it only when it fits naturally into a discussion—when it's relevant. That will be enough, usually. Unnecessary repetition or pregnant pauses as you wait for an anticipated reaction tend to make you less convincing rather than more so, less "instinctive" and more drilled and, consequently, less effective as a negotiator. So, act the part. Don't let your behavior contradict your words.

Here's a brief, preliminary introduction to the most effective tactics the astute homebuyer can use in negotiating the lowest price.

### 1. The Attractive Alternatives Tactic

From the beginning, before you find a home you like, you casually let the agent know that you have seen a home that interests you keenly. Later, when the negotiation process starts, you refer back to this "other" home reminding the agent that it is an attractive alternative. If the agent asks which home it is (the agent will want to look it up in their book), say it's being sold privately, or that you feel it would be disadvantageous to you to say more: Or both.

Your "attractive alternative" doesn't have to refer to another home you like. It could mean that you'll decide to hold on to your present home instead of buying anything. Or maybe you'll decide to rent for another six months and buy next year. Both work particularly well with a 'that's all I can afford' tactic.

## 2. The Stall And Jolt Tactic

This is where, in the negotiation, you back off to 'think over' the proposition that has been put to you. There's just the slightest hint in your tone that your response will be favorable, that you'll accept the other side's position or price. Although your hint is clear, you give no guarantee that is what you will do. Then, in your next contact, you deliver the jolt. With a show of disappointment, you reject the price or terms you've been offered and dampen the seller's and the agent's optimistic expectations. Now, you stall again and wait for the other side to try to rescue the situation. You state your "final" price calmly and restate your interest in the home. If there's a further concession possible this tactic will usually unearth it.

## 3. The Comparative Value Tactic

You inform the agent or seller that the price they are looking for is higher than a number of comparable homes sold recently and others you've seen, one or two of which you have some interest in. You might state, also, that you believe your offer is fair and consistent with the prices of homes that are largely similar. Don't let the agent draw you out by getting you to identify the homes you have in mind. Just say you've kept all the relevant details in your notebook and you have a good feel for what your money will buy (which is what you have been doing. Isn't it?)

## 4. The Third Party Tactic

This tactic enables you to prolong the negotiation while staying involved. You indicate your personal interest in the home but it's your partner (spouse, parent, attorney, lender) on whom the final decision rests. Unfortunately, that person believes the price is too high, or prefers another home or has some other reservation which you are finding difficult to get around. Much as *you* would like to buy the home, your hands are tied. The only thing that might solve the problem, that you can think of, is if the seller made the price more attractive. Then, your partner might agree to go ahead. This tactic is good any time, but best later in the negotiation, particularly as you stretch out the communication with the agent.

## 5. The No More Money Tactic

You've negotiated well but you have reached a point where the seller refuses to reduce the price any further. You make the statement matter-of-factly that your offer is genuine and that you believe it's a fair price for the home. You're already over your spending limit (here's one good reason for never revealing your true budget to the agent) and, short of next month's salary, you simply have no more money. If the seller dismisses your predicament and you're convinced they're not going to accept your last offer you can always pull one last trick out of the bag. You somehow 'find,' borrow, or 'steal' a few last minute dollars to clinch the deal. You can then consider adopting a 'walk away' tactic.

## 6. The Walk Away Tactic

Your argument here is that you're keen on the home and you've made a "very fair" offer. This new, slightly increased offer is the last one you'll make. You've now given it your best shot. If the seller doesn't accept it you'll be satisfied to know you went as far as you could go. And you'll just walk away and forget the whole idea. Perhaps you'll buy the home you saw on Sunday, which probably represents better value for money anyway, and there, you won't have to go over your budget. (This 'other' home is being sold privately. It won't appear on the agent's listings book. And you'd prefer not to give any more details about it.)

Now, you caution the agent, it's up to the seller. If the agent persists in trying to get you to increase your offer even more, you act like you're about to change your mind once and for all, like you've decided against the home. Begin making your exit. Head for the door or your car. This is the ultimate 'walk away.' If the agent makes no attempt to stop you, *don't lose your nerve!* The agent may be testing *you,* too. And he knows he can easily call you later. More likely, though, if the agent believes there's even the slightest chance of saving the deal, they won't let you get as far as the door. They'll suggest that they have 'a talk' with the seller or listing agent.

There are other tactics I could add to the list, but these will be more than sufficient, especially when used in combination. For example: your spouse (third party) is not enthusiastic because they feel the 'other' home is a little brighter (bigger, more modern, has a better kitchen, etc.) and costs less (attractive alternative).

Or, the seller has stubbornly asserted their lowest price and says that they are through compromising. You say you'll need some time to 'think it over' (the stall, preparing for the jolt). Some time later, despite the urging of the agent, you reject the seller's price. But you add $500 (perhaps) to your last offer and state persuasively that if the seller doesn't accept, you'll cancel your interest and walk away.

Throughout your association with the agent and the seller, and especially during the negotiation phase, *you're trying to influence their thinking* with subtle skills of which they are unconscious. You are steadily building an impression of yourself that will work to your benefit in the ultimate negotiation. In effect, what you are doing is shaping the agent's and seller's perspectives, shaping how they assess you, your confidence as a buyer, your interest, money, situation, poise, temperament, definiteness, your toughness, and your degree of emotional attachment to the property.

If it sounds like a conditioning process, that's exactly what it is. It's unavoidable. It will happen automatically, whether you're a smart buyer or a vulnerable buyer. Therefore, it pays, literally, to make sure the impression (the conditioning) you create is the kind that leads you to buy the home you want at the lowest price possible. The steps outlined in the following chapter will help you do that in some very effective ways.

**KEY POINTS TO REMEMBER**

- Any time you increase your offer, the size of the increase should be based entirely on the last figure you offered. It should almost never be influenced or determined by the figure the seller expects or is demanding.

- Splitting the difference or meeting halfway is rarely a good idea.

- Any offer you make must be seen to be based on one of two factors: what you believe to be a fair price for the property, or the fact that you cannot afford to pay a higher price. Combine the two, if you like, but make the 'fair price' argument your principal justification for the amount you offer.

- When you increase an offer, it is always better to do it gradually in small increments rather than in one or two big jumps.

- When a home interests you, ask specific questions and look for specific answers. Verify what you are told and accept only hard facts rather than opinions, guesses, generalizations, or estimates.

- In negotiation, it is usually the tortoise, not the hare, that wins in the end (momentum).

- Tactics are your defense against, and best response to, the tactics of the other side—especially those that aren't easy to detect or be certain about.

- Along with research and professional advice, tactics provide a solid defense against tricks, fraud, and deception.

- Tactics on their own are relatively worthless. They must be part of a strategy (an overall plan) to be most effective.

- Always let the agent think you are also interested in and are considering another home (or homes) with a different agent.

- A "third party," real or make believe, gives you more options, particularly in the later stages of a negotiation.

- When you have claimed your budget is already "used up," you can later, if you have to, make a slightly higher take-it-or-leave-it offer by "discovering" an overlooked, but believable, source of funds.

- When you have stated you will "have to walk away" if your offer is rejected, follow through! Say your good-byes, courteously and with an air of finality; make your exit, and leave. Give the seller or agent time to contact you. If the agent doesn't, contact them out of "curiosity" or "just to inquire" if they have any new listings you should know of. And be ready for what happens.

# PART FOUR

*Tactics in Action:
Buying Directly from a
Private Seller*

---

# Chapter Nine

# Invisible Negotiation in Action—Part One

*Honesty is the best policy—*
*when there's money in it.*
—Mark Twain

Most of what you learn from this book will assist you just as much when you are buying directly from a property owner as when you are dealing through a real estate agent. Sometimes, when negotiating with a private seller, you'll need to make just a few minor adjustments in your approach. In both cases, though, your preparation should be equally diligent, as there's no substitute for relevant information.

Know your facts about what has been selling and the prices obtained in your selected area. Find out what is on the market and the prices being asked. Find out what has actually been paid. (A local real estate office will gladly help. After all, you're a prospective client.) When you see a "sold" sign in front of a home, knock on the door, smile, state your intention to buy in the neighborhood, and ask questions. Alternatively, a neighbor might be able to provide as many details as you need about a home for sale. When you do this, especially if it makes you feel awkward, keep in mind that most people take very kindly to being asked for their opinions. That's a good opener and often leads to discovering facts that are impossible to get from any other source.

## A Visit with the Neighbor

Many times a nearby neighbor will know more about a seller's circumstances and the history of the property than will the agent. If the first contact you make in this way isn't productive, try a second or a third contact until you develop a feel for the situation at hand.

There are good reasons for taking this approach. Some have to do with gaining you an advantage in negotiating. Others concern your need for protection. Let's face it, homeowners might be reluctant to reveal the true reason they are moving away. Considering their objective to sell at the highest possible price, that is understandable. But it could mean a problem for you, if you act blindly.

Possibly, the seller is in debt and under time pressure to sell. Maybe the situation would be eased by a quick, unconditional deal. But maybe there is a problem with the neighborhood, or the house itself. Maybe a new highway is to be built within view or earshot of the home. Maybe there are undesirable changes happening in the neighborhood, or a new airport is being planned for where nearby green pastures now exist. It could be that area crime is rising rapidly.

These are the types of questions for which you must find answers. If the owner isn't likely to tell you, who is? In my experience, a chatty neighbor is a godsend. Cultivate conversation; listen to the neighbor's opinions and stories. As you listen, remember that your mission is to absorb; to take in rather than give out. Keep details of your interest and situation confidential, as you can't be certain the information you reveal won't get back to the seller. And bear in mind, too, that this could be your future neighbor.

Some people find it difficult to knock on a stranger's door. And many others don't know what they should say in such situations. I believe the two problems are inextricably linked. It is much easier to knock on a strange door when you have prepared your opening remarks, at least.

Here's how I generally break the ice. (It works very well.)

First, smile! It communicates friendliness and it gets the conversation off to a good start. Then, a simple introduction:

> *Hi, my name is Joseph Cummins. I'm thinking of buying the home across the street. I'm new to the area and I thought I might ask your opinion on the neighborhood. You know, the things that are nice about living here and things you'd like to see change. Would you recommend the area?*

Here again, you'll be trying to get at the specifics. That means that instead of letting the neighbor talk freely, you'll know the questions you want answered and will interject them into the conversation. Of course, be prepared to learn things you hadn't anticipated.

When you've established rapport, mention that you'll be meeting later with the owner and add a comment like this:

> *I guess you know the owner quite well. Have you been*
> *neighbors for a long time?*

You're trying to learn as much about the situation as you can. This kind of gentle prodding will usually help you achieve that goal, provided you keep the attention on what is relevant. Prior to using this tactic, I'm assuming you have driven around the neighborhood and have a good feel for the location. Along with that, you'll have your earlier research to rely on.

Here's a tip you might want to keep in mind, especially when buying from a private seller. Leave your best clothes and luxury car at home. Appear as "ordinary" as possible. Sellers often develop a sudden stubbornness on price when the buyer looks like a *money person*. Not everyone agrees with this, but I believe in it implicitly whether you're spending $60,000 or $600,000.

## A Story of Perception and Legitimacy

Before we look at how you might handle a face-to-face meeting with a private seller, you should stay aware that your task in the negotiation will be to shape that person's perceptions. That can be done in many ways, some overt, others subtle, some verbal, others visual. Your objective will be to communicate a variety of opinions, messages, and impressions that lead the seller to think in a specific way.

Let us digress for a moment to look at what I consider an excellent illustration of the power of perception. This true story also serves as an ideal introduction to the following sections dealing with how to use tactics most effectively.

One of my best friends in college was a humorous and eccentric character, Peter G., who came from a wealthy Dublin family. His field was psychology, but he certainly was no typical student. Peter had become consumed with the thrill of devising his own practical experiments and with the evidence and proofs these established. Academic theories and case histories were for those, he claimed, who were afraid of *real world* testing. Freud and Skinner had their places, but he was much more fascinated with Pavlov and particularly with the ways in which people's perceptions and behavior could be controlled and manipulated. Over the all-too-brief and often hilarious two years I knew Peter, this is what he spent most of his time working on. And this is where, he asserted, he learned his most valuable lessons—not in the classroom but out in the "world laboratory."

One warm August day as we sat in an outdoor cafe in Manhattan, we became engrossed in a conversation about perception and such matters. After a while we were interrupted by a threesome. The two girls and a guy, who had been sitting at a nearby table, had overheard most of what we had been discussing. All were students at a New England college and were intrigued with what they had been hearing. They joined us and the talk went on into the evening.

Eventually, to prove a point, Peter claimed that by using his knowledge of how humans react, often unconsciously, to different types of signals, he could program the most unlikely of outcomes. To prove his point, he accepted a challenge put to him by our new friends. Yes, he could—and would—sleep and eat in New York City for a whole week with just $20 spending money in his pocket. Not an altogether impossible task, you might think. But then came the big surprise. He would do so at seven of New York's finest hotels, staying one night in each. Our three new friends scoffed at the idea of such a feat being possible. But I knew Peter better. And I, too, knew the power of perception.

Let me make it clear, though, this wasn't an attempt to cheat the hotels. It was a genuine experiment in human psychology. It was something no amount of theory could prove. There was no other way to test it but to try it out in the real world.

The only requirements Peter had was this list of items:

- A set of casual clothes (jeans, sneakers, shirt, etc.)

- His best business suit, white shirt, tie and dark shoes, and a short bowler hat (the type you might see on an aristocratic banker)

- His diamond tie pin, gold watch and pen, and a conservative looking briefcase

- A pair of dark-rimmed spectacles

- A large Bank of New York envelope with a fictitious name, Walter C. L. Sykes, typed on it

That was all. Everything else he needed would come from within.

On the day the experiment began, we arranged that our new friends and I would gather casually in the lobby of the hotel, close enough to observe that Peter adhered to the rules and to watch the application of Peter's theories on the power of legitimacy, perception, and persuasion.

Minutes later, in walked Peter, right on schedule. His chin was slightly high; his walk was deliberate and assured, and his gaze never left the direction in which he was heading. Although barely 23, he looked as impressive and as important as any corporate executive the hotel had ever accommodated. A distinctive aura surrounded him as his demeanor exuded confidence and superiority, from the manner in which his shoes squeaked on the marble tiles to the aloof, demanding, and slightly displeased look on his face. He arrived at the check-in desk looking far from the picture of a pleasant hotel guest.

The female desk clerk greeted him with, "Good morning, Sir." That's when the fun started. To the best of my memory, here is the dialogue that ensued.

Peter:    (In a detached, slightly aloof tone) Hmmm, I wish it was. I'm Walter Craig Sykes. If you wouldn't mind, I'd like the quietest single room you have. I don't wish to be above the fifth floor and my preference is for the back of the hotel.

Clerk:    Certainly, sir. If you'll just fill in this card. May I see some identification or your driver's license?

Of course, Peter had no license, at least not for this adventure. He ignored the clerk's request and pulled his gold pen from his inside pocket, then made like he was about to fill in the card. Suddenly, he stalled, reached up and removed the bowler hat from his head and placed it on the counter almost between himself and the clerk. With an audibly deep, sighing breath he removed his spectacles with one hand and rubbed his eyes with the other. A grimace of tiredness stretched across his face. He stared directly at the clerk, and for a moment, said nothing. Then:

What an airline. It's not enough that they lose my case and overnight bag but they leave me stuck with these darn driving spectacles.

He handed his gold pen to the clerk and informed her:

You'll have to fill this in for me. I can hardly see the lines. I'll be staying for two nights, possibly longer.

The desk clerk did exactly as instructed, writing the information as Peter dictated it. He then very deliberately reached for his bowler, displaying his expensive gold watch, which he took off and reset, checking the time with the clerk. He leaned over, picked his banker's briefcase from the floor, and said:

*My bags should arrive shortly from the airport. Have them sent to my room immediately, will you? If I'm at dinner make sure my overnight bag is placed in your safe right away and send someone to let me know. I'll be in your mezzanine restaurant. What room am I in?*

The clerk hesitated insecurely then quickly motioned to the porter, to whom Peter presented his briefcase and bowler hat. As they both marched to the elevator I know Peter must have been chuckling inside. But he certainly didn't show it. It was a mighty performance.

Peter slept and ate well that night and again the following night in an equally classy hotel. At that point there was nothing left to prove, so we called off the experiment. At each of the two check-ins his performance changed only slightly to fit the prevailing circumstances. Both times he acted the part; he talked the part; and he looked the part. No one he dealt with doubted the character he pretended to be.

Once he had secured a room, he was free to eat in the hotel restaurant and place the charge on his bill. You might be wondering what was the reason for the Bank of New York envelope. Well, that was a fall back, just in case he needed the smallest piece of extra 'proof' that he was who he said he was, Walter C. L. Sykes. In neither case did he have to show it.

Why did he need the twenty dollars? Tips for the doormen and porters. Both hotel bills were paid in full later by Peter's father, who viewed the experiment as humorously as we did and considered it a valuable contribution to his son's graduation thesis, which is what it later became.

Why do I tell you a story like this in a book on how to buy your next home at rock-bottom price? Chiefly to illustrate the ways in which human perception works and how it can be controlled when you learn how to program the responses you wish for. As Peter did, you can affect people's perceptions by sending the right messages. Some of these messages are verbal, but most are *unspoken*. The two must work in harmony. With Peter, his clothing, demeanor, personality, body language, speech, and assurance all worked together to give him credibility and, consequently, the power to control what the hotel staff thought. He programmed their thinking exactly as he intended, without them being aware of it.

He had the power of legitimacy because he looked and sounded and acted legitimate. To the hotel clerk, he was an important business executive, upset, mildly cantankerous, demanding and quite stressed by the events to which he alluded. His entire demeanor demanded immediate and superior service. And in both cases that's what he received. Without money, without identification, without credit card or check book, without a job or even a business card.

No, you certainly don't have to become a Peter to buy your next home at the lowest price. Your task is much more simple. Once you have the basic know-how you need (this book gives it to you—and more), all you have to add is the key ingredient that wins negotiations—mental power. You already have that. By channeling it correctly you will achieve what others cannot.

Let us now proceed with applying some of this to dealing face-to-face with a private seller.

## Face to Face with the Owner

Let's assume you've arranged to meet with the owners, the Smiths, at their home and are about to make your first inspection. Before you do, keep in mind that it makes no sense at all to talk money at this stage, particularly if the home is of definite interest to you. If the owners emphasize how fair they are being with the price and how they could probably get more if they really tried, don't respond directly. A brief smile, while you allow yourself to be distracted, will communicate the right reaction—disinterest. That's a middle-of-the-road, neutral position but does not signify a total absence of interest.

After you've made a thorough inspection, you might want to ask the price, even when you already know it. When that moment comes, ask the question in such a way that it is part of a list of seemingly routine questions:

- What age is the home?
- What type of tree is that growing in the back yard?
- How far is it to the nearest convenience store?
- What property taxes do you pay?
- What schools are around here?
- What is the asking price?

- Where does the public transportation pick up?
- How long have you lived here?
- What's the name of this street?

The impression you are trying to give is that these are standard questions you ask in every home you look at and, consequently, don't reveal any specific interest on your part. As the owner answers, you might consider making notes in your notebook. Once again, make it seem as routine an action as possible—just as if you do it in every home you inspect (you could even mention this).

If you like what you see and hear, wander slowly around, going back over the areas you've already looked at. But, say as little as possible without seeming impolite. As we saw with the agent, don't allow your words to praise or compliment the home except, perhaps, infrequently and in the mildest way when responding to the owner's comments. Nor should you show any sign at this stage that you might be interested in making an offer, even though you are still wandering about. When you need answers, don't hesitate to ask the relevant questions, but don't help the owners by offering compliments, even when the answers are impressive. For example, let's say you ask the owners about the heating system:

Mr. Smith:    *Well, it's the top model on the market. Solar powered from twin roof panels. Cost me $6,000 just eight months ago and it's under warranty for another four years and four months. It's economical, efficient, and clean.*

What do you say? Despite being impressed, you are not there to add to the owner's impression of the value of their property. Instead, you go straight into a totally unrelated question. Better still, make a slightly negative remark about some aspect or feature of the home, but don't overdo it. Here are two examples of what I mean:

1. Buyer:    *That fencing out front seems like it's ready to be replaced.*

2. Buyer:    *I noticed the timber on the side of the house has some rough spots. It looks like it's due to be painted again. When was it last painted?*

You get the idea. You don't want to seem overly critical, but neither do you want to play up the value of the home. This type of response points out the need to notice and remember a number of faults or negatives about the home. That way, you have a ready comeback when you need it.

On the other hand, should your question about the heating system produce a less than positive response, you take the opposite reaction. Let's say the owner says, something like this:

> Mr. Smith:    *It's the original oil heater we put in when we were building the home 37 years ago. We've had it checked and cleaned a few times. It still works well.*

Here are a number of ways you might respond:

1. Buyer:    *It seems like the whole system will have to be replaced shortly. Have you had any cost estimates on having a new one installed? It's very costly.*

2. Buyer:    *The older systems, especially oil, become so problematic and expensive as they age. But the new systems cost an arm and a leg. It's really an expensive problem no matter how one looks at it.*

3. Buyer:    *I'm always concerned about the safety of older systems. And the expense. The new systems are so much safer and more economical but they are prohibitively expensive to buy and install.*

I used the heating system here simply to illustrate the tactic in question. The same logic can be applied to many other features like plumbing, wiring, fencing, brickwork, aged timber, paint work, landscaping, roof, decor, and so on. The essential point is to pass quietly over the positive features and to focus on and emphasize the negatives—simply a case of eliminating the positive and accentuating the negative.

Many owners, understandably, have an emotional stake in the home they are selling and don't take kindly to continuous, insensitive criticism. Therefore, your negative comments should reflect genuine, if exaggerated, concern on your part rather than outright empty criticism. You'll also sound more convincing.

However, far more productive than what you say is the amount of time you spend discussing the problems that concern you. In this way, time, rather than criticism, provides the emphasis and puts the desired impression into the mind of the owner. That impression should be that you are potentially interested but have a number of genuine concerns. Even if the house is difficult to find fault with, you still have points that will work for you—*your* perceptions of the home, its location, size style, the direction it faces, and so on. These are things that can't be fixed.

Maybe the home looked bigger or brighter or newer or different in some other way, from the outside. In short, it's not quite what you imagined—though it is nice. Because these are impressions—your perceptions—the owner cannot refute them and, therefore, has little defense against them. Points for you.

## How to Get Maximum Leverage from Home Inspection Reports

It goes without saying that the ordinary homebuyer is usually a nonexpert when it comes to assessing the condition of buildings and domestic systems. For that reason, you will probably want to have the home you like checked by a professional home inspector. This is particularly recommended when you have reservations about the parts you cannot see, like the roof, wiring, plumbing, heating/cooling system, and so on. Or, indeed, just for the peace of mind that comes from knowing exactly what you are buying.

In fact, a professional home inspection, just like a pest check, is something I recommend with every purchase. It should be carried out before you commit yourself to buying any property. If a Purchase and Sale Agreement must be signed first, you should insist on adding a condition (a contingency) stating that a professional home inspection, to be carried out, must produce findings that are acceptable to you and, if it doesn't, that you hold the right to rescind (cancel, revoke) the contract without incurring loss of your deposit or any other penalty. (Your attorney will guide you on this matter.)

Then, if a problem is discovered with the home, you are fully protected. However, you might choose not to exercise your right to cancel. You have other options, which we'll look at shortly.

You can expect to see the professional home inspection called by different names such as a Professional Property Inspection or a Home Condition Report. All mean much the same thing. A similar service is often known as a Structural Condition Survey. And there are other variations.

If you don't know someone personally whom you can trust to do this for you, you could consult your local Yellow Pages or a nearby architects group. However, a better idea might be to contact the American Society of Home Inspectors or HouseMaster of America, two groups that specialize in this field. Both have members throughout the country and have reputations for offering reliable service. (You'll find more details and toll free contact numbers for both in the Appendix.)

However, shop around. Fees can vary, as can the range and quality of services on offer. If comparing prices at two or more inspection companies, be sure to provide identical details of your requirements to each so that responses are based on the same work. It doesn't necessarily follow that the most expensive service will be the best, nor that the least expensive will be inadequate. Along with considering cost and value for money, go with your feelings based on the professionalism with which your inquiry is handled.

As a guarantee of fairness and impartiality, the inspector you choose should have no interest in carrying out any repairs the home might require. For the same reason, the inspector should not suggest you employ a particular associate or contractor to do the work.

When the home inspection is almost complete, be prepared to be alarmed. Whether you are having a single feature checked or a full home inspection, it can be a startling experience. Skilled building professionals are strongly motivated to find and report faults to an extent that appears to justify their fees. Occasionally, it is only by questioning their findings that you'll get the information you really need. The problem is that some home inspectors are prone to innocent exaggeration of the nature and quantity of the "faults" they find.

However, now that you are aware of this tendency, don't frown on it, as it makes for a more comprehensive report. Just keep in mind that the findings might seem more serious than they are.

In some instances, too, the jargon that some building professionals love to use can add to your confusion. This tends to push the facts about the home even further from your grasp. So, grab the initiative. Ask and re-ask specific questions until you learn, in plain English, all you need to know.

Remember too, that the unintentional exaggeration that sometimes happens is no reason to be complacent. Don't dismiss automatically, or diminish, any problems brought to your attention. Your first task will be to establish clearly whether the faults are serious and unusual, or, if they are typical of homes of that type, or in that age bracket, and of no real significance. Most important of all, make sure you understand the report's implications for your decision.

Sometimes, that is easier said than done. Here's the kind of experience I've had on a few occasions.

## All 'Problems' are Not Problems

Recently, I engaged a local architect to provide me with a home inspection report on a relatively inexpensive home. The property was 25 years old, so I didn't expect it to get a perfect rating. (Even on a new home I don't expect that.) What concerned me most were problems that might require expensive repairs in the short term. The written report given to me by the inspector contained various comments about minor defects that caused me no worry. But, highlighted at the bottom of the report, was a note that read: "Under-floor air vents blocked by construction of sunporch. Potential damp problems."

I called the architect and asked for a complete layman's explanation of what he was trying to tell me. Normally, I do this in person but in this case I was out of town and had the report faxed to me. In our telephone conversation, the architect gave me a basic lesson in under-floor airflow and why it is necessary. That was OK, but I wanted to know what it meant for the property in question. To find the answer I had to ask questions such as: "Does it mean the home has a damp problem because of this fault?" Eventually, I got somewhere.

No, he told me, he could find no sign of damp in the home, above or below the floor. Truly amazing, seeing how the cause of the problem, the sunporch, had been in place for 15 years. I then asked him if it was likely a damp problem would develop after such a long period of time. Next came the answer I should have got in the beginning. He explained that the original under-floor ventilation had apparently been more than adequate. And, despite the fact that a number of vents had been blocked by the construction of the sunporch, it was extremely unlikely a damp problem would ever develop. In other words, the under-floor condition was normal. No problem!

Despite that caution, the person who conducts the inspection is, presumably, a professional, one you have hired to do a job you are not personally qualified to do. Listen well. This advice could save you from a bad investment, and you'll pick up knowledge that may help you later in other ways.

When you hire a professional, one thing you should insist on is confidentiality—whether the report is good or otherwise. The contents should be for no one's eyes but yours. This is how most professionals work anyway, but I'd make a point of mentioning it just the same, even if only one feature, such as the roof or the plumbing, is being inspected.

Here's why I believe this is important. Because the sellers are typically, the ones who provide access to the home, they usually have the opportunity to accompany inspectors as the work is being carried out. That makes for conversation, which is likely to concern the condition of the home. While most sellers stay discreetly out of the way, I've seen some who have tried to beat the buyer to the punch by interrogating, and even challenging, the inspector.

Whatever the report contains—positive or negative—it can prove valuable to you when you make an offer and begin negotiating price. To illustrate this, let's look back at the hypothetical case of the home with the 40-year-old oil heating system and continue the story.

The plumbing and heating professional you hired informs you that the system has had a couple of quality repairs, but has a useful life of only another two to four years. At that point, a major expense will be incurred. Also, for safety reasons, a number of minor components in the system should be replaced immediately. This will cost, at most, $250.

You now have at least a couple of strategies for negotiating a lower price. Any offer you make might be conditional upon the complete system being replaced before you take possession, with the additional stipulation that the replacement must meet with your full approval. If you don't feel confident about how best to word such a condition, your lawyer will ensure your interests are fully protected.

Generally, though, sellers don't want to take on the hassle of complying with such conditions in the Purchase and Sale Agreement. Many will suggest eliminating such conditions in return for an appropriate reduction in price. Or, you can suggest it. That way, you take responsibility for replacing the system. Either option puts you in a strong negotiating position. Your concerns are legitimate and are supported by the professional's report, not just your personal opinion. Because of that, and because the seller is not a plumbing and heating expert, it is extremely difficult to dispute the existence of the problems. Consequently, in most such cases, an astute buyer wins a valuable concession.

Such a concession also draws the seller into the negotiation process, heightens anticipation of a sale and moves the seller closer to an agreement. Once involved to this extent, sellers are reluctant to break off negotiation, a distinct advantage for you.

In most cases, when an inspector's report establishes a problem of the kind we've just seen, you will maximize your advantage by showing the report to the seller. It's not a side issue any longer, but a central element in your discussion.

There is another powerful phenomenon at work here, one that is at the heart of the negotiation process. It's called the power of legitimacy. The power of legitimacy works when any communication, claim, or statement is perceived to be above dispute or challenge. It's almost a case of "if it looks official and professional and is printed and signed, it must be accepted and heeded."

The decision on whether to have a professional inspection carried out might hinge on how competent you feel about assessing the home without expert help. However, the signs that something is wrong aren't always easily detected by the layperson. In fact, many problems can be covered over and camouflaged quite convincingly by a sharp seller. That alone is ample justification for having a professional do the job.

A professional home inspection report, as we've seen, generally provides you with additional benefits like extra leverage. However, let's assume that your inspector found no serious faults. How, in such a case, is the report of value to you in your negotiating (apart, that is, from your peace of mind)? The answer lies in a point we covered earlier.

I have never seen a single property inspection report that did not list a number of actual or potential problems. The list may contain nothing but minor flaws that result from normal wear and tear. What these problems mean to you, nonetheless, is leverage. Bargaining power. If you have followed my advice you'll have discussed the seriousness of the problems with the inspector. But only you will have the precise details. The written report, however, often looks very official and has little explanatory detail, indicating only the nature of the problem and very little else. You can then inform the seller that the inspector found problems that will require attention, time, and expense to put right. Then, negotiate accordingly.

This is why I recommend not allowing your inspector to discuss the findings with the seller, even if it means you are at the inspection.

A question I'm often asked is this: "If the homebuyer has no suspicions of any kind that there are problems with a home, should the buyer still have a professional inspection carried out?" My answer is always the same. If you feel in any way nervous about relying on your own judgment, you should consider strongly having a full home inspection done. It's a job for a trained professional, not for a week-end do-it-yourselfer or even a professional qualified in just a single area, such as electricity or carpentry or plumbing.

Most inspection companies provide a comprehensive service that checks on hundreds of points within and around a home. Alternatively, you can order checks on individual features and elements, such as the roof, foundation, plumbing, and heating system.

### Professional Home Inspection—Before or After Your Offer?

Which is better: to have the home inspected before you make an offer, or after? Most commonly, you will order an inspection after you know that your offer is acceptable to the seller. If the price you are prepared to pay seems to have no chance of buying the home, paying for an inspection ($250–$350) is a waste of money. That's the conventional thinking, and it usually is sound.

However, homebuying is a flexible undertaking, and much is dictated by the particular circumstance in which you find yourself. It isn't always best to leave your professional home inspection until your offer has been accepted. You could have it carried out between offers, while the negotiation is still in progress (perhaps before you make your second, third, or final offer when it can be the catalyst in making the deal). Naturally, any offer you make before the inspection will carry a contingency clause stating that you will go through with the deal only if the results of an inspection are satisfactory to you.

A later inspection can sometimes give you even greater advantages than an early one. Let's say you have reached agreement with the seller. You have negotiated well and have won a good reduction in the selling price. The seller's anticipation is heightened. The deal seems to be a done thing. They are glad the whole process is over. Then, if the inspection reveals problems, it is much harder to back out. The seller is far more likely to agree to a lower sale price or, at least, pay for the repairs or replacements that are needed.

If you are a first-time buyer or new to negotiating, it is probably better to negotiate a price first. Then, have the inspection carried out and try to get the seller to pay for any work you consider necessary or to agree to a lower price.

### The Trap of Home Warranties

Whether you are buying a newly built home or one that has been lived in, there's a good chance that somewhere along the line someone will try to sell you a home warranty. These are usually pushed by agents and brokers because they are a lucrative source of income—for them. For you, they offer little protection and are often worthless. More than that, they steal your money—between $350 and $450 usually, for the first year—with hype and a long list of exclusions.

In existing homes, most of what you think will be covered probably won't. Usually excluded from standard warranties are refrigerators, washing machines, dryers, jacuzzis, pools, and so on. To find out, however, you'll have to read the fine print, often printed in light gray ink. Not exactly designed with homebuyer protection in mind.

And yes, you'll still always have to pay the service fee, usually $40 to $60, just for the repairman to come out to inspect a problem. Even then, a breakdown that might be included on paper—a plumbing fixture, for example—will be rejected if the repairman concludes that the problem existed before you took out the warranty (even if there were no signs of it).

If you are buying a new home, consult with a good real estate attorney about new home warranties in your state. These have been the subject of congressional and consumer investigations and have been held, in some cases, to be deceptive and fraudulent.

With existing homes, at least, a far better use of your money is to have a comprehensive professional inspection carried out before you complete the purchase. That way, the money you save by saying no to the home warranty will more than cover the cost of repairs or replacements you are likely to face in the first year.

Let's move now to another important aspect of buying from a private seller.

## Do You Know the Owner's Real Reason for Selling?

This is a question you should ask the owner directly, even if you have learned the reason from a neighbor or some other source. If the owner's answer corresponds with what you have learned, you probably need investigate no further (unless, that is, there is reason to suspect the story has been concocted to conceal the truth). This is where your judgment and intuition are called for. The only assistance I can offer you on this point is to listen carefully and stay alert for signs and hints of contradictions. And watch for explanations that sound suspicious.

When you get different stories from the seller and another source, you'll just have to probe deeper. Maybe the neighbor's account was wrong, perhaps gossip. Or, maybe the owner isn't being up front about the reason for moving. It's in your interest to find out.

An owner who is in debt is often too embarrassed to admit it, and may protect their pride with a made-up reason for moving. If you suspect this is the case, mention it to your lawyer, as your lawyer will want to take special steps to make sure you can take possession of the property free and clear.

Knowing the owner's reason for moving can give you a potential advantage that might affect the kind of offer you will make later.

## How to Respond When the Seller Offers to Reduce the Price

The *Attractive Alternatives* tactic is adaptable and extremely useful and can be applied in almost any situation. Like all tactics, though, it must be presented in a sincere-sounding way—not as an ultimatum, and never in a way that might be even mildly offensive or insulting to the owner. That would be completely counterproductive.

To get the result you desire, you need to be convincing in your delivery. The reason is simple; tactics have no inherent or automatic or magical power. They are, after all, only words. The power is in *you*. It is determined by how well you put across your chosen tactic.

Let's assume now that you are part way through a deliberately slow second inspection of the Smiths' home. The company you've hired to check the property has told you that it is largely satisfactory, with only a few minor problems. You have been careful, too, in how you conducted your own inspections, and you have followed my recommendations with regard to your conversations and comments. And then it happens. The seller makes you an eyeball-to-eyeball offer. The home can be yours at a reduced price—a bargain!

What should you do? What should you say? How should you act?

Unfortunately, most unprepared buyers in this situation react impulsively and wrongly. What is needed now are tactics.

There is one thing you *don't* do. You don't accept the offer. And, you don't do *anything* quickly, no matter how you are feeling inside. There is some chance—a small one—that you might later accept this offer. But not now. Neither, though, is it the time for a blunt rejection. So, if you are not accepting and not rejecting, what are you doing?

In the quiet moments following the offer, you will consider the most appropriate tactic or statement with which to respond. Usually, little thought will be required here, as undoubtedly you will have been following a particular line of reasoning with the seller up to this point. Still, you let the silence happen, but only for a second or two. You don't want to imply that the offer is worth your serious consideration (except with the *Stall and Jolt* tactic).

For example, you may have explained to the seller that there is another home you are very keen on for a number of reasons (Attractive Alternative). You may have stated that your partner is unlikely to go along, even at the price you offered (Third Party). You still believe their home is priced higher than comparable homes, both on the market and recently sold (Comparative Value). You have overstepped your budget with the offer you have *already* made for the home (No More Money). Or perhaps you use another tactic, or a combination of two or more.

No matter what comes into your head, you must not jump at the reduced offer—not even to attack it. Get your thoughts clear, take a few deep breaths, and respond in a courteous, genuine tone that communicates nonacceptance, or, at least, serious reluctance or doubt.

Exactly what to say will be determined by what has transpired between you and the Smiths up to that point. Most likely, you will continue with the main argument you have been using, though you may choose to add a new tactic. Conveying understanding for their situation, and even gratitude (but be careful here) for their interest in selling you their home, will usually dissuade the sellers from now terminating the discussion. At the same time, you are preparing the ground for your next move in the negotiation—closing the deal.

What follows now are ways to apply, in practice, the powerful but easily learned tactics introduced briefly in the previous chapter. Keep in mind that these can be used at almost any stage in the negotiation, not just to close the deal.

### How to Apply the Attractive Alternatives Tactic

From your initial contact with the owner your discussion will have included casual mention of other homes that have captured your interest. There is no need to sound like a broken record about this, which would only diminish your credibility anyway. Make the point once, at first, then refer only occasionally to the other homes. You can be certain the owner will remember.

On your second contact, mention the alternatives again, perhaps in comparing features. But try to work it into the conversation in a way that sounds natural. At all costs, avoid making it seem contrived as, then, the owner will see it as a ploy. If that happens, you'll have lost an important advantage and may have made your task harder.

Here are a few examples of what I mean by working it into the conversation and making it sound natural and reasonable:

1. "I'm sorry I have to rush away, but I've arranged to make a second inspection on that two-story home at 4 p.m. and I don't want to keep the owners waiting. I'm sure you understand."

2. "It's really quite a coincidence. Your home is remarkably similar—almost identical—in layout to another home my

wife and I will be seeing for the second time, later this evening."

3. "Rather than making things *easier*, finding a couple of homes you like at the same time makes the decision so much harder. My husband favors one of the other nice homes we've seen, but I'm not so sure."

Another option you have is to pick a feature that the Smiths' home does not have and incorporate that into your comments about other homes. For example:

4. "My wife is keen on a bigger home that we've looked at twice, just south of here, but yours is quite big enough for me."

5. "We've seen a couple of homes with an extra bedroom, which is nice to have—it's a feature my husband really likes—but, personally, I think we could get by here without one."

6. "We looked a few times at another nice home—one with big bright windows. We like it a lot; it's probably a tiny bit smaller than this."

Each of these last three comments keeps the owner's attention on features that are important to you, not offered by this home. Thus, you are indirectly diminishing the value of the Smith home, but you are doing it inoffensively and with subtlety.

By letting it be known that you have attractive alternatives, you are laying the foundation for a successful negotiation.

## How to Apply the Stall and Jolt Tactic

I added this phrase to the lexicon of negotiation because it describes aptly and simply the two stages of the maneuver. Plus it's easy to remember. As we saw earlier, when the proposition is put to you, you stall. Say absolutely nothing. Just fix your gaze on the ground. Your stance and body language should communicate only that something is going through your head. Your eyes-to-the-floor gaze suggests it isn't positive. Forget what you learned about the value of eye contact. This isn't one of those situations.

Allow the silence to continue as long as possible even if the atmosphere grows tense, as it should, and will, if you hold out long enough. Five seconds will seem like twenty to the seller. If you can stretch it to ten seconds, even better. Sometimes the tension will compel the seller to try to justify her price or even to reduce it still further. In either case, you react in exactly the same way. After a momentary glance up you focus again on the ground and remain silent. Because this is a deliberate stall tactic, the silent period can be stretched out for a longer time than with other tactics.

That's the stall. Now, slowly bring your attention back to the owner; it's time for the jolt. The jolt you deliver is a new lower offer accompanied by a short, slow, reasoned justification.

Here's an example: Suppose the property you want to buy has an asking price of $164,000. You are interested, though your goal is to buy for $152,000 or less. The owner has just put this proposition to you:

Owner: *Look, if you're seriously interested in the home I'm willing to take $6,000 off. You can have it for $158,000.*

Clearly, the owner is feeling the tension. You might be the only current prospect. In short, you're in control. Are you going to accept this price concession? Not a chance. The most important thing to do now is to remain *silent!* Four seconds. Six seconds. Ten seconds. You're in the *stall* stage. Then you respond genuinely and understandingly—with the jolt!

Buyer: *I like your home and I could be interested in buying it from you. But, based on other homes I've seen—and one in particular I'm looking at now—and also what my inspector tells me I'd have to spend here, the most I could pay for this property is $146,750, or possibly slightly more.'*

The seller will probably balk at this, but the chance of terminating the discussion is low. However, if you suspect that is likely, you can add a saving comment to keep some glimmer of hope alive. Be careful: The trap you can fall into here is acting prematurely. Take it slowly, then suggest that you are prepared to go over your finances and calculations again to see if there is any room to cut back on the cost of repairs and refurbishing. At that point you might open your notebook and start checking and perhaps scribbling down some changes while wearing the heaviest frown you can muster.

As you pour over your scribblings, it's a good idea to make an occasional remark to yourself in low but audible tones. A deft head scratch or two will also emphasize your difficult predicament. Your mumblings might include comments like: Maybe ... no ... could possibly save a few dollars there … hmm … maybe … maybe cut back. You get the idea.

Then, after some more mathematics, you continue (note carefully the first two words and the last sentence):

> Buyer:    *I'm sorry. Even though I would like to buy your home, the best I could do would be $148,500. Why don't you think it over and let me know tonight or tomorrow? I'm definitely going to buy something in the next day or two—before Wednesday, I hope. My financing is cleared, so I'm ready to buy immediately.*

Rather than stopping bluntly at, "…the best I could do would be $148,500," your interests are better served by sounding less urgent and by inviting no immediate response from the owner. This emphasizes again that you have options but you are still genuinely interested. You can take it or leave it. Your whole persona reflects this.

If the Smiths are prepared to compromise further, they are likely to do whatever possible to prevent you from leaving. Bear in mind throughout this exchange that, as we saw earlier, the seller usually has a more urgent need to sell than buyers imagine. Sometimes, the need is desperate. The moment you walk out the door, the seller's chances diminish steeply. Over the course of even 12 hours many things could happen to kill your interest in that house. If the sellers are going to make you a better offer, this is the safest moment to act or face the consequence of not acting.

Maybe you'll hear something like this:

> Mrs. Smith:    *Listen, we want to be reasonable. We're willing to meet you halfway. What would that be? Say, $153,000. You can't ask for fairer than that.*

But you can. You can ask for whatever you want. Where you go from here is up to you. The strongest tactic you have available now is to motion to leave. That's the last thing the Smiths want. They're getting used to having you around (really, they're getting to like the idea that they're on the brink of a sale).

Although this scenario is hypothetical and things don't generally happen this quickly, it is, nonetheless, typical of a significant percentage of property transactions when the buyer understands and applies even the most basic negotiation techniques.

## How to Apply the Comparative Value Tactic

Let's stick with the same example; the Smiths reduced their price from $164,000 to $158,000 and are staring at you waiting for an answer.

You decide to use the Comparative Value tactic:

> Buyer:    *I am genuinely interested in your home, and I am in a position to buy. The problem I have is this: I've looked at three or four other homes that compare with yours and, to me, they seem to represent better value for money, with little or no repairs or refurbishing. Still, I'm interested in your home and I'm prepared to pay what I consider a fair price. To me it's worth $146,750.*

Immediate rejection of your offer shouldn't frighten you. It's often an instinctive reaction. Equally often, it's a calculated response by the owner to embarrass you into making a *sensible* offer. Whichever you suspect, hold your ground. As the dialogue continues the prospect of losing the sale looms larger in the owner's thinking, prompting a more compromising attitude.

Then, proceed as before. You are willing to go over your figures. Here, too, you take out your notebook and refigure the costs you'll incur, a make-believe exercise perhaps, but it is important for you to understand the reason for this "refiguring." When you make a concession, your credibility and power will depend, to a great extent, on the apparent justification you find for doing so. Making an increased offer without a justifiable reason damages the perception you've striven to build in the mind of the seller.

Here are some useful justifications you can use to support your decision to increase your offer:

1.  Openly re-figuring your costs, as we've seen, to squeeze the expenses you will incur and scrape together a few extra dollars

2.  Phoning your bank (or mother, spouse, attorney, etc.) to see if you can borrow more money

3.  Having the owner agree to carry out repairs, replacements, landscaping, etc.

4.  Deciding to sell your car to add a few dollars to your offer

5.  Getting the owner to agree to pay a larger part of the closing costs

6.    Saying you are prepared to spend a little more than you believe the home is worth because your spouse thinks you should give it "one last try"

You'll have to use your own feeling for the situation to determine which of these or others is most appropriate. If, all along, you have claimed that you believe your offer reflects what the home is worth (a value argument), it would be inappropriate then to base a higher offer on being able to free up more money. Your position should be definite. Either you are offering what you believe to be a fair price, or you are claiming you have no more money to spend. One of these strategies must dominate. Otherwise you risk not being believed. On the other hand, a spouse's liking for a home is a legitimate basis for making an offer above what you personally believe the property is worth.

It is almost always better to take the approach that your offer is based on fair value. Having no more money is generally not quite as powerful, though there are situations in which it works very well.

One of the very best examples I've seen of this refiguring technique occurred when Kathy, my then wife-to-be, and I went shopping for our wedding rings. When we found what we liked I asked the clerk what discount we could expect, as we were buying two reasonably expensive rings for cash. After checking with his boss the sales clerk brought back the answer. We could deduct 12.5 percent from the price of one ring; no discount on the other. We rejected that, so off he went and brought back a better deal. This happened a third time but, working to a strategy I had devised, we thanked him and said "no, thank you." Before we reached the door the owner stopped us, asked us to come back, and said he would deal with us himself and would "work something out." Well, to cut a long story short, he made us two very slightly better offers, both of which we rejected. He "arrived" at each new price after lengthy refiguring using a legal pad and calculator. His final price, the one we accepted, took him a good five minutes of mathematics and muttering to work out. He was a good tactician and ran an extremely successful group of stores. What he didn't know was that he was dealing with a buyer who knew how to negotiate. As we saw earlier, that's a *big* advantage and it's a *quiet* advantage. One that should never be weakened or eliminated by informing the other side of your skill—even after you have sealed a good deal. Egotism has no place in negotiation of this sort.

By the way, the jewelry store owner confided to us, just before making us the offer we accepted, that he was going to "bend the rules" to find a way to get us an "exceptional price." Undoubtedly, it was a ploy (and a smart seller tactic), but one put to good use by an astute businessman. Did he make a profit in the end? Certainly he did, or he wouldn't have made the deal.

So far, we've seen the Stall and Jolt and the Comparative Value tactics. How else might you reject a reduced price offer made to you by a seller? The next one is a classic.

### How to Apply the Third Party Tactic

Look at a few statements that I'm sure you've heard *many* times in everyday life:

My bank won't go for that.

My wife has her eye on something else.

My lawyer isn't comfortable with that arrangement.

My partner just doesn't seem to want to agree.

My kids prefer to be close to the beach.

My accountant feels I should hold off on this.

The *Third Party* tactic is simple and comfortable. And it works. Like all tactics, though, it requires good judgment in its application. This is one of the most difficult tactics for the seller to argue against. The chief reason, of course, is that the "third party" is either absent or fictitious. Or, at least, the authority or guidance ascribed to the third party is fictitious. Also, he or she may be conferred with unchallengeable *expert* status (architect, lawyer, etc.), whether expert or not. When the third party is distant from the negotiation the seller has no opportunity to persuade; no opportunity to argue a case face to face.

By distancing yourself from the responsibility of making the final decision (as the seller perceives it, the third party will control the decision), you create a less competitive atmosphere between you and the other side. This allows you to offer the seller understanding and empathy, when appropriate, but not necessarily to agree with the seller's opinion on price or value. These types of situations sometimes cause the seller to tell you things he or she wouldn't have done had you been engaged in head-to-head negotiation.

Comfortable as the Third Party tactic is, it still requires you to research and prepare as you would for any negotiation. You'll have to be careful, too, not to create an overly friendly atmosphere in your discussions with the seller. In fact, your performance should not differ from that which I've recommended throughout this book. The Third Party tactic is simply that, a tactic you may choose in response to the seller making you a reduced-price offer, or at other points in the negotiation.

The effectiveness of this tactic stems from the fact that it slows up the momentum while maintaining a noncompetitive relationship between you and the seller. Usually, the more time a seller puts into negotiating with you (or even prior to the negotiation beginning), the better chance you have of achieving the lowest price. Since the seller can't talk directly (usually) to the third party, you move closer to filling the role of go-between. You can agree to discuss the seller's offer with the third party, but if he or she (the third party) is not very keen on the price or the neighborhood or the kitchen, the answer is unlikely to be a full acceptance, regardless of *your* opinion.

A spouse or partner is often the best third party. A parent or son or daughter can also fill the role effectively, as can your architect or mortgage lender or, to a lesser extent, your attorney. If the third party is a real person (your husband or wife, for example), you should try to arrange it so that person plays a secondary role in the face-to-face discussions and negotiation, particularly in the later stages. The easiest way to do that is to leave them out of the exchanges between you and the seller. As I pointed out previously, it's difficult, if not impossible, for the seller to "sell" the features or the value of the home to someone he can't talk to.

Recognizing the best moment to introduce the Third Party tactic is important and will come from your feel for the situation. Usually, it's best left until you have reached the offer stage. Up to that point, everything proceeds according to the behavior you've adopted right from your first contact with the seller—the behavior of an astute, informed homebuyer. No tactic changes this demeanor that I've outlined extensively, until that tactic is introduced into the price negotiation. Then, of course, you let your tactic dominate your position and your discussion. For example, when the third party is not someone accompanying you (perhaps your architect or electrician or mortgage lender), he or she should be introduced into the conversation only when the tactic is being put into operation. Before that point, no mention should be made of the existence of the third party.

Let's go back once again to our example and apply the Third party tactic. You are interested in the home and are about to make your second inspection. Remember, you have had no negotiation on price with the Smiths yet, but you have had your architect or home inspector compile a home inspection report. That report has indicated that the property is in reasonably good condition. Clearly, some minor repairs and maintenance are required, but no major work or heavy expense is involved:

> Mr. Smith: *Look, if you're seriously interested in the home we're willing to take $6,000 off. You can have it for $158,000.*

Remember, the owners are feeling the tension. They want a sale. Today, if possible. They're anxious, and you are their only serious prospect (seldom are sellers so lucky as to have two or more prospective buyers competing for their home):

> Buyer: *My husband and I both like your house. I'm particularly keen on the flower garden (note, this is hardly a feature that is likely to add much strength to the seller's position, if any). But I know my husband believes we can get a bigger house (or four-bedroom, newer, better neighborhood, etc.) for our money. We like another home that is very similar to yours but quite a bit less expensive. I do prefer your house, though. It's just that I haven't been able to convince my husband to consider it seriously, though, as I said, he does like it.*

Then, stay silent once more. Do not say a single word, even if the pressure reaches a point that seems unbearable. The owners are feeling even more pressure. Let it push them to respond. That might happen immediately. Or it might take five very long seconds, even longer. It is decidedly to your benefit that the owners break the silence.

Here's another way to use the same tactic:

> Buyer: *I understand you are keen to sell. And I do like your home. So does my husband. But my husband also likes another home that's quite attractive and reasonably priced—though it wouldn't be my first choice. But for the price, we'd buy yours.*

This is a softer approach, yet your message is still abundantly clear. You are interested, but not at the seller's reduced price—$158,000. And, as always, when you make a statement like this, you shut up!

## How to Apply the No More Money Tactic

Don't be deceived by the apparent simplicity of this tactic. When used at the wrong stage in a negotiation, or in an inappropriate situation, it can do more harm than good.

Almost never should this tactic be used alone. It is powerful and strongly persuasive only when used in combination with another tactic. Just as importantly, no matter how many or what combination of tactics you use, *No More Money* should generally be the last tactic introduced into the negotiation. An obvious exception to that is the Walk Away tactic, which, typically, is introduced later.

You'll appreciate, too, that claiming you have no more money is effective only when a very big gap does not exist between your figure and the seller's. It isn't effective, either, before you have made at least one increase on your first offer. In fact, the best way to prepare to use the No More Money tactic is by making a number of small increases, thereby giving the impression that you've exhausted your spending budget and are at or dangerously close to your limit. In such an atmosphere, there's a reasonable chance the seller will believe that they are flogging a dead horse—that there's simply no more money to be squeezed out of you. That's exactly what this tactic is designed to imply.

Of utmost importance, though, throughout the negotiation, is that you make it clear that you believe your offer is a fair one. You've based it on your informed estimate of the value of the home—its value to *you*. No offer you make must ever be seen by the seller to be based solely on how much you can afford. Remember, the limits of your budget bear no direct relationship to the value of a piece of real estate. The two things are totally distinct and unrelated.

For these reasons, your main negotiation argument—your estimate of fair value—should be built on factors that directly concern the home in question—value for money, size, age, condition, style, brightness, location, decor, layout, or a combination of such qualities and features.

To be most persuasive, this tactic and the atmosphere you build should communicate the following message to the seller:

> *I'm convinced that I've been fair and reasonable and that the home is not worth more than the offer I've made. I'm concerned because this figure is already over my budget. Even if the house was twice as large and had an ocean view, I simply wouldn't be able to spend more than I've offered. I just have no more money.*

While you may not speak exactly these words—at least not in one go—this is what the seller should be reading from what you do, what you say, and how you say it.

In an earlier section, I explained the importance of keeping your true spending limit confidential. Whether buying through an agent or directly from a private seller, that rule must always be observed. If you break it, you lock yourself into a position you cannot later retract. Thus, you forfeit the opportunity to claim you have no more money. The other side already knows how much you have to spend because you told them.

If you have applied the No More Money tactic and it appears to have failed, you still have a couple of positive options—even if the seller has flatly refused your highest offer. In this situation, you must appear to accept that you will *not* be buying the home. Act like you are reluctantly about to conclude the discussion. Thank the sellers, compliment them on their home and wish them good luck in finding another buyer. Then, make one or more distancing comments such as:

1. *I guess the way I should look at it is that it makes our choice easier. In a way it's a pity, because we both like your home. But then, there are others we like, too. That's how we've got to look at it, I suppose.*

2. *Well, I think we both tried our best. And that's all we can do with anything in life. Thank you.*

3. *Well, thank you, Mr. and Mrs. Smith. I'm sorry we won't be buying your home. I wish we could have reached an agreement. Good luck in finding another buyer. You have a really nice home.*

The idea here is to start pulling away from the closeness and the hope you built up during the negotiation. To the seller it will feel like everything that was warm is getting cold and final—not a good feeling. Let this atmosphere play as long as you can. Stall and delay as you prepare to leave, but don't let it be obvious that you are doing so. Write your name and phone number on a card, and hand it to the seller. Pick a few insignificant questions out of the air (for example, "How did you get the roses to grow so well?"). Make them seem like parting remarks before you bid farewell for good.

Don't show any sign that you believe a deal is still possible—not yet. For now, you've "accepted" defeat. The great warrior is working for you—time. Let it work.

Your exiting of the home is the hardest and most pressuresome time for the seller, and often will produce a concession, or even an acceptance of your offer. If you leave, the seller faces the uncertainty of a "no buyer" situation all over again tomorrow.

However, if worse turns to worst and no concession is in sight, all is still not lost. You can take it all the way. Get into your car and drive off. Whatever new offer you might decide to make can be communicated later—at least a day later. No sooner. Give the seller time to contact you first.

Another alternative is this: Just as you exit the home, or after walking back from your car, make a new, slightly higher offer. For this to work it needs all the conviction you can muster, along with a very good explanation of where the extra dollars are coming from. Just a few moments ago you claimed, very persuasively, that you had no more money. How do you now avoid being disbelieved?

Perhaps in the car your husband reminded you that he is due a couple of thousand dollars in holiday pay the following month. Or that your tax rebate check should arrive within a week or two. When you "discover" this extra money, you can make it part of your offer. The chief requirement is to be believable.

Another discovered source of money could be a decision to borrow from your brother or parents. Just a little, of course, and only if it would clinch the deal. When you seem to be bending over backwards like this, it endears you to the seller and often influences a decision in your favor.

Whatever source of extra money you discover, it must appear understandable why it didn't occur to you earlier. So make the source unusual. A few examples might be withdrawing money from your retirement fund, even if you'll be penalized for doing it; selling the 1966 Mustang you are restoring; borrowing from your kids' college fund; cashing in part of your life insurance policy (anything, in fact, that you can make sound credible). To achieve that, not only your explanation but also your performance must be convincing.

You're doing what you're doing, you explain, because you want to be certain later that you gave it your very best shot. Then, even if it should fail, you'll be able to walk away happy.

The seller might still say no but offer a further price reduction. At that stage, you're just going to have to be creative and weigh up the situation. Try to judge how much *give* is still in the seller. And remember, the more time you spend with the seller (better in person than communicating by phone), the greater your chance of a successful deal.

When you've made the new offer based on your discovered money, you can still use the Walk Away tactic. You'll walk away and forget the entire deal if your new offer can't buy the home. Then, if it comes to it and you have to follow through on your threat, there's nothing but pride and a little ingenuity stopping you from adding another small amount then, or later.

How much this might be will depend on the price of the home and on how much "discovered" money you have already added. An extra $5,000 or $10,000 might be appropriate on a $250,000 to $500,000 property. On an $80,000 or $100,000 home, $250 to $1,000 would be more appropriate. Even here, though, it's difficult to lay down hard, emphatic rules. If in doubt, err on the lower side. There's nothing that says you can't increase an offer of, say, $300,000 by a thousand dollars or two. Only the situation can tell you if such an increase is likely to move you closer to a deal or alienate the seller to the point where it puts the negotiation in jeopardy.

Before we move on, I must repeat the caution I gave earlier. You cannot use the No More Money tactic as the basis for your initial offer. That must be seen to be based on what you believe the home is worth. Then, later, you get the chance to use "no more money." And, after that, perhaps "no more money" plus your "discovered" dollars. Then, if necessary, maybe a few dollars more, until the deal comes together or is clearly out of reach.

This is a powerful tactic that requires a little more skill than many of the others. That skill is largely in your performance, particularly in how believable you can be.

### How to Answer the Question: "How Much Would You Be Prepared to Offer?"

In many cases, the seller will respond to a buyer's objection to the asking price with the question: "How much would you be prepared to offer me?"

Here, you have the opportunity to use the Third Party tactic again. Here's one possibility:

Buyer:  *Well, we hadn't actually discussed making an offer for your home. I'm pretty sure, though, that I could not convince my husband to pay more than what we can buy the other home for. That owner will accept $146,750.*

Again, don't add anything once you've made the statement. The owner will probably balk at this figure. That doesn't necessarily mean rejection, only that the negotiation is under way. If the seller persists with the view that the house is definitely worth more than your offer, put on a show of quiet disappointment but understanding that you understand his situation. Try this:

Buyer:    *I do understand what you are saying. I know it isn't easy to sell your own home. It is still a fact, though, that there are quite a number of attractive homes available around the price I mentioned.*

Then, after a pause:

Buyer:    *I do like your home, though, and I will talk with my husband. I think I'd be able to get him to pay around the same price as the other home we're considering—$146,750.*

Now, you've not only reestablished your offer figure, but you've injected an element of doubt into the proceedings. Maybe you'll be able to get your spouse to pay $146,750. But maybe not. Yet you're clearly a serious, interested buyer.

The very subtle but powerful implication in what you have said is often missed even by experienced negotiators. What you just did is put you and the Smiths on one side, and your spouse on the other. That's the reason for *repeating* your preference for the home. The sellers will like you for it and it will keep alive hope that an agreement can be reached, despite the fact that you have rejected their reduced price offer of $158,000.

By any measure, you have put yourself in a strong position. You may not buy the home for $146,750, but the next move is the Smiths. Expect a further price cut.

First, though, prepare for another recitation on the virtues of the property. And perhaps, too, a number of less-than-outright rejections: "Oh, I couldn't possibly accept that. It's just too low."

If the seller makes no mention of a compromise, you should return to your point about your preference for this home over the one your spouse favors. Then point out clearly that your spouse's leaning in favor of the other home is based solely on value for money, and that, all things being equal, he, too, "wouldn't hesitate" to buy the Smith home. The phrase *wouldn't hesitate* is an important key to persuasion in this situation. To the seller, it makes a sale seem tantalizingly close.

When determining your strategy and tactics, keep in mind that home sellers and their situations vary greatly. Your approach must be based on who you are, your objectives, and the information you have that allows you to read the situation at hand.

But what if a seller gives no hint that he or she is willing to compromise? What if the seller seems completely unperturbed by your opinion of value? Let's assume you have stretched out the discussion on the property's potential shortcomings, not least of which is your view that it is overpriced. And you've gone through anticipated expenses a new owner would incur while, at the same time, playing down or ignoring the positive features. You've been doubly careful not to offend the Smiths regarding maintenance, noting the inevitability of aging in all buildings. But still, you see no sign of flexibility. Where do you go from here?

Obviously, what you have failed to do, so far, is to alter the sellers' thinking. Your task now is to get them to consider a different reality—yours; the reality of a lower price. As you dig deeper, the statements you made earlier about the other house take on added significance. Because you referred to it *before* your interest in the Smith's home was declared, it doesn't seem like a hastily thought-up ploy. Now you must build on it.

Sellers almost without exception, price their property higher than the figure they are willing to accept. And while all sellers are flexible to some degree, some are also quite stubborn, holding tight to the belief that it is not in their interest to volunteer a price reduction. Then, you are forced to be more assertive and to "win" the concessions. You do this through the use of tactical questions, statements, and actions, and by influencing the seller's perceptions. Using a combination of the tactics we've already covered will help you do that. Here are a couple of additional suggestions.

### How and When to Use a Probing Statement Instead of Making an Offer

Let's assume the seller hasn't yet offered to reduce the asking price of $164,000. A probing statement by you pushes aside a lot of the posturing sellers go through before revealing their willingness to compromise. Here's an example you might try:

Buyer:    *Your home is similar in many respects to the other property we're considering buying. But your asking price is a lot higher. In my opinion, the other home is not quite as attractive as yours, but it's slightly larger. They've told us they'll accept $146,750 for it.*

Whether the seller responds immediately or not, don't wait long to add part two of this probing statement:

Buyer:    *We'll definitely buy something immediately—probably today or tomorrow. If I can get my husband to make you an offer it would be at the same price—$146,750.*

This is an effective probing statement because it forces the seller to respond in a way that will give you an opportunity to learn his or her thinking on price. Listen well and long if you have to, but don't help. The more the seller talks, the more likely he or she is to rethink the home's value, and the closer he or she will move to a compromise position of some kind. That's your signal to employ a tactic or two and to remember and use the negotiation techniques you are most comfortable with.

Note that you haven't yet made an offer. Not even a verbal one. So there's nothing, formally, to accept or reject. Nonetheless, the Smiths feels compelled to respond. As you wait for a reaction, avoid eye contact completely. For reasons that have to do with psychology, not generally well understood, direct eye contact in a situation like this usually works *against* you. It can embarrass and intimidate a seller into a stronger defense. What you have presented here is not a challenge or an ultimatum and nothing you do should even hint at such. The impression a probing statement communicates must be matter-of-fact conversation. In even mildly adversarial communication, face-to-face positions and direct eye contact signal a challenge. In this situation, that would be entirely counterproductive, possibly even putting your goal out of reach.

With a probing statement, you will help your cause also by sounding open, genuine, and factual. The last thing you need is an open contest of wills between you and the seller. In fact, negotiating from an aggressive or superior stance, *or one that is perceived that way by the other side,* will rarely lead to the best deal—the seller's lowest acceptable price.

Making a probing statement work effectively always requires careful judgment and a convincing presentation. More than that, it requires you to have spent some time building a good rapport with the seller. A brief encounter won't do it.

When you have made your probing statement explaining your feelings about value for money and your partner's preference for another home (and, of course, the fact that you are potentially interested in the property), start moving very slowly toward the exit. Do this even while the seller is responding. If you get the slightest hint of flexibility, slow up your departure. Allow yourself to be side-tracked by a feature that catches your attention. The brickwork on a fireplace or a built-in bookshelf are suitable distractions. Feel the texture and admire the design as you while away extra minutes.

Your casual disinterest and your avoidance of eye contact will communicate your probing statement as just that—a statement, not a deliberately disguised trick question, after which you stand waiting for an answer. Naturally, the seller's defenses will be heightened to a greater degree if you appear to be merely testing the price in preparation for making an offer.

What you are hoping your probing statement will do is throw light on the Smiths' resolve and on how badly they want or need to sell. When that happens, you, nonetheless, continue the discussion without hinting at any sudden, stronger interest in the home.

In responding to your probing statement, the Smiths have just two options: comment specifically on what you have just said, or respond in a totally unrelated manner. Either choice will tell you more about their true position, which will guide you in how to proceed with the negotiation.

There will come a point when you will tell the seller directly how much you are willing to pay. At that stage it won't be a probing statement, but a verbal offer to which the seller will have to respond. In the next chapter we'll examine 10 ways the seller can respond to your low offer, and how best to handle each one. But now, let's look at the *ultimate tactic*.

## Walking Away—The Ultimate Tactic

We've already seen how acting like you are about to terminate the negotiation can be used in combination with other tactics such as No More Money. The fear that you will walk away is always in the seller's mind. The more genuine and more interested you seem, the greater that fear, particularly as concessions are made and the gap between your figure and the seller's diminishes.

Sellers, on the other hand, enjoy no "walk away" privilege. They must persist until they find a buyer, which is to your distinct advantage. Still, the Walk-Away tactic is one you must use *carefully* and with *subtlety*. It must never be used in the form of an ultimatum but must be seen as an inevitable consequence of your inability to reach agreement—an unfortunate conclusion, one you arrive at reluctantly.

When applied in a context like this, it exerts maximum leverage on the seller—leverage that quite often leads to further concession and agreement, especially when there's been an investment of time in the negotiation and when the seller sees you as a reasonable and genuine buyer. Even the most stubborn of sellers chooses to relent, to some degree at least, at the prospect of a serious, qualified buyer walking away.

When making your exit, remember that many agreements and concessions come late in the negotiation. In fact, *most* come after a deadline has passed or when the prospect of agreement seems to have faded.

For that reason, follow through with your exit even when the seller makes no attempt to lure you back into discussion. The seller might call you later with the concession you wanted, or one close to it. Invite the seller to call you if he or she has a change of mind. Then, if that doesn't happen, you can, as we saw earlier, "discover" a few extra dollars, which gives you a reason for recontacting the seller and resuming the negotiation. Don't allow pride to stop you from doing this. A good deal is worth a lot more than any slight your ego might suffer.

Also, it's almost always best to conduct the negotiation in person rather than over the phone. If that means going back to the home a second or third time, do it! You'll be increasing your chance of buying at the lowest price possible.

Every day the home is on the market, the seller is dealing with uncertainty. Maybe the home will hard be to sell; maybe it will sit on the market for months. Are the people looking at it genuine buyers? Is the asking price too high? and so on. All this uncertainty ends on the day the house sells and turns into cash. The seller can then go ahead with his or her life and plans—a major relief. All these factors are working for you as a homebuyer, though the seller will rarely admit these feelings.

Why do I emphasize so strongly these homebuyer advantages? Because, with just a few exceptions, all the homebuyers I encounter believe the opposite to be true, that the advantages lie with the sellers. That is seldom the case. Stop for a minute and consider what sellers need. They need to sell to go on to whatever their goals happen to be; they need money (yours); they have a timetable of some kind, which they would like to stick to; and so on. In short, sellers have a lot riding on making the sale and less riding on the price they accept. Taking $5,000 less than expected won't abort a seller's plans. Holding out too long, or not getting the sale at all, *could* be detrimental, in a number of ways, to the seller's hopes and goals.

For these and many other reasons, sellers do not want to see a genuine buyer walk away from the negotiation. Taking a lower price is often a better solution than holding out and continuing to deal each day with the terrible uncertainty of it all.

### Buyers' Market or Sellers' Market

At seminars, when I speak on negotiation, one question that always seems to come up concerns the natural cycles and trends that occur in property markets. Buyers' markets and sellers' markets—when can you negotiate, and when not?

The simple answer—and, fortunately in this case, the correct one—is that you can *always* negotiate. Of course, common sense must play a part in *how* you negotiate. It goes without saying that you can negotiate harder when there are a few buyers and many sellers—when homes are not selling well. This is what is called a *buyers' market*. Sellers find it difficult to turn their homes into cash. Consequently, prices tend to decrease and, typically, have more flexibility in them. The sellers who refuse to follow this trend in the market usually have problems locating willing buyers. Eventually, most are forced to withdraw their homes or accept lower prices.

In a buyers' market, the homebuyer can, naturally, expect greater negotiating success, as a general rule. A sellers' market is just the opposite. This occurs when there is a shortage of homes for sale in a particular area, and an abundance of eager buyers. Such a 'hot' market generates competition among buyers, causes homes to sell fast, and tends to push prices higher.

Two keys to making a successful purchase in a sellers' market are, first, to secure loan approval before you go house hunting, and second, to inspect properties as soon as they come on the market.

Most of the time, though, residential property markets are at neither extreme. That is, the demand for homes isn't so low that properties can't be sold, nor so high that there are many buyers clamoring to purchase each home that comes onto the market. Generally, the demand for homes fluctuates between being slightly in favor of sellers to being slightly in favor of buyers. In a recession, demand falls, fewer sales are made and prices tend to remain stable or drop. In better economic times, especially when inflation is high, as it was in the 1970s and part of the 1980s, the opposite is true.

What a lot of homebuyers fail to appreciate is that despite whether the market favors buyers or sellers, there is a private situation behind every home for sale. There are anxious, motivated, impatient, flexible and even desperate sellers in every market. *At any time,* a good negotiation strategy can save you thousands of dollars. All you have to do is gather the facts that are relevant to your objective; recognize the signs given by sellers that reveal their true position and needs; remember how valuable nearby neighbors can be in alerting you to problems and potential advantages; and know the basic negotiation tactics that are at your disposal.

It is extremely important not to let the opinions of real estate agents or friends dissuade you from negotiating. As a negotiator, your chance of saving more hard-earned cash is always infinitely better than those buyers who choose, for whatever reason, not to negotiate. I can't overemphasize that success in the vast majority of negotiations depends *less* on external factors such as market conditions, and more on the needs of the seller and the know-how of the buyer. In particular, your success depends on your ability to select and apply the simple negotiation tactics covered in this book. And your willingness to have faith in them. Be certain—they do work!

## KEY POINTS TO REMEMBER

- Neighbors close to a home you are interested in will often be your best sources of information about that home and the immediate area. Knock on a few doors, introduce yourself politely, and soak up quality information.

- Agents and sellers make assessments and judgments based on what you do, say, and communicate. This is how they form their perception of you.

- Success in negotiation is based on what the other side perceives to be true and not necessarily on what is actually true.

- Consciously feed and dictate their perceptions in the right way, and you take control.

- Don't compliment a home in such a way that you add to the owner's estimate of its value.

- Negative comments you make about a home that interests you should relate to matters of genuine concern. However, your degree of concern, even if only minor, can be used to win concessions.

- A professional home Inspection is worth the expense, as it can highlight hidden defects and eliminate unpleasant surprises that show up after the sale. It can also provide you with an edge in negotiation by adding the power of legitimacy to your position. (See the Appendix for toll-free numbers and other contact information.)

- When you state your position to the seller, don't act like you expect an instant decision. This form of imposed urgency can be counterproductive, especially when you have put your 'best' price before the seller.

- Try to "find" a reason or a new way to make an increased offer. "Refigure" estimated expenses or repairs or come up with additional "discovered" dollars.

- An offer based on the value of the home—as you see it—is almost always a better argument than claiming simply that you cannot afford to make a higher offer.

- The Third Party tactic reduces competition between you and the seller, slows up the momentum, and puts you in the position of conciliator. Use it in the later stages of the negotiation only.

- Silence is a powerful tactic. Recognize when to shut up and let it work.

- Don't use No More Money as an equal main tactic while claiming that you are offering what you believe is a fair price for the home. The most No More Money can be, in that case, is a secondary justification for you sticking to your offer. Avoid making this tactic the sole basis for your offer.

- When working through an agent, or directly with a seller, help the seller to see a 'reality' other than the one he or she is locked in to. This other reality makes clear the logic of your position and the fairness and objectivity of your offer.

- Face-to-face positions and eye-to-eye contact work against you in many negotiation situations!

- When you find a home you like, go back and inspect it three or four times, but delay the start of the offer stage, then let the negotiation proceed slowly.

- Let no one, agent or otherwise, talk you out of negotiating, regardless of how "pointless" they try to convince you it is. In virtually all cases, this is either a tactic or it is due to inexperience. Whatever the reason, it's a line you won't fall for.

# CHAPTER TEN

# INVISIBLE NEGOTIATION IN ACTION—PART TWO

*A man who says he is willing to meet you halfway is usually a bad judge of distance.*
—ANONYMOUS

Throughout this section, I will reintroduce, apply, and explain many of the most important points we covered in earlier chapters. Even on a general reading, this will help you see the negotiation process as a whole rather than just a number of disconnected elements. Here, you will appreciate more clearly how the negotiation develops and concludes. I will match tactics to particularly appropriate situations and I will apply other points we've already covered to circumstances in which they are relevant and easy to understand.

Virtually all of the suggestions in this section can be used just as easily and as effectively when a real estate agent or salesperson is involved in the negotiation. Where adaptations or slight changes are needed, they will be simple and readily apparent.

### Dealing with Ten Seller Responses to Your Low Offer

Here is a list of the 10 most common ways sellers respond to a buyer's low offer or probing statement. On the following pages you will find what I believe are the best ways you can handle each situation so that you maximize your chances of getting the home you want for the fewest dollars possible.

First, the list:

1. I couldn't possibly sell my home for that price.

2. I'm willing to be flexible on price, but I won't come down to that figure.

3. I don't believe it's possible today to buy a home of this quality for that price.

4. The people selling that other house you mentioned must desperately need to sell. Luckily, I'm not in that position.

5. You say you're going to buy in the next day or two. Well, if you're genuinely interested in my home, I'm prepared to come down to (say) $158,000, but not any lower.

6. Look, I believe this home is worth every cent of the price I am asking. I don't want to fool around. What's the best price you're prepared to pay?

7. I'm not sure if I told you the electrical wiring was completely renewed just two years ago. And the heating system will be under warranty for another four year (avoidance).

8. When do you plan to talk to your husband? (wife, attorney, etc.)

9. I'll be as fair as I can be. I'll meet you halfway. Can we agree on (say) $158,000?

10. No way! You're just wasting my time with an offer like that.

Now let's look at how you can handle each of these, one by one. Bear in mind that in most cases where I use *husband,* you may substitute wife, boyfriend, girlfriend, mother, father, banker, or attorney with just slight alteration.

For consistency, we'll stay with the same scenario we've been using. The home is on the market at $164,000. You like it, but not at that price. You would be seriously interested at a figure in the low $150s—no higher. You have made an offer of $146,750. Or, you have just used a probing statement in which you mentioned that same figure.

Now, as you read about how to handle yourself in the various situations, imagine actually being there—not just reading the words. Imagine how you and the seller would think and feel in the actual situation. Think about the needs, desires, anxiousness, perspectives, hopes, plans, options, risks, skills, and perceptions of both sides. The better you can do this, the more you will appreciate why and how invisible negotiation puts power and protection at your disposal.

1. Seller:    *I couldn't possibly sell my home for that price.*

Your reply here should sound as factual and as reasonable as you can make it. You say:

Buyer:    *Well, based entirely on what I've seen, Mr. Smith, since we started looking some months ago, $146,750 seems to me to be about what people are paying in this area for this kind of home.*

If this line of reasoning succeeds in convincing the Smiths to reduce their price further, your next offer, and subsequent offers, should come after a show of doubt and reluctance by you. And then, only in small, spaced increases. Creep or crawl up slowly, if you must. But never leap!

But what if the seller sticks stubbornly to the asking price? In that case, inquire, courteously, how they have kept up to date with *actual* prices buyers have been willing to pay in their neighborhood. Stress the difference between prices actually paid as distinct from *list* or *asking* prices. There is a good chance the seller isn't up to date with this information. In the most sincere way you can, give two to four convincing examples that reinforce your offer, and supply brief but attractive descriptions of the homes concerned (you have done your research, haven't you?).

If you reach a stalemate, tell the sellers that, although you don't expect you'll change your offer, you will still talk to your husband anyway. Then, wish them good luck and tell them you hope they'll find a buyer. Immediately, head for the exit.

Most times, the ice breaks late—after the sun has gone down. Typically, compromises and agreements are reached at the eleventh hour when deadlines have passed and the deal seems to be slipping away. It is at that point that the party in the weaker position signals a critical concession. By getting the sellers to perceive you are in the stronger position (even when you aren't), you build the likelihood of them making the critical concession that will rescue the sale and save you money.

So, as you make what appears to be your departure, remember that, as a buyer, you are naturally in a stronger position than the seller in almost all property transactions. *You*, therefore, have an inherent advantage in the negotiation process.

If the seller doesn't stop you by the time you reach the door, pause briefly to write your name and phone number. At the same time, comment warmly but assertively:

Buyer:  *Just to assure you, Mr. and Mrs. Smith, we are genuine buyers. And as I said, we'll definitely buy one of the homes we like within the next few days. If you reconsider selling us your home, give me a call. If we haven't already bought, we might consider increasing our offer slightly, especially if we can agree on the move-in date.*

And then, you add a twist:

*'Here's my number. Unfortunately, you might have trouble reaching me. But if you leave a message, I'll try to get back to you as soon as possible. In the meantime, I'll talk to my husband.'*

Exit! You are doing two things here. One, playing hard-to-get and two, laying bait by suggesting you might increase your offer. In return, you will want a second (non-price) concession from the seller. In this case it was a suitable move-in date. It could have been almost anything of relatively minor significance (you don't want to impose an extra obstacle now that would defeat the deal). How about the patio furniture you liked so much? Or the Tiffany shade in the dining room? Or, maybe, the brass fire screen? Whatever you decide, remember, it's simply a tactic on your part. You are presenting a condition the seller will find *easy* to agree to. This underlines your interest in the home, without going too far. And it tends to increase the owner's optimism that a sale can be achieved.

Your statement that you are difficult to reach discreetly reminds the Smiths that time is running out, especially when they consider what you said about definitely buying within the next few days.

The seller will probably delay your exit by asking what is the "higher offer" you have in mind. Now, though, it is time to tread carefully. Tone down any excitement you might be feeling. Here is your best answer: "*Well, I really don't know. I'd have to get around my spouse first. Probably $147,500 or $148,000.*"

I believe you should *never* ask sellers what is the lowest price they would accept. Never! Are they really going to tell you? Hardly! The seller will pick a higher figure, possibly even unrealistically high. That figure then becomes the benchmark, and *you* have created it! Once declared, this benchmark price is going to have to be defended. After all, you just asked the seller to tell you the price below which he or she would *not* go. Now you've backed the seller up against a wall. Expect a fight—that's human nature. If the seller doesn't, they'll look like a fake.

Asking this question is a mistake made very frequently by buyers and one that's very difficult to correct. Seldom will the answer be genuine, factual, or helpful, so there's no point in asking it.

It will pay you well to remember this point: *The seller's lowest acceptable price is one that is arrived at gradually through the calculated and sequential process explained in this book.* This figure is not carved in stone. It's the product of negotiation and, despite the price the seller might have predetermined, it is dictated by the buyer's willingness and ability to negotiate. Asking "What price would you accept?" only hampers this process.

There is just one possible exception I can think of. It occurs when you are buying from a very distressed seller who stands to lose the property unless they find a buyer. Then, you might get quickly to the point. If the seller sees you as a serious and genuine buyer, they're unlikely to give you an inflated price in their circumstances. Nevertheless, it's still your prerogative to negotiate.

The figure that is imperative to your success is *your first offer*. No matter how far away that figure is from the seller's asking price, the unbreakable rule still applies: increase your offer, if you must, but only in small increments—and slowly. The seller's asking price should be largely irrelevant to any sequence of offers you decide to make.

> 2. Seller:    *I'm willing to be flexible on price, but I won't come down to that figure.*

This is quite an encouraging response from the seller, and can be handled in a number of ways. Here again, you can question the seller's knowledge of the market—the selling prices, not asking prices. And, you can also appeal to reason. For example:

> Buyer:    *Over the past few months, I've seen a number of homes similar to yours. Just about every one sold around the mid $140s. That seems to me to be as much as buyers are prepared to pay.*

Now it's up to the seller to respond. The Smiths are likely to protest that their home is unique and better than others in the area, and continue to describe its many advantages. Don't let them go on like this because they can easily talk themselves into believing even more strongly that their price is fair and attainable. Interrupt them with something relevant. For example:

Buyer: *I've had a good look through your home, and I do like it. You have furnished and maintained it very well. But it is still, essentially, comparable to many other homes I've inspected. We are going to buy immediately. Here's my number (or, you have my number). If you reconsider, give me a call. I'll be hard to catch tomorrow. If I hear from you, and we haven't already bought, we might be able to make you a slightly higher offer, provided we can agree on a move-in date.*

Here, your strategy is similar to the previous example. You've placed a tight time demand on the seller's thinking. If the Smiths don't act within a day or two they're gambling on losing a definite sale. That's a risk they might not want to take. As further inducement, you've given them hope for a higher offer, though you haven't said what figure that will be. This move makes it almost impossible for the sellers to terminate the negotiation. Instead, it draws out the discussion and leads to a bigger investment of time by them. Both strengthen your position.

Of course, your move-in date, or any other concession you request in return for making a slightly higher offer, might be totally insignificant to you. But, generally, you will seek a concession from the seller whenever you agree to increase your offer.

Your early research and checking might have told you the Smiths' time frame for moving out. Or the sellers might have revealed it to you in the course of discussion. Now, if the date you place on your new offer coincides with (or is close to) what the sellers want they will probably view this as a lucky coincidence that the next buyer (*when* he comes along) might not be able to offer. By establishing this greater degree of agreement between you and the seller, you can move closer to a satisfactory outcome.

Here is an *opposite* strategy you might consider, one I outlined in an earlier section. If you have discovered the Smiths' preferred settlement date (the date by which they would like to hand over their house and take possession of your money), you can let it be known that you require an altogether different settlement date, preferably later or earlier by at least a month. Then at the last minute, you can offer to meet their date, provided they accept your offer. If not, you'll "just buy something else." Only your own judgment will tell when this strategy is appropriate. When used well, it is very persuasive and often allows you the final "concession" that brings an otherwise stalemated deal together. It also works particularly well when you are buying through a real estate agent.

However, let's assume the seller is extremely stubborn. Despite what you say, the Smiths insist their home is unique, that you won't find another one like it. Perhaps they have put in years of work to get the property to look the way it does. Such obstinacy sometimes means they are in need of a little ego massaging and not necessarily playing just for a higher price. If you suspect this is the case, you'll have to give them what they want emotionally while holding your ground on price and value. Here's what you might say:

Buyer:   *Please don't get me wrong, Mr. Smith. Your home is very attractive. Anyone would be proud to own it. All I'm saying is, other attractive homes in the area have been selling in the mid-$140s—including the one we are considering right now. I must admit, though, your decor and flower garden are much more tastefully done.*

The two final remarks about the flower garden and decor are used to soften the primary message you have just restated; *that you can buy a comparable home much less expensively.* Those remarks are also doing something that may be even more important. They're giving what all human beings crave—acknowledgment and recognition. Any statement that satisfies such needs is potentially powerful.

But what if none of this works? Let's assume the worst. You have made no apparent progress and are about to part company. Before you reach your car, try this:

Buyer:   *Mr. Smith ... (pause) if I could convince my husband tonight to pay you two thousand dollars more than the price of the other house we're interested in, should I get in touch with you?*

Note that you have not made a formal offer. You are using your husband as the 'third party'—a person you and the seller both need to satisfy in order to make anything happen (which, as we saw earlier, makes it appear that you and the seller are on the same side). How can the seller respond? All you've asked is, if you should contact him. A blunt "no" is unlikely. You're still a real, live prospective buyer, which no seller in their right mind would reject outright. Consequently, the Smiths are likely to encourage you to contact them. They might throw in a qualification or warning, however. Here are some typical responses a seller might make:

1. "I'll be up until 10 p.m. but you're going to have to come up with more than $148,750."

2. "Two thousand? That makes $148,750. I won't sell for that. But I said I'd be flexible and I will. I'll take $154,000. But that's it!"

3. "Well, I certainly won't accept $148,750 but maybe we can work something out."

4. "I'm not going to give the house away. If you can come up with a better offer than that, let me know."

Despite the tone of delivery, all of these responses are positive. How you can deal with each is covered among the 10 seller responses in this section. Remember, these figures of $146,750 and $148,750 are no more than tactical offers by you and are part of your overall strategy. You didn't expect that the Smiths would quietly accept either figure. But, of course, they're not aware of that, so you continue the strategy.

The various tactics at your disposal are best used collectively to achieve one goal—to change the sellers' thinking, and move them gradually along a path to a point where they are prepared to reduce what they previously considered the lowest acceptable price. Your collective tactics might have included low offers, comparative values, limited time, attractive alternatives, third party problems, limited budget, investment of time, reasonableness, property condition, and so on.

As a genuine buyer you are providing the seller with an opportunity to achieve a sale. The more time you spend in negotiation, the more likely your strategy will work. Nothing happens easily or instantly in negotiation. Progress is often invisible. It happens first inside the seller's head. Sometimes it bursts out unexpectedly, turning a recurring "no" into a "maybe" or a "yes." Patience is imperative. As long as negotiation continues, change is taking place in the thinking of one or both parties. The strategy you adopt is meant to win the thinking battle between you and the other side. The tactics are the pieces, carefully chosen, that go to make up that strategy.

Here's an example of what I mean—and a question. In our hypothetical negotiation we were fairly certain the seller was going to reject our offers of $146,750 and $148,750. In that case, you might ask if there was any point in making such low offers in the first place. The answer is *yes!* It is vital to make initial low offers, as genuinely and as seriously as you can, for one very important reason—they change the seller's thinking!

Low offers, when presented intelligently and as part of a legitimate strategy, have the very real effect of causing the seller to lower price expectations. It bears repeating, though, that *low offers don't work well when they stand alone.* They must form part of an overall strategy. That is, they must be supported by the other tactics and buyer demeanor that make up an effective, overall strategy. When that is the case, low offers have a silent, and sometimes delayed, power.

> 3. Seller:   *I don't believe it's possible today to buy a home of this quality for that price.*

You handle this in a similar way to the first seller response we looked at ("I couldn't possibly sell my home for that price"). Here, though, your task may be easier, especially if you can show the seller details of the lower selling prices of comparable homes. Once again, this highlights the value of keeping a notebook with details gathered in the course of your research, even pieces of information you pick up from real estate agents. You'll be amazed at how often and how profitably you use this resource.

To combat a seller's inflexibility, whether genuine or a ploy, all the negotiation tactics we've already examined are at your disposal.

The basic tone of your approach is always respectful, genuine, reasonable, and relaxed. You will not pay more than you believe the home is worth. You are considering one or two other homes also, one of which your partner favors, while you prefer the Smiths' home. You might be able to talk your partner into offering the Smiths the same price you can buy the other home for, $146,750. You acknowledge that the Smiths are rightfully proud of their home but there are some alterations and repairs that would mean extra expense for you. You are anxious to buy right away (but you don't have to)—today or tomorrow, perhaps. If the Smiths aren't prepared to make a decision now, they can call you—but you aren't easy to reach. If you haven't bought by the time you hear from them, you'll consider making, possibly, a slightly higher offer, if you can get your partner to agree. Of course, you can't promise your partner will go along with such an offer. And so on.

Notice that you do acknowledge and address the specific reactions of the seller, but you always steer the negotiation back to the tactics that form *your* strategy. Don't allow the discussion to get bogged down in dispute, regardless of how passionate the seller becomes in defending the price. An argumentative or aggressive attitude on your part is counterproductive. The battle to be won is the one going on inside the seller's head, not any open sparring happening on the outside. By exhibiting composure, reasonableness, logic, and understanding, you'll give yourself the best chance of ultimate victory.

Winning all the minor disputes, which are inevitable in such discussions, makes you only a good arguer. Conversely, *good negotiators seldom worry about winning the trivial victories along the way.* In fact, they often concede such victories in order to build an appropriate relationship with the seller. All the time, though, their strategies and thinking are focused on the final objective, to buy at the lowest possible price.

4. Seller:   *The people selling that other house you mentioned must desperately need to sell. Luckily, I'm not in that position.*

Here, you must first dispel the notion that the other seller is desperate. Remember, though, there doesn't *have* to be any other specific seller with whom you are negotiating seriously. This might simply be part of your strategy. Here are some suggestions for how to proceed.

Buyer:   *On the contrary, Mr. Smith. The home has been appraised quite recently at very close to $146,750. While I don't know the owner's personal financial details, they don't appear to have any urgent need of cash. They just don't want the house to sit on the market for a long time and then end up having to accept a lower price.*

You continue, then, to inquire how familiar the Smiths are with the actual prices buyers have been paying in the neighborhood. Ask if they can vouch for the accuracy of the prices they have heard, reminding them that many sellers exaggerate the prices they obtain. Provide hard facts and details that support your opinion on price and value, including descriptions of specific homes. Your argument will be more persuasive if you can show wide discrepancies between the original asking prices and the prices sellers eventually agreed to accept. Then, you select and use additional, supporting tactics most appropriate to the situation.

5. Seller:   *You say you're going to buy in the next day or two. Well, if you're genuinely interested in my home, I'm prepared to come down to (say) $158,000, but not any lower.*

It is not so easy to answer this one. The seller has completely ignored (apparently) your statement that if you were to make an offer it would be, say, $146,750. There could be any of a number of reasons behind this seller response. It's possible the Smiths weren't convinced that you would, in fact, walk away and buy the other home you mentioned. More likely, though, they're going for broke, testing you to see if you really meant what you said. Or, they might believe their price concession to $158,000 is eminently fair and reasonable.

Whatever the reason, this situation calls for mental toughness. You're going to have to spell things out very clearly and diplomatically.

Reinforce the point that your objective is to pay a fair price for whichever home you buy. You are prepared to be reasonable but, equally, you will not pay more than you believe a property to be worth. This is a delicate situation and requires good judgment on your part. Not too heavy or too weak. And not too fast or abrupt. Time is your tactic of choice here.

You will recall when we set up this hypothetical example that you determined you would not pay more than $152,000 for the Smiths' home. If you still feel this way, and if you are genuinely prepared to walk away at any figure above that, now is the time to introduce the Walk Away tactic. Here's how:

Buyer:   *I understand your position. And I know it's not easy to sell your own home. We are reasonable people, but in the past few months all the homes we've seen that compare closely with yours have sold in the mid-$140s. Even the other home we're looking at right now is a good example of that. It's similar to yours—a little larger—and we can buy it for $146,750.*

Then, make like you are preparing to leave. If no further concession is forthcoming, you add:

*I'd like to assure you, Mr. and Mrs. Smith, we're not "just looking." We'll buy a home very quickly. Today or tomorrow, maybe. We might be able to pay you slightly more than $146,750. But I'm sorry; there's no way we would pay $158,000.*

*Don't* stand around waiting for a response. Keep moving as if your meeting is about to terminate. The fact that both sides have talked figures indicates that serious negotiation has begun.

Despite your low offer, the seller's anticipation of a sale has been raised. Where it goes from here will rely more on what the Smiths do now than on what you do. So give them room to act and time to think.

Initially, at least, they'll probably try to defend their price. Your task will be to listen, but not to a long monologue. Then, respond calmly and respectfully with your opinion of value once again. If the owners are willing to take less than has been stated, they will suggest a compromise and will also let you know they're not going to go any lower. Almost invariably in a situation like this, they *will* go lower, if you handle things well.

Throughout this whole exchange, you'll do whatever is necessary to avoid openly confrontational challenges or to win trivial points. You'll keep appealing to reason and logic. As the discussion continues along these lines, the Smiths' thoughts shift gradually to the risk of holding out for a higher price. The pressure inherent in that thinking causes them to review their lowest acceptable price over and over. This is why time is such an important investment in the negotiation process. The longer things go on the greater the chance the sellers' thoughts—*the ones you put there*—will cause them to set a *new* lowest acceptable price. This is what the power of a skillful negotiator produces.

When you notice your strategy beginning to work, one of the easiest traps to fall into is being too smart for your own good. Know-it-alls win few negotiations. But neither should you play dumb or naive, as that would be self-defeating. Your objective should be to maintain your composure and to ensure your character and strategy remain consistent to the end. In doing this you will enhance your image of sincerity, one of your most powerful assets, and a quality your actions and words should be transmitting from your earliest contact with the seller.

Now, back to the seller's reaction as you act like you are about to leave. The Smiths are likely to defend their price again by telling you that their home has been appraised higher than your offer. This requires you to point out a few truths.

First, the value of any property is not something that's carved in stone. Home appraisal (valuing) is not an exact science. In fact, putting a value on any piece of real estate is anything but precise. Inconsistency is the rule, rather than the exception. As any real estate agent will verify, appraisals on a single home can vary widely. What I'm emphasizing here is this: Regardless of whether the seller's asking price is based on an official appraisal or on a real estate agent's opinion of value, it is nothing more than a guide. And, frequently, it is far from being an accurate indication of the eventual selling price.

The most accurate assessment of the true market value of a home is determined by what buyers are willing to pay, not the inflated figures sometimes used by real estate agents to induce a seller to list the home with their company. On top of that, agents and salespeople are generally optimistic by nature and are more prone to overpricing than to realistic pricing or underpricing.

Second, you suggest that if the sellers were to visit some of the comparable homes on the market they would discover that even the asking prices—not to mention the selling prices—are lower than theirs. Very few sellers will take on such a challenge. For those few who do, it turns out to be a pointless exercise, because they can't be objective about what they see. They find no home they consider comparable. And, in this situation, the seller knows the risk of delaying is too high anyway. You're on the brink of buying. There's no time for the seller to start researching now. To do so would almost certainly mean losing a definite sale. You won't hang around. You'll buy the 'other' home.

Now is when your strategy becomes most effective. The Smiths know you are a genuine and serious buyer. And, from the beginning, you made it clear that you plan to buy immediately one of the homes that interest you. You have affected their perceptions to such an extent that you've narrowed the gap considerably between their position and yours. If you've been convincing, they'll try to hang on to you by one means or another. A compromise might be offered on price. Or they might say something like, "Let's see if we can work this out in a way that satisfies us both."

Judge the situation carefully, and *don't speak before you think.* Proceed slowly. Don't show any sign of encouragement unless it's necessary to keep the negotiation alive. Unless the seller suggests a very good reduction that is clearly a final concession, you probably shouldn't, in this situation, accept the first compromise offer. Instead, respond with your own increased offer, a slight addition to what you have already offered. Then, if you have to make subsequent offers, use progressively smaller increases: a first increase of, say, $2,000 followed by another $1,000, then $700, and perhaps a final "walk away" increase of $250 or $300.

From this pattern, the seller will deduce you are running out of interest or that you are overspending your budget. Either way, the implication is that you are at, or close to, your walk-away point. While being careful not to state it too bluntly, or in the form of an ultimatum, your enthusiasm level—in fact, your whole demeanor—

should imply that this is the case. This is the *deal point*. The point your strategy has carved out for you. And the point at which you are likely to reach your goal of buying at the lowest price possible. Be ready for it.

6. Seller: *Look, I know this house is worth every cent of the price I'm asking. I don't want to mess around. What's the best price you're prepared to pay?*

This is one of the most common seller responses, and one that transmits some important and unmistakable signals. Whatever the Smiths truly believe about the fairness of their asking price, they wouldn't invite you to state your best price if they weren't prepared to compromise. How far they'll come down isn't possible to determine yet, but it will be influenced by how persuasively you communicate the market information you have gathered. Especially initially, their definition of fairness must be challenged with hard evidence, but evidence presented in a sincere, interested manner, not a combative or adversarial one that embarrasses the sellers or questions their motives or judgment in a negative way.

Here, the importance of your early research work should, once again, become obvious. It's invaluable now, particularly as the rapport between you and the seller starts building.

A good response to the seller's request for your best price is similar to what we saw earlier:

Buyer: *Well, first, I do understand how difficult it can be selling your own home. It's so hard to be objective. We've seen homes comparable to yours selling in the mid-$140s. A good example is the one my husband is very keen on. It's probably slightly larger than yours, and we can buy it for $146,750.*

Then, after a pause that communicates indifference, you give a sign of hope:

*I do like your home, though, and we are genuine buyers. We'll almost definitely buy something in the next day or so. My husband would first have to agree, but I'm sure we could pay you the same price as the other house we're interested in—$146,750.*

If Mr. and Mrs. Smith react with yells and screams and emotional ranting about how wonderful their home is and how it's audacious of you to even suggest such a low figure, keep listening.

But, show as little reaction as possible. *Don't* try to answer specific remarks about value. Remember, you've got alternatives—act that way by communicating what might best be described as an interested detachment.

It's always difficult to tell when a seller's emotional reaction is a prelude to a surprise concession. Give the Smiths time to talk and protest. They might be testing you. As it goes on, a thought will come to the sellers—and it will scare them. They'll begin feeling that they are killing your interest, and they'll stop.

That's your cue to offer empathy, words of understanding, and a jolt! Why a jolt? Because seller histrionics are often either irrational or a ruse. Often, sellers are trying to conceal that they are prepared to lower the price. You continue along these lines:

Buyer:    *Believe me, I do understand, Mr. Smith. Your house is very attractive. I especially like the flower beds out front. But, thank you. I'm sorry we couldn't do business. Good-bye. (Extend your hand before moving toward the exit).*

That's the jolt. The verbal good-bye and the extended hand are clear signals of finality. The encounter is over. A buyer with money and interest is walking away. What is the seller going to do now? He'll stop you with a question, most likely. An offer to reduce the price, perhaps, or some other encouraging remark. But this isn't a moment for you to change your attitude—quite the opposite. Maintain your slightly indifferent demeanor without rejecting the new comments or price reduction altogether. Once a seller has begun conceding, it's easier to go further, especially as time and emotional investment increases. And as the gap between you narrows.

Whatever the Smiths say, you'll help your cause if you restate clearly your interest and, when appropriate, suggest that you might be able to get your partner to agree to increase your offer a little, say to $148,750, or thereabout. Then, you stress that the seller would have to be able to agree to your move-in date, let the patio furniture stay with the home, or some other demands on which you could later concede. Once again, you are using a deflection tactic (a red herring) to take the emphasis off the real target—the price. Behind it, you have little or no interest in the red herrings. However, they can serve a useful purpose. Refer back to Number 2 in this section: 'I'm willing to be flexible...' for more details on this. Also, see the case study "Making Money For A Banker" in chapter 7.

Now, here's another challenge. What if the Smiths are not the emotional type? What if they don't protest passionately that their home is worth more than your initial offer of $146,750? What if they don't rant and rave at your statement that you believe your offer represents a fair market price? Instead, they calmly reply that they have looked at other local properties for sale, and based on their research, they think their price is fair and competitive. Nonetheless they are prepared to consider an offer in the high $150s. How should you proceed? Let's see.

Remaining unflustered and matter of fact, you launch into a number of the most important points:

1.  Asking prices are not selling prices.

2.  Asking prices are very easy to find out. Accurate selling prices are not.

3.  Selling prices are often considerably lower than asking prices.

4.  It is extremely difficult for owners selling privately to place an objective value on their home.

5.  Most private sellers unknowingly overprice. They show and wait. And show and wait. And eventually often sell, when the home seems stale to the majority of potential buyers in the market, at a lower price than they could have gotten earlier.

6.  If the sellers gathered details of actual selling prices, they would see the validity of your offer. You are certain of that.

7.  Finally, in the circumstances, you might be prepared to increase your offer slightly (mention no figure at this point), *if* your partner agrees.

It is to your greatest advantage to list these points in a sympathetic, sincere way. And even more so, to *have examples that support your contentions.*

7. Seller:  *I'm not sure if I told you the electrical wiring was completely renewed just two years ago. And the heating system will be under warranty for another four years.*

This response indicates a clear avoidance on the part of the seller. The surprising thing is, it's very common. Probably because many sellers simply don't know how to handle assertive, knowledgeable buyers. For you, the problem is that it's hard to know what is going on in the seller's head. You know the seller is sidestepping your low offer. But, right now, that's all you know.

It might well be that the Smiths are just not comfortable with the task of selling a house and are unaware of how to act in the situation. On the other hand, it's possible they are hesitating out of fear of making a bad decision. Yet, behind that, they might be giving serious consideration to your offer, or to an attractive compromise. The fact that your figure hasn't been rejected out of hand indicates that he is, at least, prepared to continue the discussion and probably needs more persuading.

Your comments now should include a number of references to features of the *other* home that interests you. Repeat the price the other owner will accept—despite having to pay an agent's commission (quite a few thousand dollars). Consult your notebook, if necessary, and provide the seller with a few actual selling prices from the neighborhood (and the addresses, if you can). These extra details support your opinions on home values and will almost always influence the seller's thinking—more so, the more specific, factual examples you can cite.

But, if you are caught out with no specific properties to refer to, you can still describe homes you've inspected, giving just general addresses. However, pick close, recognizable locations that are comparable to the seller's, or better. You can use the excuse that you find it difficult to recall street names because you are not familiar with the area.

When you suspect the seller is a nervous type and is evasive out of fear of making such a big decision, don't rush it. If you move too fast you run the risk of being seen to be too slick. This can frighten sellers into backing off and deciding they need a real estate agent, or postponing the sale of his home until some later date.

What you need now is to build greater trust. It won't happen immediately. Let the sellers get to know you a little better. Show empathy for their situation and talk conversationally about the trivia of the home and the locality. Lighten the atmosphere, if you can, with a humorous remark or two. Humor, used wisely, is a remarkable tool in reducing barriers and fear. But, don't force it if it is not your style. And don't overdo it either, or *you'll* appear just as nervous as the seller feels.

The more you come across as a reasonable, genuine person, the more you stand to gain. Eventually, though, you must bring the conversation back to supporting your offer. It's a fair offer, you believe, based on what people have been paying and based on the expenses you will incur in replacing or repairing items in the home.

This is work, you stress, that would cause many buyers to reject the property. And, unlike many people who make, then break, appointments to inspect homes being sold privately, you are a serious buyer; you have the money; you're interested and you are prepared to pay what you believe the home is worth—today, if you can agree. Your time, unfortunately, is limited. That's why you have only a few days to find a home you feel good about buying. You and your partner have seen one other home that you both like (describe it briefly) but you, personally, prefer the Smiths'… By now, you know the rest.

Then lead the seller closer to settling the transaction. What move-out date did they have in mind? (Even if they've already told you, ask again.) You believe you could *probably* agree to that. It wasn't what you wanted, but you could probably agree. (Use the word *agree*. It has power.) You'd have to confirm this with your partner (bank, attorney, employer, etc.) just to be sure. If you state that you can possibly agree to the seller's time schedule, ask again if that arrangement suits them. When they confirm that it does, respond positively and optimistically, implying that agreement is close.

You'll have some more negotiating to do, but eventually, when an agreement is reached, even when it's only verbal, *never thank the seller.* Instead, talk about the work you'll have to do in the home and the expense of hiring tradesmen, and so on. This is no time to celebrate a victory. Rather, showing a few hints of doubt about your decision to buy is more appropriate. Once again, though, don't overdo it. Tearful remorse isn't called for.

If you have an Offer and Acceptance form with you, (or an alternative your attorney has approved) now is the time to introduce it. As we saw earlier, this is a simple-looking document that serves as a forerunner to a full Purchase and Sale Agreement, which you and the seller will later sign. The best Offer and Acceptance form is one that allows you to pull out of the deal later, if necessary, but locks the seller into the price and terms agreed. For that reason, it's a good idea to get this Offer and Acceptance signed by the seller before you leave. The last thing you want, when a good deal is at stake, is for the sellers to change their minds overnight, or to have their minds changed by others. (As I mentioned earlier, Offer and Acceptance documents are not in use in all states. Ask your attorney.)

In handling any seller response, it's important to remember that successful negotiation seldom proceeds without hitches, delays, or interruptions. This is especially so when dealing with private sellers directly.

Consequently, when you encounter a seller who accepts your first offer, allows you a generous price reduction to refurbish the house, offers to replace an old but functional stove with a new model, and will agree to any settlement date you propose—move cautiously. In fact, any time you don't meet resistance in a negotiation there may be reason to suspect that everything is not as it seems. Are you sure the seller is the legal owner of the property? Does the seller have the right to sell? Is the seller so badly in need of money that he or she is anxious to accept the first deal that will solve the financial problems?

None of these types of suspicions need stop you from getting an Offer and Acceptance form signed. But from here on, let a lawyer take care of the matter. The lawyer will determine if it is wise to proceed with the purchase. In the meantime, don't hand over any money to the seller, even a *good-faith* deposit. In fact, this is a rule you should follow with any private sale agreement, even when you have no suspicions about the transaction. As I advised earlier, check with your lawyer before you go shopping, particularly about the use of Offer and Acceptance documents. But make sure the lawyer really does understand real estate and is not just an expensive conveyancing clerk.

> 8. Seller:    *When do you plan to talk to your husband (wife, attorney, etc.)?*

Let's recap. You've just made the Smiths a low offer of $146,750—conditional upon your spouse agreeing. The seller's asking price in this hypothetical example is $164,000 but you have determined that you are interested only if you can buy for $152,000 or lower.

Judging from this seller's response, your offer might be accepted. It's certainly not the response you anticipated, which puts you in something of a dilemma. Should you assume your offer has been accepted and push ahead with formalizing the deal? Or should you ask the seller for clarification?

When you've recovered from the shock, you'd better tease out what exactly the seller is saying. One method of doing that is to pull back a little and create uncertainty. Here's an example of what I mean:

> Buyer:    *As I said, we're interested in buying right away. I'll discuss it with my husband this evening. I must remind you that I can't be certain my husband will agree to pay $146,750—*

> *though I feel he will go along with me. He likes a larger*
> *home we've seen. But let's keep our fingers crossed. Can I*
> *call you this evening?*

Notice, you've just made the deal seem further away and more in doubt. Also, you have given a reason for your partner's preference—more space. Despite this deliberate distancing, you have the carrot dangling in front of the seller's nose and you have restated your offer of $146,750. If you misinterpreted the seller's thinking, they will now clarify their position.

But let's assume the Smiths raise no objection and the deal looks like it can go ahead. What do you do? If you are sure you want to buy the home for $146,750—and you should be if you have made the offer—let the seller know that you have a simple Offer and Acceptance form with you. And, that you are willing to sign it there and then, subject to your husband's approval and a routine professional home inspection. Alternatively, you can make the agreement subject to your attorney's approval. If the seller goes ahead and signs this Offer and Acceptance form, you can feel reasonably sure the deal is safe.

The other option you have, particularly if you don't use an Offer and Acceptance form, is to tell the seller that you're pretty sure your husband will go along with the price and settlement terms, but that you do need to discuss it with him first. Then, say you'll contact the seller later.

However, don't let too much time pass, or your risk the seller having a change of mind (using an Offer and Acceptance form would have eliminated this risk.) After a few hours, call the Smiths again, telling them that your husband has informed you that he will be tied up with work—or may even be away—over the next couple of days and that you'd both like to drop by and talk with them after dinner tonight. Use this wording, too, especially *talk with* or *talk it over*. Don't say you'll be over to *close the deal* or *put it on paper* or *make it legal*. These are all common agent phrases that scare many sellers, though they are sometimes appropriate and unavoidable.

By saying you'd like to *talk* you continue the uncertainty that keeps the sellers on edge and tends to dissuade them from the fear that they have sold too low. Instead, the uncertainty you create will focus their thinking on whether you will come through and complete the sale. This is a far better place for their thinking to be than on the fear that they are selling too low. Until the agreement is on paper and signed the seller should never be encouraged to see it as a done deal, and you should show no signs of triumph or accomplishment.

Here's an exercise that will help you appreciate this point. Contrast the situation we've just seen with one in which the buyer, on reaching a verbal agreement with the seller, communicates a high degree of excitement and euphoria. Such behavior seems like a victory, a triumph for the buyer. What thoughts does that send to the seller? Perhaps these: If the buyer has won, then I have lost. Or, if it's such a marvelous deal for the buyer, what can it be for me? Defeat? This is an absence of negotiation skill, and is self-defeating in circumstances like we've been analyzing. Even in the situation where the other side is already locked in to a deal, your accomplishment should be celebrated outside the company of the seller. Better, if you can, to let the victory seem the seller's.

Let's get back to our example. When you and your partner come to talk with the Smiths, you may still have scope for negotiating further concessions. What if your partner is not happy with paying the $146,750 you offered? Or thinks the pool and patio furniture should stay with the house? None of this should be mentioned over the phone. Wait until you are at the Smiths' home. How far you go with this renegotiation only you can determine, based on the facts and feel of the situation.

Sellers must always be made to feel they have extracted from the buyer the highest price you were prepared to pay. By acting like every cent you have in the world, or can get, is now going for the house purchase, you'll be helping to protect the deal you have achieved. If the seller feels guilty taking 'all' your money, so much the better.

But what if the thing you dreaded most happens? What if the seller springs a late surprise on you and refuses to accept the figure verbally agreed to earlier? Your best response is to stay calm. Reason and honor may still prevail.

Explain that you are confused and a little upset. You understood that you had an agreement. Based on a list of actual selling prices, you consider $146,750 a fair price, and the seller indicated clearly that the figure was acceptable. Then, say that you are still prepared to pay $146,750, if the seller is prepared to go ahead with *their* part of the agreement. You can't afford to come on too strong here, as you could kill whatever chance still remains for making the deal. Let the seller know you understand the emotion involved in selling a home, and assure them that your offer is fair, and you are genuine and reliable.

In the end, even if you have to pay more to buy the home, the atmosphere and rapport you established in making the deal the first time around should be protected. They are still working for you.

You won't be starting from scratch as you try to rebuild a deal you can live with. And, don't count out the chance that the seller might yet honor the price that was first accepted.

> 9. Seller: *I'll be as fair as I can be. I'll meet you about halfway. Can we agree on (say) $156,000?*

You'll recall we discussed this question of *meeting halfway* and *splitting the difference* in an earlier chapter.

Here, it looks like you are doing well. The seller has offered a substantial reduction without haggling. When this happens, it's usually the result of the buyer's persuasive early strategy and the conditioning effect it has on the seller's expectations. In fact, it usually indicates that you can probably do better, maybe much better. Now, though, you must defend your offer of $146,750 as a fair one and, at the same time, show understanding for the seller's predicament. Projecting an image of reasonableness and sincerity will increase your chance of influencing the decision.

Here's how you might proceed:

> Buyer: *I appreciate your desire to be fair, Mr. Smith. And I want to be fair too. But, just about every home we've seen that was comparable to yours has sold in the low to mid-$140's. The few that were priced higher than that are almost all still on the market—unsold. I may be able to add a little, maybe $500 to $750, to my offer but first, I'd have to talk it over with my husband (bank, accountant, attorney, wife, etc.).*

If the sellers refuse to consider such a low offer, you still have room to creep up in small increments and extract a bigger investment of their time in the process. (Remember, you decided you would buy the home only if you could get it for $152,000 or less.) At least once or twice, you'll look for a concession from the seller in return for increasing your offer. You'll also continue to provide specific details of other homes now available that offer better value for money and that cast a question mark on their price expectation.

Now, let's assume you've negotiated well using the tactics and strategies we've covered. You are both tired but a little closer to agreement. He has compromised to $151,500 and you are stuck on $147,500. You continue:

> Buyer: *Unfortunately, it looks like we can't agree on a figure we can both accept. I believe I'm offering a very good price.*

> *Perhaps even more than I should, and that makes me a bit nervous. There's only one other thing I can suggest. If you can agree to a settlement date a couple of weeks later than you'd prefer, my husband and I will each have another paycheck coming in, which might enable us to add a little to the $147,500 we're willing to pay. That would mean an extra $620, approximately. That brings it up to $148,120.*

Then, proceed until the gap between you is so small that agreement is the only logical outcome. When your offer is accepted, confirm verbally what has been agreed and confirm the settlement date that will become part of your written agreement.

However, if the seller digs in and seems stubbornly unwilling to compromise any further, remember that you can still use the Walk Away tactic. After such a marathon negotiation, the seller will be very reluctant to even think about going through it all again with another buyer. That would entail going back to square one and facing all the time and effort and uncertainty all over again. That's why the Walk Away tactic is so powerful. Be careful though: it must be played persuasively.

When this tactic appears to have failed, extend your hand before you depart and wish the sellers good luck in finding a buyer. And, just as we saw earlier, smile, and don't linger. Why smile? Because if you communicate dejection and disappointment, you risk the seller concluding that all is not over and that you'll be back with a better offer. Your smile and your words should signal that that won't be the case. You've accepted that an agreement is impossible. You went as far as you could go, but it wasn't enough. Now, you'll go and wrap up the deal on the "other" house. These are the messages you should be sending out. It is often the tactic that will clinch the best deal available, so make it as persuasive as you can.

But what if none of this happens? What if the seller smiles back at you and wishes you well? What if your final tactic fails? Then, you do as I suggested previously. Leave! You can come back later if you have to. But make sure you leave your name and phone number behind. Then, wait. If the seller doesn't contact you within 48 hours, call back and restate your offer. Say that you held off signing the agreement on the other house because one of the owners will be out of state until midweek:

Buyer:    *I'm still prepared to go through with the final figure I offered, Mr. Smith, (say) $148,120. But my situation could change any time.*

*Don't* ask the seller if he or she is prepared to accept your offer. Questions that require a yes or no answer don't give the other side maximum opportunity to think or to be flexible. Usually, they provide only a trigger for the seller to defend the previously stated position. These are known as *closed questions,* and in these types of situations they do you no good.

After restating your willingness to go through with your last offer, say no more. You've placed the temptation once again in front of the seller. You're "still prepared" to honor it. The connotation in saying it that way is that you are giving the seller a second chance. Now, the seller is going to have to deliberate on it again and to struggle with all the 'what if' thoughts that will come from saying no to a definite sale. And no to the money that is there for the taking—if he or she acts now!

But, let's play devil's advocate. Let's make the challenge even bigger. Suppose the Smiths told you their minds were made up—your offer is too low, period. What options should you try? Here are a few to consider:

1. Say you might be able to borrow between $500 and $1,000. You'll have to do some checking. But, if you get the money, you'd be prepared to add it to your offer. You ask, "If that happens, should I call you?"

2. Even though the sellers don't seem willing to accept your offer, ask if you and your partner can come by to talk with them. If they say there's no point, say you might be able to make a new, slightly higher offer, but *don't talk figures,* even if they press you.

In the first case, you haven't, in fact, made a new offer. After all, you may not succeed in getting the $500 or $1,000 loan. At least that's your message. What it does is prompt the seller to fall into a particular pattern of 'logic' that can best be described like this: "*If you do x, the least I can do is y.*" Note too, that you aren't asking for a binding commitment from the sellers, which might cause them to back away from your proposition. All you're asking is if you should contact them, something that seems much safer to agree to. Then the contact, when it comes, should, preferably, be in person. That way, you once again have the best circumstances in which to continue negotiating toward your goal.

The second example skips the 'I might be able to get a loan' approach in favor of an unconditional resumption of face-to-face discussion. It will be much harder for the Smiths to turn you away again, even if your increased offer falls short of their expectations, particularly when you are sitting in front of them. Stretch out this meeting, and make it so congenial and personal that to disappoint you would make the Smiths feel they are rejecting a genuine, sincere, likeable person. Like turning away a close friend.

10. Seller:    *No way. You're just wasting my time with an offer like that.*

This is a tough one. Or is it? This slightly aggressive response is sometimes a bluff, one the seller hopes will shock you into a much higher offer.

At other times, it's just an initial nervous reaction from a seller who feels insecure about selling the home without the help of an agent. Still, it's likely to mean just what it says—the seller is less than impressed with your offer.

Difficult as the challenge might seem initially, you must engage this seller in conversation if you are to make headway. It's an ideal opportunity to display your qualities of calmness, sincerity and, in a subtle way, your knowledge of local real estate prices.

As you listen attentively, don't allow yourself to be railroaded or your opinions to be dismissed without consideration. Letting the seller dominate the exchanges prevents you from being able to make a convincing case based on factual information, which is exactly what you need to demonstrate if you are to get the sellers to soften their stance.

On top of that, it's also true, as we saw earlier, that allowing the sellers to talk unchecked is likely to add to their conviction and stubbornness on price. Words have a self-influencing power that you must challenge with logic and facts.

Any time a seller dominates the conversation, he's in control. Generally, this is something you can't afford to let happen. In particular, with this type of seller, your case might never get presented or your strategy applied unless you are prepared to be assertive. It's only by doing this that you'll be able to exert any negotiating influence.

Any seller who dismisses your initial offer as 'wasting their time' needs to be won over on a personal level before being likely to heed the facts you present. By this I mean that your early conversation should focus on things that are neutral, beyond dispute (such as small talk of real estate and the home in question). You must find common ground, the things you agree on, and build on that before returning to the hard business of price. This foundation enables you to introduce gradually the facts you must get the seller to consider.

- How familiar is the seller with the properties that have recently sold locally?

- How many did the seller see personally?

- Is the seller aware of the gap that exists between the asking prices of those homes and the prices the sellers eventually accepted?

- Are the sales the seller can cite really relevant?

- Does the seller know that real estate agents are often guilty of placing unrealistically high valuations on homes in order to secure listings?

- Does the seller know that many buyer inquiries and home inspections are made by people who are not in a position to buy, but are simply curiosity seekers, dreamers, or worse?

- Is the seller aware of how too-high a price hurts a home in many ways, condemning it to sit on the market and eventually seem stale and suspicious to buyers?

You can also add comments and questions specific to that particular home, the neighborhood, local taxes, nearby developments, prices, and so on, in congenial conversation. Eventually, you'll reach the point where you must make your case for the second time. You consider your offer of $146,750 to be very fair, based on actual prices paid for local homes by real buyers, homes that were largely comparable to the Smiths'.

It is time to remind Mr. and Mrs. Smith, again, that you are not a "looker," unlike many who respond to a home being sold privately, that you are interested, ready to buy, and prepared to pay what you consider a fair price. From this point, you proceed as we've seen before. There is another home ... maybe your partner would agree to pay ... you'll make your decision almost right away ... and so on.

Depending on the kind of reactions you get from the seller, you can conclude your conversation with a suggestion that you might increase your offer:

Buyer: *That's where I stand, Mr. and Mrs. Smith. I do favor your home over the other one and I might be able to increase my offer just a little.*

If you don't already know how the seller's thinking has changed, this kind of comment will generally make that clear. Then, keep moving toward the best deal you can arrange.

Never dismiss the possibility that the seller is moving closer to your figure than you are being told. That's an important reason (another one) to keep your increases to small increments.

And, finally, stay aware that it is very difficult, if not impossible, for a seller to maintain an attitude of aggressive stubbornness for any length of time, especially in the company of a calm, genuine, and reasonable buyer. As you persevere, these are the qualities that will bridge the gap, leading to a communicative atmosphere in which your negotiation skills can produce the results you are seeking.

# BUYER BROKERS: WHAT YOU SHOULD KNOW

*I not only use all the brains I have but all I can borrow.*
—WOODROW WILSON

For homebuyers who are reluctant to take on the task of negotiating, there may be an exciting alternative—hiring an *exclusive* buyer broker. Buyer brokers, who are also known as buyer representatives or buyer agents, have been around for quite a few years. However, it is only recently that their value has received the wide recognition it deserves. The trend is still in its early stages in North America, but it is spreading fast in many areas. In other countries, it is established to different degrees and generally seems to be gaining wider acceptance as the need for homebuyer protection gains support. In effect, the exclusive buyer's broker will do for the buyer what the traditional real estate agent (the seller's agent) has been doing for sellers throughout the years. That is, he or she will represent the homebuyer's best interests by searching out suitable homes and negotiating the lowest purchase price and best terms. Naturally, the broker takes his instructions solely from his client, the buyer, and owes no loyalty or confidentiality to the seller, unlike the traditional agent.

The best part of all this, typically, is that the homebuyer gets protection *and* assistance with the negotiation, at no extra cost. The agent who listed the home for sale shares the sales commission with the broker who represented the buyer. The net result is that the homebuyer's interests are fully and exclusively represented without any additional cost or a separate fee being paid.

So, neither the seller nor the buyer pays extra because a buyer broker is involved.

This *no cost to the homebuyer* arrangement is in operation in a large majority of buyer agencies. However, a very small percentage of buyer brokers operate differently. They ask for a flat fee payment directly from the buyer. Or, more likely, an upfront retainer fee of 0.5 to 1 percent of the buyer's target price. Almost always this retainer fee is returned to the buyer at closing, or is applied to the purchase price. Do you have a financial obligation if you don't buy? Ask! There is no standard practice on this.

These arrangements are generally less preferable, as I see it, than the usual and straightforward no cost to the homebuyer arrangement. However, they are not to be avoided automatically, especially where a top agent-negotiator might be available to work for you. Whatever arrangement you choose, be sure to get all details of fees and responsibilities spelled out clearly before you sign any document or engage a broker.

## Study Shows Significant Savings

In 1993, U.S. Sprint announced the results of its own study into the effectiveness of exclusive buyer brokers. The study, mentioned in an earlier chapter, concentrated on 232 of its employees relocating to different parts of the United States.

The findings were impressive for a number of reasons. The employees who bought in the conventional way paid, on average, 96 percent of the list price of the homes they purchased. Those who employed a buyer broker, paid just 91 percent. The first point this study supported very clearly is that all prices are indeed negotiable. A significant and more revealing point, though, is that the know-how of the buyer broker saved buyers thousands of dollars.

How much on average? Well, you'll remember that the U.S. median home price in late 1994 stood at approximately $106,000. So, let's assume that the U.S. Sprint employees bought average priced homes. In that case, those who bought in the conventional way paid 96 percent of $106,000. That's $101,760, a saving of $4,240 per home. Not bad.

But those who used an exclusive buyer broker paid just 91 percent of $106,000. That's $96,460, a saving of $9,540 per home. A lot better!

Keep in mind also that these savings are cash in the hand and are, in virtually all cases, worth more than they seem! As we saw in chapter 2, over the life of a mortgage, any amount borrowed—or saved—multiplies. For example, that saving of $9,540 at the time of purchase, over 30 years at 10 percent interest rate, saves the buyer more than $30,000! In other words, the buyer would pay back $30,000 less by taking a smaller loan ($9,540 smaller). That's like an automatic saving of $1,000 every year for 30 years.

For many, savings such as these represent a small fortune. This is the power—*the power to save money and make money*—that *Not One Dollar More!* places in your hands. It gives that same power to the buyer broker. The methods explained in these pages will work for anyone who uses them wisely, ordinary homebuyer, experienced investor or buyer's agent.

## Types of Buyer Brokers

More and more homebuyers are discovering that buyer brokers offer a worthwhile service that deserves serious consideration. One problem you might run into, though, is that the idea is only now starting to mushroom and, so far, is not easily accessible to all who might benefit from it. If you choose not to negotiate on your own behalf, you may be lucky enough to find a professional buyer broker in your area who has read this book and has otherwise been well trained in representing buyers' interests.

Most importantly, you need someone who is a competent negotiatior. Not simply a traditional agent who decided to catch the wave and call him- or herself a buyer broker while ignoring the special tuition and training that is necessary to serve the best interests of the homebuyer.

The first rule is to ensure the broker you engage will be representing you *exclusively.* You don't want a broker who assures you they can function as a *facilitator* or *go-between,* acting for you and the seller at the same time. This is like a lawyer representing the plaintiff and the defendant in the same case. It just can't work, in my view. Yet it is legal in real estate when properly disclosed. And there are agents who seem to believe, genuinely, that it's possible to play a 'neutral' role in buyer–seller transactions. This neutral role means two things.

First, the broker is practicing what is known as dual agency, which brokers are legally bound to disclose to you and to the seller (undisclosed dual agency is illegal), and for which they must have the consent of buyer and seller. However, how and when that disclosure is made and how and when consent is sought and received is often very loosely regulated and is the concern of many consumer protection advocates. For example, it's hardly fair for an agent to wait until the negotiation is in progress—or completed—to tell you that he or she is also 'representing' the seller. By that time, you will probably have revealed personal and confidential information you would not have done had you been aware of the agent's double role.

Second, it means that the broker is not, in fact, representing your best interests or the seller's best interests, but is simply conveying information between both sides. On the surface, this might sound like a fair arrangement—and it can work if you're a very astute deal maker and otherwise experienced with real estate, and, if you know exactly what you are doing. But, for the vast majority of homebuyers, using a dual agent is, I believe, unnecessary and potentially risky and I recommend strongly against it.

The best advice I can give you is, be safe. Stick with someone who will pledge their loyalty and expertise to protecting only *your* money and only *your* interests. Choose an exclusive buyer broker who will work hard for *your* goal of getting the home you want at the lowest price and on the best terms possible—one who will listen and advise sympathetically, then act faithfully on your instructions.

### Choosing a Buyer Broker

First, where do you find such an agent? Buyer brokers generally work in smaller real estate companies and, naturally, in exclusive buyer agencies. The latter usually have words similar to *buyer* or *buyer agency* in the company name and don't engage at all in selling real estate. Other companies practice what is called *single agency*, which means they will represent the buyer or the seller but never both in the same transaction.

The best way to find a reputable exclusive buyer broker in your area is to contact one of the state or national associations of buyer brokers. (For more information, see *Miscellaneous Recommended Services* in the Appendix). Buyer broker associations usually offer advice and helpful educational literature to potential homebuyers. They will also provide the names and phone numbers of their buyer broker members closest to the neighborhoods you have selected. Alternatively, a search of the Yellow Pages or a call to a local real estate company will probably turn up a few prospects.

Just as with sellers' agents, though, not all buyer brokers are created equal. Many have accumulated a range of selling skills and will be able to offer good advice on such things as local property regulations and financing options. Another big plus is that almost all can assist you in applying for and securing a suitable mortgage, if you have not already done so.

However, because of the work they must do for the buyer, they also need something more—negotiation skills that are at least as sharp as the competition's. That means they must be at least as sharp as the selling agents with whom they will be negotiating on your behalf.

This emphasizes once again why it is critical for you to be familiar with the basic how-to of negotiation, even if you decide against negotiating personally.

So, how do you go about choosing an exclusive buyer broker? Well, getting a reliable recommendation from another homebuyer is one way, but make sure it is reliable; not everyone is a good judge of such things. Or, you can call on one of the professional buyer broker associations. Otherwise, you'll have to spend sufficient time with a broker to get a feel for how effective he or she can be, before you hire the broker. Even when one is recommended to you, it is a good idea to have a getting-to-know-you meeting in which you can make some kind of evaluation. You'll find a lot of the material in this book will be very helpful in making your selection. Keep in mind that the broker you engage is just as likely to be female as male. Here are some criteria on which you might base your decision:

- Does the company also represent sellers' interests? Or is it an exclusive buyer agency?

- Does the broker, personally, also represent sellers?

- How long has the broker represented buyers' interests? Exclusively?

- What special negotiation training has the broker had in getting the best deal for buyers?

- Will the broker give you specific details of recent purchases in which the buyers got the best deal?

- Will the broker give you those and other buyers' names and phone numbers? And permission to contact them?

Then, see what you can find out about the broker's specific skills:

- How well does the broker understand tactics and timing?

- What does the broker know about setting the mood and building credibility?

- Is the broker aware of the importance of control and the power of perception?

- Does the broker know how to make use of concessions and capitalize on home inspection reports?

- Is the broker aware of the power of relevant factual research?
- What type of relationship does the broker advocate with sellers and sellers' agents?
- Can the broker pick and mix tactics to make up a good strategy?
- Can the broker "sell" a strategy convincingly?
- Can the broker communicate the right impression and create distance when it is necessary?
- Is the broker aware of the subtlety of persuasion and how it is based on an understanding of psychology, motivation, and interpersonal communication?
- Can the broker leave his or her ego aside when getting a good deal depends on it?
- Can the broker adapt to different agent and seller personality types and select an approach that will get you the best deal?
- Can the broker use probing statements and read between the lines?
- Does the broker appreciate the importance of verifying seller information and the power of legitimacy?
- Is the broker prepared to listen and take specific directions from you where appropriate?
- Does the broker understand the value of 'alternatives' and the use of power?
- What is the broker's philosophy on how offers should be made?
- Does the broker believe in the value of good legal advice and in ensuring that you are fully protected?

Naturally, you won't be able to get answers to all these questions in a preliminary, getting-to-know-you talk. But you don't need to. What you should be looking for, primarily, is an overall impression of the broker's experience and resourcefulness, the name and code of ethics of the association with which the broker is affiliated, and a verbal commitment to getting you, exclusively, the best deal possible.

But, even in an arrangement like this, remember, you are still in control. All the strings are still yours to pull. In fact, what you learn from this book is yours to use in any situation in which you stand to gain or lose anything of value.

It is most important, as we saw earlier, never to put your financial fate blindly and exclusively in the hands of someone else. Using a buyer broker should be a collaborative exercise, one in which you stay involved throughout—and one in which your new know-how can play a major part in securing a very desirable outcome.

Should you decide to use a buyer broker, most of what you learn from *Not One Dollar More!* will serve you well and profitably, not just in selecting a broker, but in instructing your agent wisely (after all, this one really is yours!) as the agent searches for a home that is just right for you, then negotiates for the lowest price and best terms possible.

Finally, for the homebuyer who feels inclined to try his or her luck at house auctions, but lacks the necessary know-how and experience, all is not lost. Finding a buyer broker who has experience with auctions may well be the ideal solution. First, though, read the following chapter on auctions, and you'll get a general idea of what can happen. At least, you will understand better how to select a bidding strategy and how to instruct your agent.

One final caution: As buyer representation gains momentum and popularity, some traditional real estate companies have been pushing buyer broker services to homebuyers. The result is confusion. Even dual agents—who cannot and do not exclusively represent the buyer—frequently claim to be buyer brokers and buyer representatives.

A dual agent, however, is not what you need. Your goal should be to engage an agent who will represent only *your* interests, not just a buyer broker, but an *exclusive* buyer broker. Make sure that is what you are getting.

Also, it's important to keep this in mind: Dual agents, facilitators and transaction brokers do not provide you with the safe, exclusive representation I recommend. That's understood. However, out of the purchase price you pay comes their commission—usually the same as or higher than what an *exclusive* buyer broker gets paid. Hardly a good deal for the homebuyer. Reduced services and less protection, to my way of thinking, call for reduced fees. So, stay alert! And remember the key work—*exclusive.*

In the Appendix, along with the list of buyer broker associations, you will also find information on prominent buyer agents in different parts of the country.

# PART FIVE

## Auctions

# CHAPTER TWELVE

# BUYING AT AUCTION

*What is wanted is not the will to believe*
*but the wish to find out, which is the exact opposite.*
                                    —BERTRAND RUSSELL

While residential property auctions are well established in parts of Europe and in Australia, the idea hasn't yet become a routine method of selling real estate in the United States. Most commonly in the United States, it is employed in the selling of distressed and foreclosed properties. However, this is not exclusively the case.

This chapter is intended to give you just a basic introduction to the auction process. It is not meant to equip you with all the know-how you will need to participate confidently and safely.

The way government-regulated foreclosure auctions work is very specialized. I generally advise ordinary homebuyers to steer clear of this field. Unless you already have the required know-how, or are prepared to acquire it, leave it to the professional speculators who can better afford to take the risks.

Foreclosure regulations change from state to state and sometimes even from city to city. Those hoping to buy in this way need to be clear about how the system works and be prepared for the hassles that sometimes ensue. If you are interested in buying a foreclosure property, one of the best books on the subject is *The Smart Money Guide to Bargain Homes* by James Wiedemer.

From time to time you might also come across builders' auctions. These can be either public or private auctions. However, both call for a level of expertise and familiarity the average homebuyer usually does not have. When they are private affairs, buyers are often required to register beforehand and even to demonstrate their genuineness by placing a deposit with the auctioneer before entering (or bidding).

Clearly, builders' auctions and foreclosure auctions are not for the ordinary homebuyer. A high degree of knowledge, familiarity, and caution are called for, particularly with regard to the various rules and regulations that apply. If you are determined to learn about and participate in either of these types of auctions, the best advice I can give you is to discuss the matter with knowledgeable professionals. A suitably experienced buyer broker or local auctioneer is a good starting point. After that, read as much as you can on the subject. You would also be well advised to attend as many auctions as is necessary to gain the required confidence.

The third type of auction is the more conventional house auction, which the public is invited to attend. These are not popular everywhere though, and in places feature only higher priced homes, sometimes in the million-dollar-plus bracket. Nonetheless, these are the auctions that probably are most relevant to the nonprofessional homebuyer.

Now that you are aware that I advise against auctions for the inexperienced or uninformed buyer, I am going to make a few assumptions. I'll assume that if you are attracted by the possibility of attending and buying at public auction, you appreciate the importance—before you bid or buy—of learning the ropes and becoming thoroughly familiar with how the process works. Having said that, my remarks from here forward relate to conventional public auctions, not necessarily to private auctions or foreclosure auctions, though some of what I have to say is relevant in all cases.

### Know the Property Before You Bid

This is an obvious starting point. However, it means knowing more than just the location and the condition the property seems to be in. You'll need to have a reliable estimate of the value of the home— with the emphasis on reliable. If your own knowledge of local home prices is insufficient, consult with area real estate agents and perhaps a few neighbors close to the property. Ask about recent sales nearby. Then, contact the auctioneer's agent and ask if a recent appraisal (valuation) has been carried out on the home. If so, was it made by the agent's company or by an independent appraiser? And how recently? If an independent appraiser was involved, find out the appraiser's name and contact them. Tell the appraiser you are potentially interested in the home and ask if he believes the appraised value is still valid.

When no recent independent appraisal has been made, you'll have to rely on your own research and your knowledge of the local market. Or, alternatively, hire a professional appraiser to tell you what it is worth. Unfortunately, this can be difficult—and sometimes even impossible—to arrange with certain types of auctions. Ask the agent, if you are unsure. If you have a lawyer (one who understands real estate), call and explain your situation. It is essential for you to understand your legal rights and obligations before you commit yourself.

At that stage, if you are still determined to go through with it, contact the selling agent and request copies of relevant documents and *as much information* as he or she can give you or show you. Ask also about the bidding. What can the agent tell you about it? What reserve price has been set? (This is the price below which the property will not be sold. The agent may or may not know this figure before the day of the auction. Or, they may know it and not tell you). When the agent seems to be hedging, push for an estimate of the selling price, based on his experience. You'll sometimes be surprised at how quickly such a simple question can unearth needed details (the Feed-the-Ego tactic).

Buying at auction requires special care for a number of other important reasons. To begin with, you'll be buying without some of the safeguards you get with a conventional purchase. Auction contracts are usually drawn up by the selling agent and must be signed immediately when the sale is made. The right of the buyer to impose conditions on the agreement is either severely limited or entirely prohibited. That can mean no escape clauses and no opportunity to make the purchase subject to your partner's or attorney's approval, or even conditional upon a satisfactory professional home inspection.

Nor can you, typically, buy the home conditional upon your lender approving your loan application. You are expected to have that sorted out before you bid. Before the day of the auction, you should also seek assurance from the selling agent that the title to the property is guaranteed. When the agent can't provide this, your alternative is to have a title search conducted, something you are well advised to discuss with your attorney as early as possible.

I'm going to further assume now that you have carried out all the research and checking that are called for and that everything meets with your satisfaction. You are sitting or standing in place as the auction is about to begin, and you have a clear understanding of the value of the home to be sold. Most important, you have also determined the limit to which you are prepared to bid, the point at which you will quit bidding and leave the property to another buyer. And you won't be swayed from the position in the heat of the moment.

## On the Day of the Auction

After calling the auction to order, the auctioneer is likely to present an exaggerated description of the value and beauty of the home, and then invite someone to start the bidding. At this stage a smart buyer will make only one type of response—total silence. Leave it to a less astute buyer to get the process moving. Your aim is to do nothing that will contribute even slightly to advancing the momentum of the auction or the bidding.

From your point of view, the slower things move, the better. Most inexperienced auction buyers I've observed are too anxious to become involved and to throw out early, low bids believing they are doing their cause no disservice. Of course, that's what the auctioneer would like everyone to think. The most common phrase that illustrates this point, and one you'll hear often, is: "It doesn't matter where we start. It's where we finish that counts." Auctioneers are very fond of using remarks like this to fire up the bidding. Ignore them every time.

Even more dangerous is the temptation in the early stages of the auction to outbid another buyer. Such competition plays into the hands of the auctioneer and drives up the eventual price you will have to pay to buy the home. Keep in mind, the aim of the auctioneer—to get the highest price possible—is the opposite of your objective. That makes the auctioneer your competitor, despite any "nice guy" image that is projected.

Does what I'm saying mean you should restrict yourself to just one, or possibly two, late bids? No, not at all. When to start bidding will be dictated by how the auction progresses, how the price builds, how many buyers are actively interested, and whether the auctioneer will actually sell when the bidding slows up or stops. If a reserve price has been set by the owner but has not been reached, the auctioneer can request the reserve to be lowered, in which case it might then be made clear to the audience that the auctioneer *is* going to sell. Alternatively, the auctioneer can terminate the auction without accepting the highest bid, and then list the home for conventional sale at a higher price.

Short of learning the auctioneer's style from repeated observation, it is quite difficult to recognize the stage at which they are genuinely going to bring down the hammer. If the auctioneer is good at their job, they will employ calculated dramatics and speech to convince interested buyers they are about to sell to the then-highest bidder. This usually happens long before the auctioneer has any intention of actually doing so. The aim is to generate competitive bidding, especially from buyers who might be interested but who have not, up to then, entered the fray. This is where having observed the auctioneer previously gives you an advantage. You'll be aware of the signs to watch out for. Failing this, a colleague of the auctioneer might be willing to offer you some guiding signs before the auction, particularly if you present yourself as a potential future client or a source of referral business.

Staying out of the bidding until a sale is imminent won't endear you to the auctioneer. But, if it upsets them, let it be *their* problem, not yours. I've watched—and have been the subject of—occasional attempts by auctioneers to intimidate the smarter, low-profile buyers into playing the game *their* way. Once again, the best defense against such tactics is to totally ignore them in the knowledge that the auctioneer deprived of a response will soon look foolish. By sticking to your game plan you'll avoid the risk of being lured or cajoled into making decisions you might later regret. This is called putting the pressure back on the auctioneer. That's exactly what your expressionless response will achieve.

The keys are to know the rules of the game and to make your own decisions. How the auctioneer feels toward you is *completely irrelevant* to your goal to buy at the lowest price possible. Keep that thought firmly in mind.

### How to Bid Wisely

Let's build a hypothetical scenario to illustrate a few key points about bidding. Suppose the auction has been rolling along with buyers bidding up the price in $5,000 bids. But now, at $110,000, no one seems willing to go any further. However, the limit you have set, and one you are prepared to pay if you have to, is $125,000. What do you do next?

Do you raise the bidding by another $5,000 and make your offer $115,000? You could. But let's examine the situation more closely and see if you should.

You can be sure that the auctioneer wants nothing more than to sell the home. Perhaps they've given the owner the understanding that a sale is all but certain. But now, the excitement has faded. That tells the auctioneer a resistance point has been reached, indicating they are at, or close to, the maximum price the market is prepared to pay. The auctioneer's experience will prompt them to put on a show of disbelief. But behind it, they'll be well aware that further bids, if any come, won't come easily. In fact, the auctioneer may need to work very hard to get even a slight increase in the bidding. From here on, they'll be struggling.

Now, in light of these facts, do you still believe it would be a good idea to offer another $5,000? Not on your life! I would now bid $116,000, an increase of just $1,000. Because the size of the bid is being changed (from $5,000 to $1,000), the new bid would have to be spoken very clearly—"one sixteen." A nod or hand gesture alone could be taken as a bid of $5,000 and could result in an embarrassing situation in which you are forced to explain what you intended.

At first, the auctioneer might appear to reject your $1,000 bid while pressuring you to make it $5,000. The auctioneer might even try to tell you they haven't got authority at that point to accept bids lower than $5,000. By focusing attention on you, the auctioneer hopes you'll be persuaded to escape the pressure by giving in to their demands. Eventually, though, when you answer these tactics with nothing but stoic silence, they will accept your bid, unless another buyer offers more.

It is tactically important for you not to be drawn into an open exchange with the auctioneer. Don't see it as a conversation — and leave your best manners at home. I'm not suggesting you be rude, but this is a battle of wits. Silence and stubbornness can be the most effective tools at your command.

As the bidding stalls, the auctioneer is likely to lapse into another flowery description extolling the virtues of the property and the rare value-for-money opportunity that's available. This is called "talking-up the price" and can go on for many minutes. However, don't let it affect your resolve. Your bid is *still* $116,000, whether they have accepted it or not. Keep in mind that if there are no further bids it would be foolish to sell to the $115,000 bidder and thereby deprive the owner of your higher offer of $116,000. That, simply, won't happen.

However, if there are still two or three buyers in the bidding when the auction builds to a climax, you're going to have to call on your instinct, your research, your knowledge of the property, and what you've learned about auctions. Whatever the situation, the principle of *inactive bidding* will generally serve you best. You stick with your plan of bidding only when you have to—only when it looks like the auctioneer is about to sell the home for the price offered by another buyer. This assumes, of course, that any new offer you make would not exceed the spending limit you have set for yourself.

Inactive bidding—bidding that tends to suppress the auction's momentum and, consequently, the price—leaves the competition to other buyers in the earlier stages. That's exactly as it should be. But what if you are the only interested buyer? Then, you will be forced to open the bidding (after letting the auctioneer plead as long as possible). In such a situation, your opening bid may be all you need to buy the property. This isn't a common occurrence, but it does happen. So, keep your bid low and, if you have to, negotiate up from there in small, drawn out increases.

### Understanding the Blast Bid

This is a tactic you should be aware of, not necessarily to use it, but to recognize when it is being used by a competing buyer. Although it's certainly not as safe a tactic as inactive bidding, it can work well when used intelligently.

You might hear this referred to by other names such as *shut-out bidding* or *power bidding*, but the objective is always the same, to kill the interest of the other buyers who are hoping to buy the home.

Let's return to our example to illustrate this tactic. You've decided you'll pay a maximum of $125,000 for the home, but only if you have to go that high. The bidding, which had been creeping up in $500 bids, has stalled at $102,500, though it is clear that there are at least two, maybe three, buyers interested. This is the kind of situation in which a blast bid can win the property. You decide to make a blast bid of $106,000 (an increase of $3,500) in the hope of killing off further interest from the other buyers.

Perhaps $106,000 would not be sufficient to accomplish that objective. Maybe you'd have to go as high as $108,000 or higher. Only the situation will tell you that. The message you're hoping to send is one of intimidation, that you want the home enough to outbid all those offering $500 increases, and that anything they might offer, you'll beat.

You'll have noticed, too, there are risks attached to this tactic. If your blast bid buys the home, you won't know if you might have got it for less. Maybe the inactive bidding tactic would have resulted in a lower price. Or maybe a smaller blast bid would have been sufficient. For these reasons, I don't recommend blast bidding, unless the buyer is very confident about the property's value and is certain the blast bid, if successful, would represent a bargain buy.

This is where good research and auction experience come into play. You need to be certain of the accuracy of the information on which you are basing your decisions, just as with any form of real estate buying. Most of all, though, you need to have an accurate and objective assessment of the value and condition of the home.

### Case Study: When Things Go Terribly Wrong

Here is an account of an incident I witnessed recently at a suburban auction.

I investigated a Victorian-style home on behalf of a client but recommended against the property after my first inspection. That recommendation was accepted by my client. The size of the home, coupled with the amount of work it required, made it unsuitable, though it was a very salable piece of real estate and would very likely be an ideal buy for another type of buyer.

My estimate of the value of the home was $175,000 to $185,000. I talked with the agent handling the auction, and he confirmed my figures by telling me he expected the selling price to be a minimum of $180,000 on the day of the auction.

Purely out of curiosity, I attended the auction on a beautiful Saturday morning in the middle of summer. I fully expected the auctioneer would ask for an opening bid of around $120,000 just to get the ball rolling and get the interested buyers involved. (Many auction buyers, incidentally, know nothing about smart buying or the wisdom of inactive bidding.) If two or more active bidders had come to buy the property, I felt the selling price could possibly be pushed to $190,000 to $200,000. After going through a lengthy description of the home and all its attributes, the auctioneer asked for the opening bid to get the auction under way. He had no sooner uttered the words (he hadn't even yet asked for a specific opening bid) when a man at the back of the audience shouted "$280,000." Everyone gasped, particularly the auctioneer, who paused, then enquired nervously: "Could you repeat the bid please, sir?" The man said it again, "$280,000," this time more strongly and articulately.

No need to tell you, that was the only bid (a disastrous use of the blast bid), and it bought the home. Unfortunately, the buyer had either been very badly informed or had gathered no research or information at all. He paid $100,000 more than the property was worth! It was painful to watch. I felt like offering my advice, but it was too late to do anything.

Subsequently, the auctioneer's agent told me the buyer discovered the magnitude of his mistake a few days later. But there was no way out. He was forced to go through with the purchase.

I don't want you to take from this that the blast bid has no validity. But, like any tactic, it can be used wisely or unwisely. Had the unfortunate buyer followed the steps I outlined earlier in this section, he could still have bought the home with about $100,000 left over to spend on anything he wished.

It was this, more than any other single incident, that prompted me to write this book.

## Recognizing When the Auctioneer Is Going to Sell

You need to be able to predict when the auctioneer is about to sell in order to maximize the effectiveness of your bidding. The problem is that most auctioneers bluff continually that they are on the verge of bringing the hammer down. This is designed to elicit last-minute bids and to ferret out previously undisclosed interest.

Without experience of auctions, and of a particular auctioneer, it isn't easy to determine accurately when such a bluff is taking place. Some auctioneers use specific phrases only when they are about to sell. A few examples: "I'm going to sell," or "the property is now on the market." And, of course, sometimes but not always, "going once, going twice..." When the hammer hits the gavel, the buyer holding the highest bid has bought the home.

But a bid can be made right up to the moment before "sold" is called. Having the experience and familiarity that enables you to time a very late bid gives you a number of potential advantages over other active bidders. You achieve maximum advantage when the buyer holding the highest bid is prematurely confident that he or she is about to become the owner of the home. In this situation, your deliberately timed late bid can produce a major psychological victory and can cause the other bidder to throw in the towel.

It isn't necessary to cut it so fine that you wait to the very last second. It's much better to ensure you get your bid in, even if it is slightly earlier than you would have liked, than to risk waiting until the hammer is on its way down for the final time. A less than fully observant auctioneer frequently misses last-second bids. So, take advantage of late bidding but don't leave it so late that you run the risk of being overlooked. You'll do better if you can spot when the auctioneer is bluffing and when he or she is genuinely about to sell the property.

### Shills, Stooges, and Conspirators

I'm often asked if *stooges* or *shills* are still used in auctions today. Stooges and shills are individuals who work secretly with an auctioneer, but pose as legitimate, ordinary buyers.

The role of these conspirators is to force up the bidding by offering fake bids, especially when several genuine buyers are actively competing for the property. They are also employed in the opposite situation, when bidding is sluggish. Then, their job is to get things moving, to fire up the bidding.

Not all real estate auction companies use stooges. In fact, it may be only a small percentage. But it's a figure that is impossible, because of its nature, to determine accurately. Nonetheless, it does happen, more in some parts than in others.

To get the stooge to bid, the auctioneer uses a set of pre-planned signals, such as certain phrases or hand gestures. Even the size of the bid the auctioneer wants can be communicated in much the same way.

The big problem for the genuine buyer is that stooges are difficult to spot, unless you've been around auctions for a while, and even then there's no guarantee. The most an experienced buyer can usually hope for is to be able to spot likely suspects and observe their behavior closely. If you notice a particular individual turning up and bidding, but not buying, at a number of a company's auctions, it's time to be suspicious. You may have discovered a stooge. Unfortunately, there isn't a lot you can do, except stop bidding. Even when you feel sure the bidder is not a genuine buyer, open challenge or confrontation is unlikely to produce a satisfactory remedy.

An alternative move is to reduce dramatically the size of the bids you make. For example, follow an increase of $5,000 with $500, or an increase of $1,000 with $250 and at the same time, fix a stare on the suspected stooge. When the auctioneer sees what is happening they'll very likely signal the stooge to back off. Protecting the company reputation is far more important than the outcome of any single auction.

In some special situations, you may be entitled to ask for evidence that will establish the genuineness of prospective bidders, before the auction begins. However, that involves your legal rights and is outside the scope of this book, not least because legal rights vary from place to place. Once again, an attorney familiar with real estate law is your best source of advice in this regard. An experienced buyer broker familiar with auctions is likely to know the whole process even better.

This is as good a place as any to repeat my warning that auction buying is not for the unknowledgeable, inexperienced homebuyer. However, if you decide you want to participate, then attend, as an observer only, as many auctions as you need to learn how the system works in your area. At the same time, talk to real estate auction professionals. Tap into their expertise, ask a lot of questions and learn the ground rules. How do you get the most complete, factual description of the home before you bid? What is specifically included and excluded in the sales agreement? What do you need to know about the method of payment required? Is settlement fixed or flexible within limits to suit the buyer? These questions and others help eliminate the risk of unpleasant surprises.

When you are sure you know what you are doing, you can expect to find some real bargains from time to time in the auction arena.

### Finding Out Where the Auctions Are

This task isn't very different in most cases from how you go about locating non-auction properties for sale.

Just about all metropolitan newspapers publish real estate auction notices, usually in the weekend editions, though sometimes during the week, too. If you are new to an area, you might call the real estate section of the largest local newspaper and inquire about the best day for auction ads. This is also a good opportunity to find out the names of the leading auction companies and if the paper has run any recent features on auction buying. In my own experience, I have found this kind of contact extremely valuable. Real estate writers and editors are frequently a fountain of good, relevant information, which they provide freely and objectively in most instances.

Not all ads, though, will give the full address of a home to be auctioned, or even a detailed description. Instead, you'll often find a phone number to call and, possibly, the name of a contact person.

The Yellow Pages probably lists real estate auctioneers in your area and will often indicate whether they specialize in commercial or residential properties. These companies will usually send you a list of upcoming auctions along with property descriptions, at least.

Your best sources of information will be buyer brokers who participate in auctions and local real estate agents. Either will give you pointers on the auction industry in the area, often even in cases where they don't handle auctions themselves, and will direct you to sources of further information, if necessary.

### No Time to Let Your Guard Down

In one way, there is no difference between buying at auction and buying in the more conventional manner. The auctioneer is just as much your competitor as the real estate agent or salesperson. Their objective is clear—to get you to part with as much money as possible. To get the highest price they can—for a particular home—out of you!

For that reason, in both cases, you must protect yourself in exactly the same ways. All the protective strategies I advised you to take in the earlier sections are just as necessary when buying at auction. Keep your cards close to your chest and reveal only what you have determined is in your interest to reveal. The points you should remain vague or noncommittal about include the degree of interest you have in the home to be auctioned; how much you are prepared to bid; whether, in fact, you will even attend and bid at all; the size of your budget; and any details of your personal circumstances that can, in any way, disadvantage your chances of buying the home at the lowest possible price.

At all times, keep in mind that however you buy real estate, you will always be up against an opponent who is trying to *stop* you from achieving your goal. Nobody is more strongly motivated or potentially more capable of protecting your savings and your wealth than you are.

The difference between those homebuyers who pay too much and those who buy at the lowest possible price is usually nothing more than the general know-how contained in this book—nothing more than a little inside knowledge of how the game of real estate is played and the simple negotiation skills that tilt the odds in your favor.

## KEY POINTS TO REMEMBER

- Learn how auctions operate in your area. Attend, and observe what happens, how, and when.

- Thoroughly investigate the property for sale and confirm all information given to you before you decide to participate in the auction.

- Get a reliable assessment of the value of the home. Don't rely totally on what the auction company tells you.

- Make sure the title is guaranteed. Consult your lawyer if you are in any doubt.

- Set your spending limit before you start bidding. Then, stick to it!

- Stay out of the early bidding. Don't fuel the momentum of the auction.

- Don't allow yourself to be intimidated, embarrassed, or pushed to action by the auctioneer.

- When the bidding slows dramatically or stops, offer a significantly lower increase than the auctioneer had been accepting up to that point. State it clearly, and sit tight. Ignore pressure to follow the size of the previous bids.

- Inactive bidding (not bidding at all until the final stage) is often the safest and most beneficial way to participate in public home auctions. But auction familiarity and specific experience is still strongly recommended.

- A blast bid calls for experience, care, keen judgment, and thoroughly accurate information about the home.

- Your attendance at an auction is not to win friends or gain the approval of the auctioneer.

- A suitably experienced buyer broker may be the ideal way of buying at auction, particularly if you have little or no auction experience. (See chapter on Buyer Brokers.)

# PART SIX

*Different Strokes…*

# CHAPTER THIRTEEN

# FIVE REAL ESTATE AGENT PERSONALITY TYPES

*We know but few men, a great many coats and breeches.*
—HENRY DAVID THOREAU

As you go about your task of finding and buying the home you want, you will face one last challenge—the variety of agent personality types you'll encounter and deal with.

Each of these broad types is different in important ways. Each has revealing traits, distinctive characteristics, and particular motivations. It is certainly not possible, though, to categorize all agents in this way. Nonetheless, when you know and can recognize the main types, you immediately know more about the individual concerned. This can give you a profitable edge in negotiating.

So, that's what this section is about—personalities and behaviors. It is not the result of a professional, scientific study and shouldn't be taken as such. But, having said that, it is based on serious research I conducted over a number of years. To an even greater degree, it comes from my own in-the-field encounters with—and diligent observation of—people who sell real estate for a living.

It is undoubtedly true that there is an infinite variety of people in our world. Nonetheless, I have identified five broad categories of personalities into which many real estate agents and salespeople seem to fit. I believe it's helpful to learn earlier rather than later the types of agent you are likely to encounter on the other side of the negotiation divide, and to know the slight shifts and gestures you might use to increase your chances of ultimate success.

Real estate agents and salespeople have jobs to do, and the majority of them do those jobs effectively and professionally. That doesn't alter the fact that they are *never* working for you. They are paid by and are committed to the seller—always! It is a fact, though, that most of the time they are working to bring about a sale—to pull a deal together. However, the seller's interests remain primary. Your interests have one defender, one protector, you! Agents promise the seller to get the highest price possible. That's exactly what they'll be trying to get *you* to pay. The agents referred to here are the typical agents who list and sell homes. Exclusive buyer brokers (buyer agents) are excluded from these remarks.

You might not find it easy to place a particular agent into one category. Some will exhibit traits that seem to be divided between categories. Just stay alert for additional clues that will give you a better understanding. Also, it is important not to rush into labeling an agent. Sometimes two, possibly three, contacts will be needed. At other times, a conclusion may not come at all. Of course, face-to-face contact is most revealing, by a long shot. But the telephone may also provide you with valuable clues, especially if you develop an open dialogue. Remember, though, that people can speak in generalities all day long without really saying anything at all. That is socially acceptable. But the task of buying a home at the lowest price possible requires specific, current facts and relevant, detailed information. When an agent or seller overloads you with history or the future profits you can expect from owning real estate, it's time to call a halt. Turn the discussion back to what is current and pertinent. Responding to a buyer's questions on price with rosy projections of future value is a ploy commonly used. Don't fall for it.

It's not that historical price increases in a particular neighborhood or projected growth in property values are not relevant or worthy of consideration. They certainly are. But when you find a home you would like to buy, you are dealing primarily with today; with the here and now; with the price you are going to have to commit to today; with the value of the dollars in your pocket today; with the seller's needs today; with your own needs and aspirations today; with the thousands of dollars you are trying to save today. It's easy to be lulled into figuring what a home will be worth five years or ten years into the future. Such optimism has led many buyers into bad decisions. Guard against it by staying firmly rooted in the present and by ensuring there are no negatives affecting the property or the location that would tend to diminish the potential of your investment over time.

The better prepared you are, and the better you know what it is you want and can afford, the more you will be able to stay in control of any buying situation. When you develop even a reasonable familiarity with the principles and methods in this book, personalities become much less consequential to the success you can expect.

However, by recognizing the main real estate agent and salesperson personality types, you can often give yourself a critical time advantage. This allows you to react quicker mentally and to tailor your performance to suit the situation at hand.

Negotiating to buy the home you want at the lowest price possible is exactly that—a performance. And, as with convincing performances of all kinds, the single most important key is good preparation.

Before we look at the individual personality types, I should point out that the characteristics and recommendations I describe apply equally to male and female agents and salespeople except where I indicated otherwise.

## The Gentle Intimidator

This personality type merits the tag of *the Gentle Intimidator*, first because of his or her admirable manners and friendliness. Both are natural to how the agent feels and functions. In females, it often shows through as likable sweetness. And in males, it frequently manifests as downright chivalry.

The problems arise when their pleasant, courteous natures lull you into complacency, and from there into quick and complete trust. It's almost as if something inside you wants to reciprocate the perceived personal qualities of this agent, allowing the business of buying a home to become almost secondary. As the endearing compliments roll softly off the Gentle Intimidator's lips, you are distracted by enjoyable charm and "no problem" efficiency. You are seduced by what you decode as obvious sincerity. Such agents thereby dictate the atmosphere and begin to consolidate control. It's important for you to remember this agent is not a rogue or a fake, but is genuinely sincere. Gentle intimidators have bad days like everyone else, when performance suffers.

The real trap is that the intimidating side of their personality is rarely evident in the early stages of your contact with them. They're very adept at putting the best foot forward. That remains so, usually, until you stall in making the "right" decision, which, typically, is when you say no to a property or an offer. The intimidating part might also show up when your opinions or questions cast doubt on the agent's "genuine" or "expert" point of view.

More than any other agent type, except perhaps for the Determined Persuader, whom we'll encounter shortly, Gentle Intimidators need to impress you with their declared absolute honesty, integrity, and the reliability of their advice. They don't generally shout these out for the world to hear but are more subtle and confidential. In extreme circumstances, and this is far more true for men than women, such agents are not beyond swearing on some sacred symbol or even the grave of a dead relative to convince you that he or she wouldn't steer you wrong or that the agent's intentions have never wavered off the path of sincerity and truth.

For all their deliberate attempts to sell you on their credibility, what is ironic is that their advice and information are usually highly accurate and their opinions perfectly sound. Gentle Intimidators make it a point to know their business and the market very well.

Like many real estate salespeople, Gentle Intimidators are short on true empathy for the buyer's sensitivities and concerns. If they could detach themselves more from the obsession with their own objectives, they would provide a better service and would, undoubtedly, make more sales. But, without the right kind of sales counseling, they are probably never going to achieve their true potential. Still, it's a positive experience to encounter such a likable individual. Just don't let the agent push the buttons that control your thinking.

### How to Handle the Gentle Intimidator

The majority of unwary homebuyers will always find it difficult to deal effectively with Gentle Intimidators. Their entire demeanor tends to throw buyers off guard making it embarrassing, or even impossible, to challenge them or openly offend them. Their mere presence dominates.

However, the informed buyer will find the answer in a seldom discussed fact of negotiation—manipulation. You must become something of a manipulator to handle this agent type successfully. But don't let that frighten you. You've been doing it all your life. You just don't call it manipulation. In many situations in daily life, if you're not prepared to defend your interests by using *positive manipulation*, you're likely to end up the one manipulated.

The secret is simple. This agent has a hungry ego. Certainly, all egos crave feeding, but this one is special. A good start is to bestow one or two appropriate compliments. Let the agent know how much his or her pleasant manner and helpful nature pleases you. Or emphasize how much you appreciate such professionalism and trustworthiness. But don't overdo it, as your intentions could be misread for blatant patronizing. Talk about how you feel comfortable dealing with the agent, who is doing a great job in helping you find the home that's right for you. These tactics will have the agent reacting to *your* strategy. Then, *you* are winning.

You might go even one step further by saying you'll gladly refer your friends and business associates to the agent, when buying or selling. And if everything does go well, do it, but recommend that your friends read this book first.

If openly complimenting another individual is not your style, you could find the whole experience with the Gentle Intimidator quite frustrating. That would be unfortunate because, when handled well, this agent can be your most powerful ally and can help you in many unforeseen ways. Problems that might stop many other agent types in their tracks will not defeat this individual. A strong desire for success (sales) and unquestionable determination enable this agent to resolve difficulties quickly and efficiently.

The key, as I've stressed, is to play this agent's game. As the agent packages and presents reasonable, charming and authoritative intimidation, you respond equally convincingly with your own positive manipulation techniques. If you reach an impasse, remind the agent that you have faith in his or her ability and experience. You're sticking at the offer you have made and you accept that the agent will do his or her best. Then stand back and watch the Gentle Intimidator perform.

The two most important things to remember is that Gentle Intimidators have huge egos and are task driven. By complimenting their professionalism and ability to get things done, you increase your chances of receiving a more abundant supply of those qualities.

But, stay constantly alert, for fear you might slip silently and unknowingly under a seductive spell. It might sting a little, but keep this terrible thought in mind—*the agent is on the other side!*

## The Dispassionate Expert

In the business of selling real estate, where warmth and amicable relationships are essential, the Dispassionate Expert survives, ironically, without ever understanding the value of empathy. Sometimes, not even the value of a warm handshake or an engaging smile or the courtesy of addressing the buyer by name. The majority of agents in this category are male, though it is not without its equally dispassionate female disciples.

Fortunately, as professional sales training methods develop and give more attention to an understanding of human psychology, the

Dispassionate Expert is becoming a less common phenomenon. Nonetheless, many are still to be found throughout the industry.

Dispassionate Experts are usually not intentionally angry or condescending, though you'd be forgiven for thinking otherwise. This impression is stronger from a distance than up close. Their detachment and informed business-like manner is more suited to those buyers who have a low reliance on salespeople and favor a less personal type of service. These include homebuyers who for one reason or another want to get the whole affair over as soon as possible. I'm sure you'll be aware by now that such an approach seldom leads to buying at the lowest price. (In this case, using a buyer broker makes a lot of sense.)

With such an impersonal style, you might wonder if Dispassionate Experts are capable of making a living in the business. They are—usually by relying on tireless energy to maintain a flow of listings, which they are expert at getting. Often, they focus on professional investors and developers instead of ordinary homebuyers. This type of agent, in larger real estate companies, is often a top performer or part of the management team.

Recognizing Dispassionate Experts is seldom a problem. Your first encounter might well include some or all of the following impressions: (1) The agent is having a bad day and is somewhat agitated; (2) The agent doesn't value your business; (3) The agent doesn't like you (Perhaps because of your race, or appearance, or maybe it's your budget or your smart-buyer approach. You just don't know.); (4) The person is probably unhappy or even depressed with life.

With some agents, one or more of these might be correct. However, the reason for such aloofness and the dispassionate attitude is usually that the agents believe this is the way business should be conducted, at least at the level on which they see themselves operating.

On the positive side (yes, there is one), Dispassionate Experts are business oriented rather than people oriented, which has its own advantages. Their efficiency and dependability are usually exemplary. If the agent promises to call you at 4:30 on Tuesday, you'll get a call at 4:30. What a pity that of all the personality types, this is the one on whom interpersonal communications training is most often wasted. They miss entirely the indisputable fact that the most successful sales people are communicators—those who listen, understand, and cater to buyers' emotions. Nonetheless, the Dispassionate Expert is just that, an expert, and it is this quality that results in success.

Their usually emotionally empty conversation is precise and measured. But, they will get all the facts and figures you need, and then some, demonstrating their knowledge of regulations, financing, legalities, and many other aspects of real estate. It's hardly ever necessary to doubt their facts. Accuracy and efficiency are two of their chief providers of status, which, along with credibility, they take very seriously. All too often, they take life the same way.

### How to Handle the Dispassionate Expert

Right away, allow me to save you a lot of effort by assuring you that no amount of warm pleasantness or friendliness will change such an agent's demeanor. He or she is not the Gentle Intimidator or the Caring Conversationalist and will not respond in the same way to tactical compliments or assurances that you have trust in the agent's integrity.

Still, it's in your interest to work as harmoniously as possible with the agent. Keep in mind that your chance of buying at the seller's lowest acceptable price is *just as good* with the Dispassionate Expert as with any other type. Start off by playing to their strengths—facts, figures and information about local properties, trends, and so on. Ask specific questions related to your goal rather than small talk meant only to maintain pleasant conversation. Dispassionate Experts love to show off all the knowledge at their fingertips.

The answers you'll get will generally be short, to-the-point, and for the most part entirely dependable. This is particularly beneficial but it doesn't relieve you of the need to verify other types of information. Nor does it mean you should concede when you are told that there's another interested buyer in the wings or that the seller will "definitely" not sell below a certain figure, or that the seller will simply let the deal die rather than compromise any more. Dispassionate Experts are very capable of sounding persuasive when dishing out such tactics in defense of their clients' interests. But, as a smart buyer, you won't be so easily convinced or dissuaded. Based on your own judgment and what you have learned from *Not One Dollar More!*, y u'll be able to recognize such tactics and negotiate confidently.

Dispassionate Experts go to great lengths with their logical approach, calculating your mortgage payments for you (precisely!), contrasting the advantages of buying a particular property against anticipated increases in home prices, and highlighting the capital appreciation you can expect if you make the only sensible decision there is—the one *the agent* wants you to make! It's not hard to see why they are such effective salespeople, or why they can turn people off the homebuying process.

What you won't hear are beguiling comments and questions about where you might put the television or furniture. Nor will you get suggestions about colors or patterns or how you might transform the mood of a particular room. And not in a month of Sundays will you be encouraged to imagine the coziness of snuggling up with your partner in front of the fireplace after a hard day at work.

— Dispassionate Experts are, essentially, nonromantics (while at work, at least). They feel safer and more effective treating this business of selling homes exclusively as that—a business.

For many buyers, this is a godsend, an agent who isn't hovering a half step behind their every move; an agent who isn't interrupting every thought and comment; and one who doesn't presume to have answers to every private superficial concern. In fact, in many ways, handling the Dispassionate Expert can be a breeze, especially for buyers who don't need handholding. The real test comes, however, when it is time to negotiate.

— Your most effective preparation for that stage is to adopt the agent's style and unwordy, unemotional approach, even an air of assertive impatience. Do this from the moment you recognize the personality type, which will usually be in your first communication. Keep the agent in the dark about what you are thinking by suppressing reactions to his or her answers and comments. The agent will find this unusual, being accustomed to buyers wilting and fawning under the agent's power and superior air.

Remember too, that Dispassionate Experts want the sale just as much, and often more, than any other type of agent. Their reputation is built on effectiveness, both at work and in their own minds. Negotiate strongly, as detached and as unemotionally as you can. Use the Comparative Value tactic as the primary justification for your offer. This is the kind of language they understand best. These agents will use all their persuasive and pragmatic skills to get the other side to accept your offer.

## The Caring Conversationalist

Most homebuyers find the Caring Conversationalist the most enjoyable type of agent to deal with. It's rare not to warm to this agent from the very first contact. When in person, this will almost certainly have been graced with a sincere handshake, obvious enthusiasm, and a broad smile.

Is it too good to be true? That might easily be your first impression, as this, clearly, is not how most buyers think of real estate salespeople. Your suspicion puts you on alert. But that suspicion can often be exaggerated simply because the agent doesn't fit your preconceived picture. So, initially at least, don't rush to a judgment, negative or positive.

A reasonable percentage of agents and salespeople fit broadly into this category, although the purest form of this type is quite rare. The Caring Conversationalist is equally likely to be male as female. But caution is still called for, because *no* agent, regardless of gender or personality, is working for *you!*

Caring Conversationalists constantly bombard you with warm messages, physical, verbal, and emotional, all accompanied by animated expression. In my experience, when this trait is genuine, as it nearly always is, you'll have encountered a professional who truly cares for the welfare of others. This quality of empathy can lead them to the top of their profession. Or, out of it. They are the agents people refer others to in large numbers.

Buyers and sellers feel equally attracted to and well served by them, a result of their excellent diplomacy and interpersonal communication skills. Although this personality type is frequently held up in training programs as a model for other agents to emulate, without the genuineness of the Caring Conversationalist that is a very difficult task.

For all these reasons, Caring Conversationalists are one of the easiest agent types to identify. They always have a story to tell you, listen intently to your comments, and address you by name. Generally, they aren't likely to be able to match other agent types, such as the Dispassionate Expert, for detailed knowledge of regulations or financial data. Statistics and bureaucratic procedures are not their style, nor will they try to persuade you otherwise.

They can sell—and sell well. When it's time to put your home on the market, you couldn't do better than employ this agent type. But when you are buying, it's a different story—watch out! Such agents are convincing, secure, and confident. You might even find yourself tempted to confide in the agent, which many homebuyers do. But that is never recommended. Even though it might not feel like it, you are still dealing with someone who represents the other side. Real estate is *always* a game; the agent and the seller are always your competition. Any overlooking of this by you compromises your chances of buying at the lowest possible price.

*How to Handle the Caring Conversationalist*

You'd almost be forgiven for thinking there's nothing to handle here. But there is.

In getting the best out of Caring Conversationalists, compliments won't be wasted, but don't be patronizing. That's not their motivating fuel. And, anyway, their people skills are highly developed and can see through most manipulative comments. Your personal genuineness—though certainly not defenseless disclosure—will encourage such agents to make special efforts on your behalf. No matter how comfortable you feel, though, always disclose only that information which you decided on before you met any agent. Don't alter your decision to keep secret such things as how high a price you are capable of paying, the urgency or anxiety of your circumstances or thinking, or how much you have fallen in love with a particular home. This caution applies with all agent types, without exception.

Caring Conversationalists are engaging, caring and communicative, and when free to practice these traits, they are at their best. They thrive on the opportunity to eliminate difficulties, to make things possible, and to respond positively. They prefer less formal, equality-based relationships than, for example, Dispassionate Experts or Gentle Intimidators would welcome. These qualities will flow to the extent that you reciprocate such an agent's warm disposition. Continued obvious distrust by you, or an attitude of abruptness or superiority, will close down his or her personality and present you with a much more formidable opponent, perhaps the most formidable of all agent types.

Make no mistake about the Caring Conversationalist. You are up against an efficient, goal driven, hugely resourceful individual—a masterful salesperson and an astute negotiator. Such is the agent's mastery that these two traits will rarely be obvious, which underlines the fact that the finest negotiators are not those who bang tables and demand concessions. Instead, they are natural psychologists who operate with a caring style and an almost undetectable effectiveness. Their greatest strength is that their power is invisible. So it is with the most skillful agents and salespeople who belong in this category.

Stay alert to the fact that negotiation is happening even when you don't think it is. It's there in *every* contact and communication when a real estate agent wants to sell you a home. The Caring Conversationalist is no exception. As long as the agent considers you sincere, the Caring Conversationalist will find the answers whatever it takes, without looking for commitments or promises in return.

Above all, let the agent know that you trust his or her integrity. Ethics and integrity are pillars of this agent's self-image. In fact, I've known Caring Conversationalists who felt it necessary and proper to always explain clearly at the outset that their loyalty and first responsibility was to the seller. Such openness isn't common. Sometimes it can be used as a ploy to win the buyer's trust. But this is never the case with the true Caring Conversationalist.

— When it comes time to make an offer or to stand by an offer you've already made, the Third Party tactic deserves strong consideration ("I really like the home but my wife won't go along with it because she believes the price is too high compared with others we've seen. Apart from that she likes this home as much as I do!").

The Comparative Value and No More Money tactics can also be used successfully, as long as you use a collaborative approach. Then, the agent will try hard to solve the problem, not just for the agent's own ego or income, but also for you.

— Ultimately, the Walk Away tactic might pull the deal together ("I'm sorry, if the seller doesn't accept this offer I have no choice. I'm just going to have to forget it and buy something else. I know you understand"). Once again though, it has a collaborative ring to it. It's not a hard, stern ultimatum, but more of a problem that the agent might well be able to fix.

### The Noncommunicator

There are two main characteristics to this personality type. First, Noncommunicators talk much less than most salespeople, forcing you to dig harder for information. And second, their answers may show uncertainty and a disregard for the degree of accuracy you require. This is by no means always the case, though. Some Noncommunicators (a smaller percentage) will surprise you with their knowledge on a variety of real estate matters.

The Noncommunicator will greet you pleasantly and will drive you around, but what you learn will be dictated largely by you. Be prepared to extract information. Yes and no answers seem to suit this agent just fine in responding to questions. Of course, the agent will promise to search out answers to specific questions, but don't hold your breath.

Noncommunicators sound relatively uninformed, at times, and seem not to mind if that comes across. You'll get a lot of *probablies* and *I guess sos* and more *I don't knows* than with other types. You might prefer this low profile approach if you know well what you are doing and prefer to rely on your own resources. Ultimately, though, if you pin a Noncommunicator down strongly enough, there is a good chance the agent will produce the specific answers you find difficult to get on your own.

The Noncommunicator is the least common of all agent types. Personalities like this tend not to remain in the industry for very long. Their presence in the first place is probably due to the huge turnover of real estate salespeople in most companies. Many stick it out no longer than a few months, or possibly a year or two (90 percent of all individuals who enter real estate selling leave the industry within five years). Overall, your experience with the Noncommunicator will be predominantly neutral but still one that is reasonably workable and potentially productive.

*How to Handle the Noncommunicator*

As a homebuyer, your decision to purchase a particular property will be based on two types of information:

1.  What is obvious, such as asking price, location, features, size, and so on.

2.  What is not so obvious, such as structural condition, the owners reason for selling, the age of the home, local planning, and so on.

Much of this second type of information—that which is not readily apparent—can be provided by the seller (but won't necessarily be accepted by you without checking or verification).

However, in this case, between you and the seller stands the Noncommunicator. That can be a problem. But it's a problem you handle in the same way as with all real estate salespeople, regardless of personality type. You establish firmly that you require specific answers and are not prepared to accept guesses, assumptions or casual estimates. And that you want answers, where appropriate, to come directly from the seller. This won't guarantee you accuracy or completely reliable information, but it is, nonetheless, an important requirement to make, particularly with the Noncommunicator. If you set down these ground rules diplomatically, and early in the relationship, you are more likely to get a positive response. Alternatively, ask the seller yourself, if possible, for the information you require.

Sometimes the Noncommunicator is basically a worthy person who, for one reason or another, may not really like the work. But whether the agent is just passing through the profession or has other motives for being uncommunicative, a relationship in which the agent feels genuinely appreciated will get you the best service.

The most important caution I can offer you with the Noncommunicator concerns the price negotiation stage. You must be certain that whatever tactic you are using gets communicated accurately to the seller and seller's agent *as close as possible to the way in which you expressed it!* Clearly, the Noncommunicator isn't the best type of agent to do this, which means you will have to repeat and emphasize your specific position. Ask the agent to be sure to convey what you feel in the way in which you have expressed it. This is another reason an informal, appreciative relationship works best.

## The Determined Persuader

This is the agent type many buyers fear, and avoid, often unnecessarily.

Don't confuse Determined Persuaders with the often arrogant, unprofessional, high-pressure salesperson. Although that type is still to be found in small numbers in real estate, Determined Persuaders belong in a very distinct category. They certainly don't merit the tags of being unprofessional or arrogant, though pressure does have a place in their arsenal. When you learn how to recognize and handle them, their tactics become nonthreatening. Contrary to what you might expect, the breakdown between male and female agents of this type seems to be about even.

Although almost all agents and salespeople use *persuasion*— and I'm not attaching any negative connotation to that term— some, particularly Determined Persuaders, make it an obsession. This agent personality type is, I believe, made up of two slightly different subtypes. The first shields a core personality and can be very suave and subtle—at first. Only later does the need to persuade surface. The second type is courteous and professional, but doesn't beat around the bush. The persuasion is up front. This second type is more common.

Determined Persuaders are easy to recognize. As you would imagine, they spend a lot of energy and time trying to do just that— persuade. They have some similarities with Gentle Intimidators, but lack that type's chivalrous charm and endearing pleasantness, preferring instead a businesslike demeanor that stresses magnificent opportunities, unbeatable deals, and the agent's role in creating and providing them. The implication is that no other agent would be able to get you such a steal. However, if you dilly-dally, the agent will have to let it go to another agent or buyer—you understand. Routinely, Determined Persuaders don't seriously consider most buyer objections but overpower them with more passionate and more "sensible" arguments. However, when forced to acknowledge a problem, one that stands in the way of a sale, they are capable of coming up with one innovative solution after another.

For many years, I trained salespeople to overcome objections, make sales, and solve problems for buyers. Such training is ethical and a necessary part of providing good customer service. But, to overcome objections, it is necessary to listen well to what the buyer is saying. This is where Determined Persuaders commonly fall down. Even when their ears seem open, their brains are often closed—a type of unemotional listening.

Their arguments are typically convincing and difficult to refute, due to their wide knowledge of their profession and the information they seem to be able to access at will. Their stubborn, absolute faith in their own viewpoint contributes significantly to their high-flying success. In their thinking, the perfect match between product and buyer doesn't exist. They conclude, therefore, that the buyer's thinking must be changed to suit what is being sold. In real estate, that's not essentially an incorrect or illogical notion. On the contrary, a good agent can point out important advantages and potential a homebuyer doesn't see. The problem, though, is that Determined Persuaders frequently carry this philosophy to the extreme, trying to push a home that plainly isn't suited to the buyer's needs.

Be prepared, too, for sequences of staged questions. This is where you find yourself answering yes six or seven times in succession, as if you are being programmed—which, of course, you are. Determined Persuaders want you to agree on minor points until a sea of affirmatives carry you along to where saying no to a major point seems illogical.

I referred earlier to the Determined Persuader who isn't easily recognized as such at the outset. This agent exudes a benign, personal style. But not for long—only until he or she introduces the "this-is-definitely-the-perfect-property-for-you" spiel. That's when the persuasive tactics kick in and leave you in no doubt as to what personality type you are dealing with. Many agents of this subtype act almost like a family friend, referring to you with such endearments as *my friend* or *sir,* delivered with an inflection intended to warm your ego. The agent is captivating and difficult for you to reject, because the agent is on *your* side, fighting for *you.* The problem is knowing when you should believe the agent, as almost everything is said with conviction. One giveaway, however, is when there is an *urgency* story for each home that seems to interest you.

In spite of their tricks and persuasive personality, Determined Persuaders are willing to put lots of effort into showing you many homes. For as long as their instincts say a sale is likely, they'll go out of their way. They have a large group of contacts, just as much from their social style of personality as from their business reputation, and they can pull lots of strings when necessary, especially to impress you. They work tirelessly in extracting seller compromises in order to pull a deal together, especially when they're convinced that if they fail they'll lose you—and the sale.

### How to Handle the Determined Persuader

There are four keys to handling the Determined Persuader effectively: firmness, exclusivity, acknowledgment, and the promise of referral business. Let's look at these one at a time.

From the beginning, you can create the most beneficial atmosphere by establishing your seriousness as a buyer and your readiness to make a decision—but not until the situation is to your liking. This firmness dictates that you will have to maintain some distance, at least initially, from the agent.

The early ritual Determined Persuaders go through is part of how they assess your seriousness about buying. They have zero patience with what they consider lookers and talkers, but positively welcome buyers with a "let's get down, to business" demeanor. If you are going to take up the agent's time, he or she will want to be certain you're ready to buy when the right home is found. Your business-like demeanor will bring out the best in such an agent and will prevent your being taken for a naive and impressionable pushover.

Although you might want to relax your business-like attitude as the relationship develops, it's a good idea to maintain a level of seriousness, as this will add power to your position when it comes time to negotiate price.

Exclusivity is relevant, because the Determined Persuader is so strongly money-focused. When not selling, the agent is generating leads and searching for other opportunities. This agent will go to extremes, and sometimes beyond, to avoid losing a definite buyer (a source of income) to another agent. You can capitalize on this by saying at your first meeting that you will, at least for a while, rely exclusively on the agent to help you find the right home at the right price. Here's where you can send another clear message by emphasizing the *right* home at the *right* price.

Acknowledgment, the third key, comes in when you have seen a number of homes. It's then time to compliment briefly, but openly, the agent's efforts and interest in your needs. Few homebuyers offer such compliments to the Determined Persuader, but when done in the manner I suggest, they result in the cementing of that *special buyer* status.

The fourth key is the promise of referral business. This is a major goal of all real estate agents and salespeople. However, Determined Persuaders strive constantly for personal contacts who are prepared to send buyers and sellers their way. Capitalize on this by making a matter-of-fact comment that if everything goes well you will happily refer your friends and associates to the agent.

When the agent finds a home that interests you, there's one tactic you will almost certainly hear from the Determined Persuader. Let's call it the "make an offer now because someone else is seriously interested" tactic, an extreme form of the *other buyer* tactic. Your defense is clear and unambiguous; you simply won't make a hasty decision on *any* property.

Then, in as casual a manner as you can, ask the agent to call you in a day or two and let you know if the home in question sold to the "other" buyer. That's your "I can take it or leave it" tactic. Stand back and watch it work—but *only*, as I've pointed out a number of times, if you are willing to risk losing the home should the other buyer prove to be real. This is rarely more than a very small risk. If you decline to make an offer, and the other buyer was fictitious, the agent will call very soon with an explanation of why the home is still available. In that case, when you are convinced you were baited, proceed as if you are none the wiser. But, of course, you are. And you now have another major advantage that will benefit you as you negotiate strongly.

## Agent Personality Types—Summary

Although a knowledge of the main real estate agent and salesperson personality types will be of interest to readers, (as far as I know, such profiles have never been done before) the average homebuyer does not need to carry around an intimate familiarity with each type.

Also, it would be naive to expect that every agent will fit neatly into a single category. People and personalities are too complex for that—a point worth celebrating. What I've done here is give you personality types and characteristics I have found most common in my work in selling, training, management, and research. In each category I've highlighted dominant traits to help you stay at least one step ahead in protecting your money. But also, I've shown you how to deploy the agent's skills for *your* benefit.

If you've already been out shopping for a home, you'll probably recall one or more of the personality types I've described. If you are new to homebuying you will, no doubt, find Gentle Intimidators, Dispassionate Experts, Noncommunicators, Caring Conversationalists, and Determined Persuaders.

However, far more important than concentrating on personalities is to gain an understanding of the fundamental know-how presented in this book. Then in the face of pressure, nervousness, and excitement, you can stay focused on your goal of buying the home you want at the best price possible.

As more and more homebuyers are discovering, that is a very attainable goal. *Not One Dollar More!* brings this goal well within your reach.

# PART SEVEN

# Finding the Money

# CHAPTER FOURTEEN

# SHOPPING FOR THE BEST MORTGAGE

*Almost any man knows how to earn money
but not one in a million knows how to spend it.*
—HENRY DAVID THOREAU

To the average homebuyer, shopping for the best mortgage (home loan, home financing) appears complex and intimidating. Worse, some professionals in the industry seem to prefer to keep it so. Their logic, apparently, is that if you don't understand what they do you are less likely to be discriminating about the loans and services they offer. And that's exactly how it seems to be working. The majority of home loan seekers are not well informed about mortgages or how to shop for a loan. They take a back seat, confused by the jargon and posturing of the industry. In that atmosphere they become compliant and unquestioning, and they surrender important and very costly decisions to loan representatives, mortgage brokers, and real estate agents. In the anxiety and excitement of buying a home this state of mind might be understandable, but it's naive. And it's dangerous to your financial well-being.

Just as with shopping for the right home at the lowest possible price, finding the right mortgage requires your active participation and some basic know-how. Your reward for being diligent can mean tens of thousands of dollars to you, and priceless peace of mind for many years into the future. Often, finding the right loan can save you more than you are likely to negotiate off the asking price of an average home. And conversely, the wrong loan can take an equally big chunk of money out of your pocket—and can go on doing that every month for as long as you own the loan.

But it doesn't have to be that way. Mortgage shopping is not as complicated as you might have imagined or been led to believe. In this chapter I'll try hard to set you on the right path. I'll explain at least the basics of smart mortgage shopping, know-how you simply cannot afford to do without. You won't learn everything there is to know about mortgages, but you'll get enough financial self-defense to begin protecting your money and getting good, honest service from lenders. Then I'll tell you about sources you can turn to for more help.

The first key point to keep in mind is this: Mortgage lenders need you and your business! The industry is extremely competitive; lenders are eager for more and more buyers. Gone are the days when the typical homebuyer almost pleaded for a loan from the local banker, then went home and waited anxiously, then rejoiced when approved as a worthy borrower. Today, nearly all homebuyers can expect to get a loan. Even borrowers who have had financial problems, erratic employment and income histories, and delinquent debts can usually be matched with loans and programs designed especially for them.

Before we explore your options as a borrower, I want to re-emphasize two of the best moves I believe a homebuyer can make. The first is, call on the resources and services of an exclusive buyer broker, a source of invaluable information as you go about conducting your mortgage inquiries (and often one of the best sources of information on loans and lenders).

— Second, engage the services of a real estate attorney, one who knows how to protect your interests. A good buyer broker probably won't be hard to find; just check the resource information and toll-free numbers later in this book. However, finding a suitable attorney might require more research. Here, again, ask a buyer broker for at least a couple of referrals. And always stay aware that it is not just any attorney you need, but one who has solid experience in real estate transactions. Some will tell you they do when, in fact, they only dabble in it.

So, have a preliminary talk with two or three attorneys, or however many it takes until you feel satisfied. Get a clear account of what the charges will be (the brief initial consultation should not cost you anything). And negotiate for a discount! Attorneys want your dollars just as much as anyone else and are usually willing to be flexible, especially if you can take care of some of the simpler information-gathering tasks.

But the time to hire an attorney is *before* you sign any documents or make any binding commitments—not after! You'll want a legal opinion on all your loan agreement forms and on your home purchase contract, and specific assistance with the settlement procedures.

### First, Know What is at Stake!

As a smart mortgage shopper your first and most critical goal is to understand clearly what is at stake. That, almost certainly is an awful lot more dollars than you realize. So much, that it might shock you to discover (below) how costly a wrong loan decision can be. When you know this you will understand why you need to keep your wits about you.

Note that over the past twenty-five years 10 percent is the average mortgage rate, though as I write, with the year 2000 looming, 30-year fixed-rate mortgages are available at around 7.5 to 8 percent. When it is time for you to commence your own search, you'll need to find out early what the then-current best mortgage deals are (rates and fees). That means research—perhaps nothing more initially than reading lenders' newspaper ads and a half-dozen phone conversations with different lenders, and certainly talking about mortgages with your local exclusive buyer broker. Then, when you begin to shop actively for a loan, you'll be able to recognize a good deal from a come-on.

Now, let's illustrate what exactly is at stake. What follows are a few straightforward examples of home loans. Pay attention to the huge amount of interest paid in each case. Also, keep in mind that interest rates go up and down. As you read this, rates may be lower or higher, but the principles explained here always hold true.

> *Example 1.* Suppose you take out a $100,000 mortgage at 10 percent for 30 years. If you stay in the house for the full term (30 years) you will pay back, in total, $315,909. That figure includes your $100,000 loan (the *principal*)—PLUS interest of $215,909!

> *Example 2.* Let's look at the same loan of $100,000 over 30 years, but this time at just 8% interest. Over the full term of the loan your payback amount will be, in total, $264,149. That includes your $100,000 loan—PLUS interest of $164,149!

> *Example 3.* Now let's see what shaving just one half point off that 8 percent rate will do. Loan: $100,000 over 30 years at 7.5 percent means you'll pay back, in total, $251,712: the $100,000

you borrowed—PLUS interest of $151,712! So, cutting just one half point off the rate saved you $12,437 over the life of the loan ($164,149 minus $151,712).

Notice that even the lowest priced loan here (7.5%) required you to pay back more than two and a half times the amount you borrowed (borrowed $100,000, paid back $251,712)! It doesn't seem like a mere 7.5 percent interest rate would whack you that hard, does it?

And the 10 percent loan hits you a lot harder, requiring you to pay back more than three times the loan amount (borrowed $100,000, paid back $315,909). Total payback figures are far too seldom spelled out for borrowers, but when they are, they usually come as a shock.

Now let's make all this more understandable. Let's put it into concrete form. How do these and other loan features affect your monthly paycheck? Here's what you would pay each month in principal and interest (P+I) payments for each of the three loans.

*Example 1.* $100,000 loan at 10% for 30 years   $877.58 per month

*Example 2.* $100,000 loan at 8% for 30 years    $733.77 per month

*Example 3.* $100,000 loan at 7.5% for 30 years  $699.22 per month

Notice that the half-point difference—between the 8 percent loan and the 7.5 percent loan—turns into $34.55 saved every month. That equals $414.60 in *your* pocket every year—after taxes!

Now let's widen the comparison. What if an unwary homebuyer pays 8.5 percent when the same loan might have been available from another lender at 7 percent? This is not uncommon; it happens much too often! Here's the outcome:

*Loan A:* $100,000 at 8.5% for 30 years. Payback amount over full term:                                                   $276,800
You pay back the $100,000 loan (the 'principal'), plus interest of:                                                     $176,800

*Loan B:* $100,000 at 7% for 30 years. Payback amount over full term:                                                   $239,502
You pay back the $100,000 loan, plus interest of:      $139,502

With Loan B you will save ($276,800 minus $239,502):   $ 37,298

But that's an overall figure, and it's based on the loan running the full term (30 years). More practically, what's the difference between what you would pay on these two loans each month (regardless of how long you hold the loan)? Here's the answer:

*Loan A:* $100,000 loan at 8.5% for 30 years:    $768.92 per month.

*Loan B:* $100,000 loan at 7% for 30 years:    $665.31 per month.

Loan B saves you $103.61 every month. That's $1,243.32 per year. If you stay in the house 10 years, you save $12,433.20 And, as we just saw, over 30 years you save $37,298!

I hope you now have solid evidence of how imperative it is to shop wisely and find the best loan for your particular circumstances. Simply, it's your money that's at stake, lots of it, often tens of thousands of dollars that can be saved or lost, plus priceless time and your peace of mind.

However, interest rates are not your only consideration. When comparing some loans it may not even be the most important feature. There are also points, fees, special conditions and loan terms, and lock-ins to consider. We'll look at all these as we go on.

Before that, however, you'll need at least a basic understanding of the types of loans that are available, and how to choose one that is right or best for you. Later we'll explore also the loan application process, what it requires of you, and how and where you can get help. And I'll suggest ways to keep your out-of-pocket expenses to a minimum.

And finally, like it or not, mortgages require us to deal with math. I'll show you how the figures work, but I'll keep it as basic and as simple as possible. So, even if you're a math hater, stick with it. All the figures are worked out for you and explained, and it really isn't as confusing as it might at first seem.

### Fixed-Rate Mortgages (FRMs)

Most homebuyers are somewhat familiar with what has come to be seen as the conventional mortgage, the *30-year fixed-rate mortgage* (commonly abbreviated to 30-year FRM). The logic is simple: The amount borrowed is paid back with same-size monthly payments over 30 years (the *term* of the loan) at a fixed rate of interest. However, one lender's FRM might carry a rate of 8 percent, while another lender is offering a similar loan on the same day at 7.5 percent or 8.5 percent. That's just one reason why you must shop around to get the best deal.

Another FRM is the 15-year loan, which, obviously, is designed to be paid off in half the time of a 30-year loan. But, although less common, FRMs can also be for 10 years or 20 years. There are even 40-year FRMs, which I don't recommend because very little is saved on the monthly payment, and the total amount you pay back is extremely high. So, short or long, all FRMs are based on the borrower making equal monthly payments over the life of the loan.

### Risk and Interest Rate Variation

Here's another variation in FRMs. Mortgage lenders deal in risk, and price their loans accordingly. What worries them most is that they might not get their money back. What if you default, or fall seriously behind in your repayments? That spells trouble for the lender. These risks, they believe, are higher on longer loans. To compensate, they charge a slightly higher interest rate on a 30-year loan than on a 15-year loan. As I write, the following rates are being offered:

*Loan A.* 30-year FRMs up to a loan limit of $240,000 available at 7.5 to 8%

*Loan B.* 15-year FRMs up to a loan limit of $240,000 available at 7 to 7.5%

At such historically low interest rates, FRMs make very good choices and are, rightly, by far the most popular home loans (remember the historical home loan interest averages 10%).

But, FRMs are not your only option, nor are they the right choice for all borrowers. Since you may be in the latter category, or may be reading this at a time when those very low FRM rates have passed, I will shortly explain some interesting alternatives that are worth your consideration. But first, let's examine some of the fundamental facts of loans in general.

### How Does the Length of the Loan Affect Your Repayments?

As you might imagine, the longer the term of the loan the smaller the monthly repayments for any particular amount borrowed (despite the longer loan's interest rate usually being slightly higher). And, although your income level will determine how big a loan you can borrow, it is the term of the loan that will set the size of your monthly repayment. Longer-term loans mean lower payments but, of course, a greater number of payments. This is an important consideration to keep in mind. A 30-year mortgage's monthly payment might be well within your ability to repay (according to the lender's qualifying criteria), whereas a 15-year loan's repayment might be too high. This is not to imply, however, that the 30-year mortgage is inherently better; it's not. Any loan you take must be matched to your individual circumstances and your feelings about debt.

To illustrate this point, let's compare two FRMs side-by-side, with only the term being different. Note: I am using $100,000 as the loan amount, but the effect of changing the term holds true for any amount you might borrow. Also note that *P+I* stands for principal plus interest—more on this later:

*Loan A.*    $100,000 borrowed at 8% over 30 years. Monthly P+I repayment: $733.77

*Loan B.*    $100,000 borrowed at 8% over 15 years. Monthly P+I repayment: $955.66.

In reality, as we saw earlier, that 15-year loan would typically carry a slightly lower interest rate than the 30-year loan. So, here is the real thing, two actual loans advertised this weekend in my local newspaper:

*Loan A.*    Amount: $100,000. Term: 30 years. Rate: 7.5%. P+I repayment: $699.22

*Loan B.*    Amount: $100,000. Term: 15 years. Rate: 7%. P+I repayment: $898.83.

Note that the 15-year loan at these rates will cost about $200 more per month, but might still be the better loan for your circumstances. And understand, too, that although longer-term loans carry lower monthly repayments, that does not mean you will pay back less in the end—quite the opposite, in fact. The total interest you'll pay on a 30-year loan is significantly greater than on a 15-year loan. We'll look at examples in more detail shortly.

### Adjustable Rate Mortgages (ARMs)

First, how do you recognize an ARM? Here is how different types of ARM loans are written (for now, don't worry about deciphering the meanings): 1/30 ARM, 5/1 ARM, 3/3 ARM.

Adjustable rate mortgages are different from FRMs in a number of ways. First, as the name implies, the interest rate applicable to the loan can move up or down, depending on the economic climate. And your repayment can change according to a set period or schedule. How frequently such a change can be made will depend on the type of ARM you have.

For example, with a one-year ARM (1/30 ARM), your rate and payment can be changed (adjusted) annually by the lender. The rationale for this change is that each ARM's interest rate is pegged to one of the lending indexes used in the industry, and as the index goes so goes your loan repayments (an index is simply a fluctuating scale indicating the cost of money to bankers and other lenders). Also, ARMs can be of any length, but the 30-year loan (1/30 ARM) is common.

The way an ARM is written and described (1/30, for example) tells you two things: The 30 is the length of the loan in years. And the 1 tells you how frequently, in years, your payments can change. So, a 1/30 ARM is a 30-year loan with payments that can be adjusted by the lender once every 12 months.

The popularity of these 1/30 ARMs has decreased in recent years. More common today are 3/1, 5/1, and 7/1 ARMs. We'll look at these in more detail shortly. For now though, understand that with a 3/1 ARM, the 3 means that the initial interest rate remains unchanged for the first three years of the loan. And the 1 means that the rate thereafter can adjust once per year. ARMs of 5/1 and 7/1 operate by the same principle.

Let's take a closer look at how these loans work.

*Important Features of ARMs*

Every ARM has the following features:

1. Initial interest rate

2. Interval (period) for changes in interest rate

3. A lending index to which the loan is pegged

4. A margin added to the index by the lender (the lender's profit)

5. Periodic cap, a limit on how much your loan can be adjusted in each period

6. Life cap, a limit over which your loan's interest rate can not be raised in the course of its life

Time to de-jargonize. Here's what all that means.

*1. Initial Interest Rate*    This is the interest rate the ARM loan starts out at. It is always lower than comparable FRM loans. For example, a 30-year FRM might carry a fixed interest rate of 8 percent, while a 30-

year ARM might start out at 6.5 percent (of course, it will not stay at 6.5%). In this case, that 6.5 percent is the rate on which your loan repayments are based during the first period of the loan. When the adjustment date comes along (commonly once each year, on the anniversary of the loan being issued), the lender may, and typically does, change the rate. So, on the adjustment date, your initial 6.5 percent ARM might become a 7.5 percent loan, or even a 6 percent loan.

Naturally, if interest rates are rising, your loan will be adjusted to a higher rate, and you'll pay more each month. The opposite is true if rates are lower in the market—your payment will reduce. No one can foresee what interest rates are going to do in a year's time. However, general trends are sometimes predictable. So, if you are considering an ARM, talk with financially savvy people whose views you trust. If you conclude that interest rates are likely to move in one direction or the other, this will become one of your considerations in choosing a loan.

Two advantages of ARMs are that the initial lower interest rate makes it an easier loan to qualify for, and the lower payments at the beginning are easier on your household budget. In fact, ARMs frequently work out cheaper overall if you plan to remain in the house for a shorter time—three to seven years, for example. But that depends, also, on the difference between the ARM and FRM interest rates when you take out the loan, and how the ARM rate changes along the way. Does that mean ARMs are a gamble? Yes!—but only when you stay beyond the initial fixed-rate period. Over shorter terms the gamble often pays off. Plus, there are safeguards on all ARMs, which we'll examine as we proceed.

Let's now consider a common situation: We'll assume you want and can qualify for a $100,000 loan at the higher FRM interest rate (higher than an ARM's initial rate). Your loan options might look like this:

*Option 1:*   $100,000 FRM 8%, 30 years. Monthly payment (won't change): $733.77

*Option 2:*   $100,000 ARM 6.5%, 30 years. Monthly payment (will change): $632.07

As you can see, this ARM will save you $101.70 per month in the first year. After 12 months you'll be ahead by $1220.40 ($101.70 × 12). That's $1220.40 after taxes, equal to $1,500 to $1,600 gross.

Now let's assume this ARM's interest rate fluctuates moderately over the first four years. Here's how your monthly expense, annual loan cost, and your total out-of-pocket costs will differ between the two loans:

| | |
|---|---|
| *Year 1:* FRM 8%: $733.77 × 12 = $8805.24 | ARM 6.5%: $632.07 × 12 = $7584.84 |
| *Year 2:* FRM 8%: $733.77 × 12 = $8805.24 | ARM 7.5%: $697.84 × 12 = $8374.08 |
| *Year 3:* FRM 8%: $733.77 × 12 = $8805.24 | ARM 8.0%: $731.01 × 12 = $8772.12 |
| *Year 4:* FRM 8%: $733.77 × 12 = <u>$8805.24</u> | ARM 7.5%: $698.50 × 12 = <u>$8382.00</u> |
| Total Paid: $35,220.96 | $33,113.04 |

So, in this hypothetical comparison, after the first four years the ARM will have saved you $2107.92 ($35,206.96 minus $33,113.04). The average annual interest rate you paid on the ARM was 7.375 percent, as against 8 percent on the FRM. Bear in mind, also, that the ARM was easier to qualify for, and that the monthly repayments were lower in three of these first four years.

But now let's make some further assumptions about how the ARM interest rate fluctuates over the next four years (years 5, 6, 7, and 8), and review the situation at the end of the eighth year.

| | |
|---|---|
| *Year 5:* FRM 8%: $733.77 × 12 = $8805.24 | ARM  9.0%: $795.52 × 12 = $ 9546.24 |
| *Year 6:* FRM 8%: $733.77 × 12 = $8805.24 | ARM  9.5%: $828.23 × 12 = $ 9938.76 |
| *Year 7:* FRM 8%: $733.77 × 12 = $8805.24 | ARM 10.5%: $893.62 × 12 = $10723.44 |
| *Year 8:* FRM 8%: $733.77 × 12 = <u>$8805.24</u> | ARM 10.5%: $893.62 × 12 = <u>$10723.44</u> |
| Total Paid: $35,220.96 | $40,931.88 |

As you can see, after year 8 the ARM's earlier advantage has been wiped out, due entirely to interest rates rising as they did. It's quite possible, of course, that rates might have fallen, or remained around their initial low level (unlikely). But it's also possible they might have risen even more steeply. However, in this example, as it stands at the end of year 8, the FRM has cost you $3,603 less than the ARM. Let's see the figures side by side:

| | |
|---|---|
| Cost of ARM, up to end of year 8: | $74,044.92 ($33,113.04 + $40,931.88) |
| Cost of FRM, up to end of year 8: | <u>$70,441.92</u> ($733.77 × 12 months × 8 years) |
| Difference: | $ 3,603.00 |

Look closely at the math in this example and you'll see that it is only in the seventh year that the ARM becomes more expensive overall. By adding the first six years of payments for both loans you'll see they work out virtually the same. And that the average interest rate on the ARM over those first six years is exactly the same as the FRM rate—8 percent. This shows why ARMs are often a better choice for homebuyers who plan on holding the loan for three to seven years.

But this argument also assumes you'll be able to get a 2 to 3 percent lower initial interest rate on the ARM. That has typically been the case, but as I write the differential is just 1 to 1.8 percent. The other assumption here is that interest rates do not suddenly shoot up, sending your ARM rate sky high. The extent to which an ARM's interest rate can increase is limited by *caps,* which we'll get to shortly.

When home loan interest rates are low, the difference between initial ARM rates and FRM rates shrinks, making fixed-rate mortgages more popular. However, as interest rates rise above 8 percent, the spread between ARM and FRM rates increases again (the difference is often 3%), and ARMs become more attractive.

For all these reasons, if you tend to be overanxious about risk, an ARM might cause you more worry than it is worth. Your psychic happiness must figure strongly in your decision. For many borrowers, predictability and peace of mind cannot be sacrificed, even when the risk is low or moderate.

*Note:* With one-year ARMs (1/30, 1/15, for example), keep in mind that lenders do not use the ARM's initial interest rate when qualifying the borrower (that is, determining the borrower's ability to make the repayments on the loan). Instead, they use a higher rate, for extra security for the lender. Here's an illustration: On a 6.5 percent ARM, the lender will expect the borrower to qualify as if the loan was at 8.5 percent (6.5% plus 2%). In other words, in the qualifying calculation, the lender pretends the borrower's initial interest rate and monthly payment will be higher than is actually true. The rationale is that the borrower might, in year 1, be able to handle the initial low monthly payment (at 6.5% in this example), but might not be able to pay a higher monthly payment in year 2, when the ARM's interest rate could increase by 2 percent (to 8.5%). This qualifying method is typically not applied to multiyear ARMs: 3/1, 5/1, or 7/1 ARMs, for example. More on this shortly.

For most borrowers planning to hold a home loan for longer than six or seven years, a low-interest-rate FRM will usually be a better choice. The problem, of course, is that most new homebuyers cannot predict how long they will stay in a particular home. National surveys report that, on average, homeowners terminate their loans within the first 7 to 10 years (they pack up and move on to another home). So, be sure to get a lender or mortgage broker to show you comparison payment projections for different types of loans over varying periods of years.

One group of borrower's to whom ARMs are often particularly appealing are those with very large loans. On loans of $300,000 and up, a borrower can often save more money by frequent refinancing when their current ARM's initial lower rate is due to end. Refinancing is not cheap, but the money saved with this strategy can cover such costs, with a tidy sum left over. But, as is always the case when loan shopping, you must first run the numbers side by side.

*2. Adjustment Period (Interval)*    With a 1/30, as we've seen, the adjustment date comes along once each year, typically on the anniversary of the loan's issue date. That's when the applied interest rate (and your repayment) can change. Some weeks ahead of the adjustment (if the rate is going to change) you can expect to receive a new payment coupon book from your lender.

One-year ARMs can be for 10 years (1/10) or 15 years (1/15), or just about any length of time up to 1/30. What's common to each of these loans is the single annual adjustment. Later we'll look at variations on this type of loan.

*3. The Index*    This is the underlying scale, or financial measure of interest rates, that a lender will use to determine the rate to charge on a particular ARM. For example, a one-year ARM will usually be pegged to the One-Year Treasury Securities Index. Whatever happens with that index will be transferred to your loan's interest rate. There are at least a half-dozen indexes used to set interest rates on ARMs of various lengths. Only some ARMs have a one-year adjustment period. Others adjust to different time schedules.

*4. The Margin*    The margin is a percentage the lender adds to the index to create the rate you pay. If the index to which your loan is pegged has a rate of 6 percent, the lender might, for example, add a margin of 2.75 percent, making the rate on your ARM 8.75 percent. See it as the lender's *profit*. Margins are becoming more uniform across the industry. However, if you can find a lender that imposes a lower margin, you might be able to save money.

*5. Periodic Cap*    Even if interest rates rise three or four points in a short time span (a steep increase), the lender does not have a free hand in what you can be charged when your loan's next adjustment date comes around. The reason is that all ARMs come with *caps*. If your 1/30 ARM's *periodic cap* is 2 percent (quite common), the interest rate you pay can never be increased (or decreased) by more than 2 percent in any one year.

Let's say your initial interest rate was 6.5 percent and your loan has a 2 percent periodic cap. And let's pretend interest rates rise 2.5 percent in the year after you take out your loan. That 2.5 percent increase cannot be added to your ARM rate on your loan's next annual adjustment date. The lender in this instance cannot increase your rate by more than the 2 percent annual cap. This provides you with some consolation, but perhaps not as much as you think. For instance, if your ARM has a 6.5 percent initial rate on a loan of $100,000, your first year's monthly P+I payment will be $632.07. But, when your rate rises to 8.5 percent (6.5% plus the 2% increase) your monthly payment in the second year goes up to $766.12, a jump of $134.05.

Note: Your loan balance at end of first year will have gone down; so your new payments at 8.5 percent interest will be based on this lower *principal outstanding* figure, not on the original $100,000. Also, at that stage, the term remaining on your loan will have reduced to 29 years, which will also be a factor in determining your new payment amount.

6. *Lifetime Cap (Life Cap)*    As we just saw, on a 1/30 ARM with a 2 percent periodic cap the lender is restricted in how much it can increase your interest rate in a single year (for a loan with a one year adjustment period). The *lifetime cap* works the same way, except that it sets the highest point to which your interest can ever be increased above its initial rate. For example: On a 6.5 percent 1/30 ARM with a 2 percent periodic cap and a 6 percent lifetime cap, the maximum interest rate you could *ever* be charged is 12.5 percent. That's your initial rate of 6.5 percent plus the 6 percent lifetime cap. So, even if mortgage rates soared to 15 percent (as has been the case), you won't ever pay more than 12.5 percent on that particular loan. It's not that you would welcome your rate climbing to that point, but it does give you a way of understanding a worst-case scenario.

On longer-term ARMs, (3/1 and 5/1 ARMs, for example—discussed later) many lenders offer a 5 percent lifetime cap. This should be a consideration when you are comparing loans.

## Other Types of ARMs

There are many varieties of ARMs, and new ideas are introduced all the time. However, in the following more common variations, you'll recognize the fundamental characteristics we've already seen.

### Hybrid ARMs

These loans, which we touched on earlier, have become popular for the same reasons we've already explored. First, they typically carry a lower initial rate than FRMs. And second, they do so for more than one year. A 5/1 ARM or a 7/1 ARM means that the loan holds its initial interest rate for five years or seven years (there are other lengths, too, such as 3/1 and 10/1).

Sometimes called *multi-year ARMs*, these loans do not generally carry as low a rate as the 1/30 or 1/15, simply because the lender cannot adjust the rate as frequently as market conditions change.

For the buyer who plans to move within the loan's initial lower-rate period (5 years or 7 years, for example) these newer type loans are worth serious consideration, chiefly because they can work out cheaper than FRMs, and offer stable payments for an extended period (not just for one year, like other ARMs).

With a 7/1 ARM, after seven years the loan turns into a one-year ARM for the rest of its life, and can then adjust annually, just like a 1/30 or 1/15 ARM. All hybrid ARMs work this same way.

Caution: Ask your lender (then confirm with your attorney) if there is an early payoff penalty clause with any loan of this type—and what it means.

### Convertible ARMs

As the name implies, this loan allows the borrower the option of converting to a FRM at some future point. Commonly the fee for converting can range from $250 to $600, but that certainly beats the thousands of dollars a refinancing would cost. A Convertible ARM's initial rate is always lower than the conventional FRM. And the restricted period in which the switch over to a FRM can be made is always specified in the loan's terms and conditions. Typically, you cannot make the switch within the first year, nor after the fifth year, though this can vary.

Converting would make sense only if, during the allowed period, you can take advantage of a lower FRM rate, which would reduce your monthly payment. Naturally, if the FRM rate remained higher you would stay with your ARM's lower interest rate. In practice, convertible ARMs do not typically convert to the current FRM rate, but to a rate about 0.25 percent higher.

### Comparing ARM Features

What are the most important features to evaluate when shopping for an ARM? Many mortgage experts advise that you watch the indexes and choose your loan according to how interest rates are headed (remember, the interest on your loan is pegged to one particular index). There are just two main types of index you need know about, a leading index (leads the interest rate trend) and a lagging index (stays behind the trend).

The rationale is simple: If interest rates are falling, the leading index will take you more quickly in that direction (reduced payments). If rates are rising, the lagging index won't take you there so quickly (higher payments). One popular leading index is the One-Year Treasury Bill Index, and a popular lagging index is 11th District Cost of Funds Index.

How do you find out what direction the indexes are moving? Ask lenders or mortgage brokers to tell you. And ask which indexes their loans are pegged to. Alternatively, log on to one of the following websites: www.freddiemac.com, or www.hsh.com, www.loan-shark.com, or www.microsurf.com.

Another important feature to inquire about is the lender's margin. As we saw earlier, this is the profit added by the lender to determine the rate you'll pay. When you know the index rate, you add on the margin rate to arrive at the loan's market rate (the lender has already done this). Your initial ARM rate will typically be a few percentage points below the market rate, a move designed to win your business (often called a *teaser rate*). Low initial ARM rates, attractive at the beginning, can rise steeply in the course of a few years.

For example: Index rate 5.5 percent; Margin rate 2.75 percent; market rate 8.25 percent (add index and margin). However, with this ARM you might start off paying only 6.25 percent (2% lower than market rate), which will rise at its adjustment, after one year, perhaps by 2 percent. Usually, however, it is still best to go with the lowest-margin loan, but you must consider this feature in combination with the index, because an attractively low margin coupled with a high index might not be such a good deal, whereas a higher margin and a lower index might overall be a less expensive loan. You need your lender or broker to work with you in comparing these features.

The third feature you'll need to compare and understand is the initial interest rate on the ARMs available to you, and what can happen to their rates in the short term and long term. I mentioned earlier that typically there has been a 2 to 3 percent difference between initial ARM rates and conventional FRM rates. So, here the important questions to ask include: How often can the loan be adjusted? By how much can it be adjusted periodically? What is the lifetime cap on the loan?

### Points, Fees, and Closing Costs

When you go for either type of home loan you are presented with a litany of fees. Some are hard to understand but are small enough not to have to worry too hard about. However, one fee that can be significant, and that you'll see again and again as you compare mortgages, is *points*.

In truth there are two different fees referred to as points, and you need to be able to distinguish them. However, either type of point is always 1 percent of the loan amount. On a loan of $100,000, one point is equal to $1,000; on a $90,000 loan, it's $900.

First, many lender's charge an *origination fee* in points, commonly 1 point. This is simply a fee that goes to the lender for processing the loan, and it is usually paid at closing (settlement). It might be negotiable. Try.

The second kind, better known, is called *discount points*. But this is a misnomer; it isn't a real discount at all. The term was created by lenders, who see charging this fee as a way to discount the interest rate—keep it lower than it might otherwise be. You may see this figure quoted along with the loan rate. When a lender advertises an FRM loan at "8%/30 1+2" you are being offered a fixed rate mortgage with an 8 percent interest rate over 30 years, plus one point origination fee and two discount points. So, if you borrow $100,000 with this loan, you'll pay $1,000 to the lender as the origination fee, plus $2,000 to the lender in discount points—a points total of $3,000. Some lenders put these two points fees together. In this case it would be presented simply as "3 Pts".

The number of points charged varies from lender to lender and from loan to loan. It is an important criterion to keep in mind when shopping around. And always it is wise to question lenders until you feel certain you understand all the fees you'll have to pay.

Even before you make a formal application, ask lenders for a Good Faith Estimate of Closing Costs (all lenders use this form). At this early stage such a request might seem premature to some lenders, but many will provide preliminary estimates for most of the costs involved. The form in question details all the various fees you will be responsible for. Later, when you make the loan application, the lender has three days to send you this and other required forms, including Truth-in-Lending information, and the HUD booklet *Buying Your Home*. But it makes better sense, I believe, to get this information early, long before the lender is required to give it to you.

Again, points and lender fees are not carved in stone. When dealing with mortgage brokers or mortgage bankers, especially, these costs are almost always negotiable to some degree. A broker or lender might well decide to give up part of the profit in order to get your business, particularly when you make it known that you can get as good a loan—or better—elsewhere. Some loan professionals are tough; others are willing to make concessions, even on interest rates, but only for borrowers who bother to demand the best deal.

What's more, you frequently have the option of paying extra points in return for a lower interest rate. For example, with the loan we looked at earlier, you might well be able to get the lender to reduce the 8 percent rate to 7.75 percent if you offer to pay one more point (an extra $1,000). This is called *buying down* the rate. Ask about such options. But also ask the lender to reduce the lender fees, just as an incentive to get your business.

### Closing Costs

These costs are many and varied. That's why, typically, you should expect to spend an additional 5 to 7 percent over the loan amount. Closing costs are generally considered to include the fees paid to the lender *(lender fees)*, such as points and lender's attorney fees, but include also fees that are unrelated to the lender, such as title insurance and homeowner's insurance fees.

When making your application, I advise that you question the necessity of each individual fee, and ask for a waiver on each one as you go down the list. Of course, some cannot be waived, but others can, and they often are, for borrowers who will negotiate. And, when faced with the risk of losing a pre-qualified borrower, hardly any lender would be so dumb as to reject all your requests.

The following list will give you approximations of many of the fees for which you are likely to be responsible: Loan application (sometimes negotiable—$0–400), origination fee (negotiable; usually 1% of loan amount; some lenders don't charge this as a separate fee), appraisal ($250), credit check ($50–$75), lender's attorney ($300–$500; ask for this to be waived completely), title insurance ($650), survey ($600), homeowner's insurance ($350), recording ($75), tax service ($75), state transfer tax ($0–$750). Discount points (negotiable—0–$4,000), homeowner's attorney (negotiable—$400–$1,250). And there are others.

### Loan Lock-ins

Locking in (a *lock-in*) means getting a guarantee from the lender that the interest rate, terms, and costs you've been quoted will be honored for a certain period of time. I advise you to get this guarantee in writing. The reason you would want to lock in is because you don't want surprises later, especially if you suspect interest rates are headed up.

Lenders policies on lock-ins differ, so ask, and get a clear explanation. Most importantly, keep in mind that the rates and terms quoted to you at application (including points) may not be the ones you get when you go to settlement—unless you have a lock-in. Lock-ins, as you would expect, have a life; they expire after 30, 45, or 60 days, typically (though some lenders offer a ridiculously low 10-day lock-in). A 45-day lock-in period should give you and the seller sufficient time to settle. But 60 days is better than 45, and 90 is better than 60. However, if you suspect that interest rates are falling, you may not want to lock in the loan until you are ready to go to settlement (when rates might be lower). Solid research, and informing yourself well about conditions in the market, are your best ways to judge such things.

On your first contact with a lender it is a good idea to ask for a blank copy of the lender's lock-in form. Then, show it to your attorney. Some such forms are worthless; they contain escape clauses that allow the lender to get out of the obligation if certain market changes occur. Your attorney should easily spot these clauses.

On this same point, there is another important reason to seek out and engage a good real estate attorney. Such attorneys can advise you on financial aspects of a loan (conditions, points, closing costs, etc), not just on the loan contract's terms of purchase. But, borrowers rarely use or question their attorney in this way—a wasted opportunity that carries no extra cost!

Unfortunately, lock-ins aren't always free. Many lenders will charge you a fee to lock-in. This can be a flat fee or a percentage of the loan amount. Whether or not you have to pay for it, ask if the lender will honor a drop in interest rates. That means that if rates go down, the lender will allow your locked-in rate to *float down*, too. Some will do this, some won't. Most won't, unless you request it.

## Applying and Qualifying for a Mortgage

In my view there is little sense in shopping for a home until you are pre-qualified by a lender, or until you prequalify yourself. With most lenders pre-qualifying costs you nothing. This is not a loan application; it is simply the process in which a lender (any lender or mortgage broker will do for this step) considers your financial situation and other details then tells you how large a mortgage you can afford. It typically takes less than half an hour and no documentation is required.

However, you must be sure to get an accurate pre-qualification; therefore, do not inflate your income or understate your debts and expenses as this will skew the loan figure you'll be given. Such an error could cause you later to be turned down for the loan amount you need, perhaps when you're already set on buying a particular home. When you have an accurate estimate of the size of the loan you can get, this figure will determine the total amount you can pay for a home.

If for some reason you do not make an application for loan pre-approval before finding a home, you are likely to have to endure some anxious days or weeks—the time it takes the lender to process your application. If you find yourself in such a situation, you can speed up the process by talking with the lender ahead of time, finding out what is required, then on the day you apply, bringing with you as many of the documents the lender will need.

In the application process all mortgage lenders seek to learn certain specific information about prospective borrowers. This enables the lender to assess the risk you present.

*What Lenders Want to Know*

The three chief questions lenders want answered are as follows:

1.  Is your income stable, and sufficient to pay back the loan you are seeking?

2.  Is your credit history that of a person who pays bills on time?

3.  Is the home you are hoping to buy adequate collateral for the loan?

If your income has been fairly stable over the past few years, despite several changes of jobs, you are likely to get approval. Also, a consistent saving record can make up for some minor lapses in employment. Job switching is more common today and is less an indicator of credit risk than it was once considered to be.

If you think your credit history will show late payments and other problems, the best thing you can do is start cleaning up your credit file well in advance of loan hunting—months or even a year ahead. If creditors have made errors on your accounts—quite likely, according to many borrowers—or if problems or disputes have been resolved satisfactorily to both sides, ask the creditor to have the entry removed from your credit file. Better still, get a letter from the creditor confirming the dispute's resolution, or noting the error. Then contact the credit reporting agency and ask to have the file amended.

Of course, you won't know what's in your credit file unless you get a copy. There are three main credit reporting agencies. Each will provide you with a copy of the credit file they have on you.

Experian (formerly TRW) 1-888-EXPERIAN ($8 per copy)

Equifax 1-800-685-1111 ($8 per copy)

Trans Union Corp. 1-800-916-8800 ($8 per copy)

Once you have that, your next step is to go over the report and make sure there are no errors. If there are, you must begin immediately to have them remedied. Call the reporting agency and ask for help in doing this. You might also call the National Foundation for Consumer Credit 1-800 388 2227 for free advice on clearing up credit problems, or log on to www.dca.org.

Keep in mind that the short credit report you obtain from any of the reporting agencies is not the report your lender will use. Instead, the lender will obtain what is called a *merged report,* a more comprehensive document combining individual agency reports. Whether or not you have had credit problems, you might begin by obtaining a copy of your merged credit report ($25–$35). Scrutinize it! It may surprise you—even by what it *doesn't* show—but that's a lot better than being shocked later, when you've invested time and energy and emotion in the home buying process. To obtain a merged report, call First American Credco ($30.95, including shipping and handling) at 1-800-443-9342, or log on to this company's website at www.confidentialcredit.com, where you'll discover interesting facts and services, and lots of helpful credit advice. Another source is QSpace at 1-888-893-1002; website www.qspace.com. Or try www.quickenmortgage.com (see Resources section, later).

The last of the three questions is whether the home you want to buy provides adequate value to protect the lender's investment. But that's outside your control. The lender will organize an appraisal of the home (for which you will pay). If you managed to negotiate a good purchase price, and presuming the home was not grossly overvalued by the real estate agent (unlikely), this will present no problem.

### Where to Shop for Your Loan

Just as in other areas of homebuying, I believe the consumer too often is badly served when shopping for the best loan. There is much misleading lender advertising being printed and broadcast in every state. Even worse, there are many people in the mortgage loan industry whose training does not qualify them to advise the borrower—yet they presume to do so. Many are just sufficiently experienced to fill out application forms, and often don't know when the loan they are offering is unsuited to the borrower's needs.

Your best recourse is to find a trustworthy advocate, a professional whose integrity and knowledge you can rely on. But where do you find such an ally? Well, first, let me endorse here what most people discover through life experience: Good ideas often take a while to catch on. Here are two.

*Models of Service Worth Every Borrower's Attention*

One innovative service I can endorse is Loan Search, a company that offers solid and much needed assistance to mortgage shoppers. This service, located in Upper Montclair, New Jersey (1-800-591-3279), covers that part of the eastern seaboard, and provides mortgage shoppers with valuable information—free! In a truly equitable marketplace this quality and type of service would be available everywhere, to all home loan seekers.

Loan Search searches its own database of 20-plus lenders and finds the lowest-cost financing based on each borrower's circumstances and objectives, then directs the borrower to the most suitable loans. The search is completed in the course of a 5 to 10-minute phone call and, in most cases, the caller gets an instant "best loan" quote. The service provides full disclosure of lenders' fees, rates, and terms, explains other relevant features of various loans, and reveals lenders' hidden fees. Perhaps the most valuable part of all this is that the company matches the loan to the individual borrower, without sales pressure of any kind, or quotas to fill. The company will even put its quotes in writing (in plain English), along with providing amortization tables that enable you to compare different loans. What's more, Loan Search's service is courteous and efficient. The phones are staffed by real people (no voice mail loops) and the service offers Sunday hours. The company's website is www.loansearch.com.

If you don't have such a service in your locality—and it's a good bet you don't—you still have an alternative. A similar service with a lot to recommend it is offered by HSH Associates, located in Butler, New Jersey, the nation's largest publisher of mortgage information. Its Mortgage Report (interest rates, terms, fees, etc.) is accurate and always current, and is available for $20 (plus $3 shipping and handling). That fee will get you *The Homebuyer's Mortgage Kit.*

In the kit is a copy of *How to Shop for Your Mortgage,* a 56-page booklet I highly recommend, and a Mortgage Report that lists loans offered by 24 to 80 lenders in your area (1-800-UPDATES). Reports cover all areas of the United States and are thorough and easy to read. HSH also offers a number of other worthwhile products, including the Mortgage Report alone via email (minus the 56-page booklet) for $11. Finally, the company has an excellent website filled with valuable information and many useful links. It is well worth numerous visits: www.hsh.com.

### Banks, Mortgage Companies, and S&Ls

When shopping for a mortgage your goal should be to find a loan professional with competence and integrity. That person may be working at your local bank, or may be a mortgage broker or mortgage company representative. However, I do not recommend that you simply walk into your nearest bank and accept the first loan product you are offered. Your responsibility to yourself is answered only by your being discriminating, by assessing and comparing different loans, different lenders, different sources. To do that well, you'll first need a sturdy notebook, as you'll want to record names and contact numbers and clear details of loans, right from the start of your search.

When you use a mortgage search service like Loan Search or HSH Associates (see Resources section) you certainly gain a head start. But if you decide to begin by checking on loans offered by local banks, it is prudent to avoid dealing with the least experienced loan officer or clerk, which may well be the person staffing the loan desk. A talk, first, with the manager could be more rewarding, perhaps even saving you from the wrong loan, or from an unjustified disapproval. Ask to deal with a loan officer with more than a few months experience, someone who has handled loans for a sizable number of borrowers. Then, when you meet this person, weigh up whether your styles and personalities gel. If not, the better decision is to go elsewhere. Also, while it is true that many banks do not routinely charge a loan origination fee, unlike many mortgage brokers and mortgage companies, that gain—and more—can quickly be wiped out by an inexperienced bank employee. (The origination fee, when it is charged, is usually 1 percent of the loan amount.)

*Note:* Inexperienced and uninformed salespeople do not just work in banks; mortgage companies have their share also, so stay constantly cautious.

A good mortgage broker can save you not just the personal time it takes to shop around, but often, too, a chunk of money. That depends, here again, on competence, not to mention integrity. Most brokers will do their best to get you the loan that is right for your circumstances, but it is still smart to assess brokers individually. Their commissions are higher on some loans than on others, which creates a temptation to push these loans even when they might not suit a particular buyer, or might not be the least expensive loan available.

When you interview a broker, ask these questions: How many loans has the broker placed in the past year? What percentage of the broker's loans are approved (look for 90%+)? What types of loans does the broker specialize in? How is the broker paid—commission taken from the fees you pay at closing, or with a separate fee paid by you? Are there recent clients you can talk with for references? Are there recent loans placed for clients whose situations resemble yours? For many borrowers an honest, up-front, hard-working mortgage broker is a blessing. This is especially true if your employment, credit history, or current financial situation make a loan hard to get. The best mortgage brokers offer quality advice, and can solve problems your bank or mortgage company may not be able—or even willing—to tackle.

At S&Ls and savings banks, loan applications and processing are usually handled by salaried employees. But here, too, you'll need to be diligent in your approach and questioning. If you find your specific questions are being carried to someone in an inner office for answers, ask to deal directly with that person, rather than with the messenger.

Obtaining a loan from the bigger banks requires extra caution. They often have their own subsidiary mortgage companies where you are likely to find yourself dealing with commissioned reps. You'll need to ask all the interview questions we've already looked at, those that apply to bank loan officers and mortgage brokers, and perhaps a few more! Does the rep make a higher commission on certain types of loans (maybe a type *not* right for you)? Are the rep's personal commissions higher for loans made *above* a certain interest rate? In other words, are there salary incentives for the rep to get the most out of you? You need to know.

What you require and are searching for is someone who will place your best interests first, someone who has the experience and competence to follow through and get you the best loan possible. That frequently comes down to personal integrity, expertise, and the bond you establish with a particular loan professional.

By the time you are ready to get down to the serious business of making a formal loan application you will have talked with a number of lenders or brokers, at least by phone. And you will have a good idea of the loans and rates being offered in the marketplace. This preparation is invaluable, and it doesn't all have to be done out on the street. If you have access to a computer you can check rates and get reliable advice at a number of different websites, including a few of the best: www.hsh.com, www.freddiemac.com, and www.microsurf.com.

## Pre-Payment Clauses

A number of lenders have recently taken to imposing pre-payment penalties on borrowers who pay off a loan ahead of schedule—as 95 percent of buyers do. Some lenders have always imposed these penalties on ARMs paid off in the early years, but now a few banks and mortgage companies are planning to include these pre-payment penalty clauses on fixed-rate mortgages (FRMs).

The sting is that homeowners with such mortgages may have to pay 1 to 2 percent of the original loan amount, in some cases after being in the house for 5 or 10 or more years. My advice is simple: Before agreeing to anything, make sure the mortgage you are offered does not have such a clause (unless, of course, you can accept it). When you find such a clause, ask the lender to remove it. If the answer is no, you may be well advised to refuse the loan. The last thing you need is having to hand your lender another big chunk of money when it comes time to sell.

*Note:* This type of penalty is aimed at homeowners who pay off a mortgage when they move to another home, as most homeowners do within the first 10 years. Later we'll look at pre-payment penalties that can affect borrowers who send in extra payments simply to get their loans paid off ahead of schedule (and save thousands of dollars in interest charges).

## What You Need to Know About APR

No doubt you will have seen the term *APR* in lenders' ads and pamphlets. Something like this: *Interest Rate 7.25%, APR 7.36%*. Lenders are required to disclose and display the APR (Annual Percentage Rate) for every loan, ARMs and FRMs. The objective is to help borrowers compare a variety of loans having differing rates, points, and fees, and arrive at a 'true rate' for each. On a surface level it seems to achieve that goal, but underneath it is often a misleading and inadequate measure.

APR is always a higher figure than the loan's interest rate because it takes into consideration the interest rate plus additional fees you will have to pre-pay (including points). All these fees are extras; they make the loan more expensive than the interest rate alone would have you believe, which is the problem APR is supposed to correct.

However one major shortcoming of APR is that it is calculated on the assumption that the borrower will hold the loan for its full term. So, if you take out a 30-year loan, the APR is accurate only if you hold the loan for that period. But, in fact, only about 5 percent of home loans run their full term. For all the rest, the 95 percent, APR is invalid.

My best advice is to pay heed to APR initially only, when you are scanning lenders' offerings. But when you find particular loans you feel might interest you, dig deeper. Compare their interest rates along with estimates of all fees payable. Then, with the help of your lender, mortgage broker, attorney or exclusive buyer broker, work out total costs for each loan, for different periods of time. This is even more important the shorter the time you believe you might hold the loan. Tell your lender you'd like to see comparison figures that enable you to make accurate side-by-side evaluations. If your lender balks at such a request, move on; there are genuine professionals out there who are willing to do this for you.

### Loan Prequalification and Preapproval

Here's a critical distinction that is often misunderstood by homebuyers. Prequalification is not preapproval!

Preapproval is a much more involved process, one that requires you to submit lots of documentation and usually commits the lender to giving you a particular loan. Prequalification, on the other hand, carries no such promise from the lender, and is simply a guide to how big a loan you'll be able to get, based on verbal information you provide. Not until a later stage, when all your documentation is submitted, will the lender preapprove you—make a commitment on your loan (preapproval).

Here is the best advice I can offer homebuyers: Start the loan process early—three to six months before you envision buying a home. And don't settle for prequalification. Gather all the paperwork you'll need, and get preapproved. Then, when you go house hunting, you'll do so in confidence, without the worry of whether you'll be able to get financing. And you'll have given yourself a powerful negotiating advantage over nonpreapproved buyers in the market. This is even more an advantage if you are a typical first-time homebuyer with little money to put down. But, you can capitalize on this only if you let sellers know, through the broker, that you are a mortgage-preapproved buyer.

### What Size Loan Can You Afford?

The mortgage industry uses two figures in determining each borrower's loan limit—28 and 36 (referred to as 'qualifying ratios'). These ratios are not inflexible. With most lenders, if you are close to the mark, there is usually something that can be done to push your approval through. In fact, at certain times it is common for lenders to use more libral ratios—33 and 38, for example, which can enable you to qualify for a significantly bigger loan. Nonetheless, let's stay with the more conventional ratios as we explore how they affect you.

The 28 is the percentage of your gross income (before payroll taxes or other usual deductions) that lenders will allow you to pay monthly toward your mortgage. Therefore, a good idea is to try to prequalify yourself before your loan hunting begins, and it's easy to do. In computing both figures, couples are allowed to combine their incomes.

Here's an example; I'll keep the math reliable and accurate, but simple:

If your monthly gross income is $2,500, your mortgage payment can be a maximum of $700 ($2,500 × 28%). But bear in mind that by 'mortgage payment' your lender means: Principal, Interest, Taxes, and Homeowner's Insurance (PITI).

*Note:* When the Private Mortgage Insurance (PMI) premium is payable with your mortgage, that, too, will form part of the monthly expense the qualifying ratio must cover. You will typically pay all these items together in one check. However, for simplicity, whether PMI is payable or not, let's continue to refer to your combined monthly mortgage payment as PITI.

So, back to our example: That $700 you are qualified to spend each month would have to cover all parts of PITI.

As you can see, to compute this figure you'll have to find out how much property taxes are likely to be in the neighborhood you've targeted, and the cost of homeowner's insurance. Probably the easiest way is to call a real estate broker in the selected area, explain what you are doing, and ask about local property taxes. All brokers will have this information. If the broker insists you come to his office, decline; it is too early to do that. Plus, as a general rule, I do not favor buyers being prequalified by real estate brokers' in-house mortgage services. Instead I believe you should do your own initial research then 'shop the market' for loans. And when you are ready, talk with at least three lenders (more on this later).

Here's how the figures might work for a hypothetical couple:

| | |
|---|---|
| Combined gross incomes (monthly) | $ 4,500.00 |
| Maximum mortgage payment | $ 1,260.00 ($4,500 × 28%) |
| Monthly property Taxes (T) | 165.00 |
| Monthly homeowner's Insurance (I) | 50.00 |
| | $215.00 |

⎯⎯⎯▷

So, the combined T and I of PITI will cost $215. Now take this from the $1260 and what's left can go toward the monthly principal plus interest payment (P+I) – $1045. (Keep in mind, too, that figures here are rounded to avoid dealing in fractions and decimals; this will alter some computations very slightly.)

Naturally, the couple's next question will be: What size loan can $1,045 per month qualify them for? To answer that question we'll need to make another assumption. We'll assume 30-year fixed-rate mortgages (FRMs) are available at 8 percent. Now the question becomes: What size loan at 8 percent can be paid off with $1045 per month? If you don't have mortgage payment tables that will allow you to calculate this (I'll tell later where to get these), or if you are not mathematically inclined, any lender will instantly provide you with the answer. Here's how the couple's figures work out:

Monthly payment of $1045.00 at 8% over 30 years will pay for a loan of $142.000.

Let's take it to the next step. The couple now know the size of loan they can qualify for. Next they must consider the cash they have for the downpayment. We'll assume that their savings plus a recent inheritance adds up to $24,000. So their budget becomes $142,000 (loan) plus $24,000 (cash)—a total of $166,000. On the surface it appears they can afford a home in the $160,000–$166,000 price range. However, first they must take additional miscellaneous costs into consideration. In fact, closing costs (settlement costs) and other fees are likely to run as high as 5 to 7 percent of the loan amount. That will reduce their budget by approximately $7,000–$10,000. To be safe we'll use the higher figure, which makes their new budget approximately $156,000 ($166,000 minus $10,000).

Continuing this scenario, let's follow the couple through a hypothetical purchase (and let's give them a name: the Browns). Just because their budget stretches into the mid-$150,000 range, does *not* mean they should spend the total amount. You'll recall I advised in an earlier chapter that you set two budget figures: Your *comfortable spending limit* and your *upper spending limit*. The latter figure need not be the maximum you are free to spend.

Let's suppose the Browns find an ideal home listed at $158,000 but, through smart negotiation techniques learned from this book they manage to buy the home for $145,000. Here's what their situation now looks like:

Cash downpayment (10%+) $15,000

Reserve for closing costs, etc. $ 9,000. The couple's $24,000 is now accounted for.

Price paid for home        $145,000
Less downpayment           15,000
Loan required              $130,000

An 8 percent fixed-rate mortgage of $130,000 for 30 years will cost them $954 per month. (In actuality, the Browns would also have to pay a mortgage insurance fee, as their downpayment is less then 20%.)

Now we can put the four parts of the PITI together to arrive at the monthly payment:

Monthly P+I payment on $130,000 FRM    $ 954 (P+I)
Monthly taxes and Insurance            $ 215 (T+I)
Monthly mortgage payment               $ 1169 (PITI)

You'll recall that the Browns were qualified for a monthly mortgage payment of $1260. As it turned out, they ended up with a lower payment of $1169. So, clearly, they did not commit themselves to the maximum. Had they wished, they could have bought a more expensive home, taken a bigger loan, and had a bigger repayment. However, in this hypothetical example, their finances are not stretched to the maximum, plus they got the house they wanted.

I mentioned earlier that lenders use two standard ratios in determining how much they will lend you—28 and 36. Both figures are computed the same way, with one important exception. The 36 is also a percentage, but it applies to your monthly gross income plus your long-term debts. With this ratio your PITI payment plus your long-term debts cannot exceed 36 percent of your gross income.

The Browns had a monthly gross income of $4,500. Here, 36 percent would equal $1620, which is their maximum monthly outlay allowable—for mortgage payment plus long-term debts. This $1620 must be sufficient to pay for their mortgage plus all debts which have ten or more months still to run. Typical examples of long-term debts include car loans, student loans, and other mortgages. Credit card debts, unless excessive, usually do not count. Nor do household utility bills. So, in this instance, PITI and long-term debts cannot exceed $1620, 36 percent of the couple's combined gross incomes.

All borrowers are expected to satisfy both ratios—28 and 36. Fortunately, although most lenders won't volunteer this fact, these percentages are not carved in stone. But they are a good guideline. Thankfully, there is some flexibility in the qualifying process, especially when lenders are greedy for market share — which is just about always.

*Negotiating for the Best Loan Terms*

With every lender you talk to, and with each loan you feel might be right for you, always ask the lender to trim the rate, waive some of the fees, and sweeten the terms offered.

The point here is that there are other lenders eager for your business, and the industry is, as I said earlier, extremely competitive. No serious lender who wants your business will let you walk away when there is still room to be flexible. Saving even one quarter of one point in fees on a $100,000 loan will put (keep) $250 in your wallet at closing. Plus, saving one quarter point off your loan's interest rate could easily put another $200 every year into that same wallet. After 10 years: $2,000. After 30 years: $6,000! So, emphasize that you'll be shopping aggressively for the best rate and terms—and you'll accept nothing less!

You're likely to find that if you have a good relationship with your present bank the manager will be especially eager to keep your business. Therefore, based on your market research results, state clearly what rate and terms they will have to beat to get your mortgage business. Mention other lenders by name, better if they're the bank's competitors. And let it be known that you are fully aware that many of the typical closing costs can be reduced or waived altogether. The lender's attorney's fees and document-preparation fees are just two such fees that are often eliminated—but only for those borrowers who ask. Ask!

If you are using a broker, ask for personal assurance that the loan being offered to you is the best then available. That is, that the loan in question is overall the lowest priced loan the broker can offer for your particular circumstances, and the terms and fees cannot be bettered by the lender concerned, or with another known lender. Then wait for an answer. And watch. If you are not fully convinced by the broker's response, sleep on it, and in the morning, if you are still not convinced, do some more checking. Before you commit to any loan you must be as satisfied as possible that the broker or lender is advising you in your best interest. If you are pressured to sign quickly, don't! In fact, such pressure might be the only warning sign you'll need. The market is not short of lenders!

One final tip: In your home hunting, if you plan to engage an exclusive buyer broker (a smart idea), now is the time to talk to him or her about the loan you are considering. Ask if it falls in with what the buyer broker knows is currently available. Very likely you will pick up the confirmation you need for your peace of mind, or you'll get a referral that might deliver an even better deal. The principle here is simple: Make use of the professional resources available to you. A genuine exclusive buyer broker (also known as a buyer's agent or buyer representative) is always legally committed to serving your best interests.

### Downpayment and Loan-to-Value (LTV) Ratio

For many homebuyers one of the hardest challenges is to come up with the cash downpayment. Often, however, a buyer need put down as little as 5 percent of the purchase price, and take a loan for the other 95 percent. There are even loans that will allow as little as 3 percent downpayment.

But a larger downpayment has certain advantages that should not be ignored. The first is that it lowers the monthly loan repayment (P+I). Second, it establishes equity sooner (your percentage of ownership in the property). Third, when the downpayment equals or exceeds 20 percent of the home's value, you pay no private mortgage insurance (PMI) fees.

When you make a 20 percent downpayment the lender funds 80 percent of the home's value (purchase price). This is referred to as 80 percent LTV ratio. All it means is that you have 20 percent equity in the home. Had you put down just 10 percent and financed 90 percent of the home's value, the LTV (at the inception of the loan) would be 90 percent.

The concept of LTV is important for one particular reason. When the downpayment is less than 20 percent of the purchase price, the buyer has no option but to pay PMI. To add insult to the expense, this insurance (similar to a life insurance policy) does *not* cover the buyer! It protects only the lender in case you default on the loan.

What does PMI cost, and how do you pay it? The cost varies somewhat from lender to lender. Here's an example: On a 30-year loan with 10 percent down (90% LTV), some lenders require an upfront cash payment at closing, typically 0.4 percent of the loan amount, to cover the first year. On a $100,000 loan, 0.4 will mean $400. In subsequent years the PMI renewal premiums on the same loan can range from $300–$350 and are paid with the monthly payment. Other lenders combine PMI in the monthly payment, from the beginning.

However, when your equity in the home reaches 20 percent through your repayments plus the home's appreciation in value, these payments should, in theory, stop. If the homeowner doesn't shout loudly, they often don't.

Caution: Be careful with how long you pay PMI premiums. Policies and payments do not automatically expire when your equity reaches 20 percent of the home's value. However, you may have the option of paying this fee separately from your mortgage payment, which gives you more control. If so, it is worth considering. Then stop paying when your equity reaches 20 percent of the home's value.

*Note:* Your lender will probably require a reappraisal of the value of your home before agreeing to cancel the PMI policy. So research well ahead of time, before you suspect you have 20 percent equity in the property.

### Other Important Things You Need to Know About Loans

In considering any mortgage loan there are other key points to keep in mind. The loan interest rate will determine the maximum amount you can qualify for. All other things being equal, you will qualify to take a bigger loan amount at 7 percent than you would if the loan were going for 8 percent.

In the case of the Browns, based on the 28 percent qualifying ratio, each month they could put $1045 from their combined incomes to their P+I payment. Consequently, with an 8 percent interest rate, they qualified for a loan of $142,000. But, had they found a similar loan with an interest rate of 7 percent , they would have qualified for a loan of $157,000.

### *Hard Facts About Shorter-Term and Longer-Term Loans*

Another factor determining the maximum loan amount available to you is the term of the loan. A 30-year loan is the most affordable fixed-rate mortgage (FRM), and it is right for many buyers. However, that does not mean this loan is the best value for money. It takes a very long time before the buyer builds up equity (percentage of ownership in the property), because just a tiny part of every month's payment goes to paying off the principal. Believe it or not—incredible as it might seem—after 10 years of paying off a 30-year FRM, the buyer, typically, will still owe around 90 percent of the original amount borrowed! At that stage, 90 percent of the dollars that have been paid have gone to the lender in interest charges.

For that reason, my advice is simple: Compare different length loans carefully. With shorter loans, equity in the home builds up faster, and the benefit of that comes back to the homeowner no matter when the property is sold. Shorter-term loans also mean that you can be out of mortgage debt sooner, possibly in half the time. You'll also own your property free and clear at a younger age. Then the monthly dollars that once went for mortgage payments will be yours to spend however you wish (kids' college, vacation home, travel, retirement, etc).

Of course, a shorter-term loan also means higher repayments, but when the extra expense is manageable, a shorter loan makes good sense. Even better news: A 15-year loan is not twice as expensive as a 30-year loan, as you might have suspected. To illustrate this point, let's return to the Browns. Here is their situation:

Their monthly payment of $1045 at 8 percent over 30 years will pay for a loan of just over $142,000. For extra clarity, and to be precise with the figures, let's state that same information another way:

Loan of $142,000 at 8% over 30 years will cost the Browns $1041.95 per month (P+I). (After 30 years they'll have paid back a total of $375,096.)

Now compare with this (note the shorter term):

Loan of $142,000 at 8% over 15 years will cost the Browns $1357.03 per month (P+I). (After 15 years they'll have paid back a total of $244,264.)

As you can see, shortening the loan term to 15 years added only about $300 to the monthly payment ($1,041.95 to $1,357.03). But the 15-year loan builds their equity in the home much more rapidly, and is almost like paying the extra $300 every month directly off the principal.

In these examples you may also have detected another advantage of the shorter loan. Here's a closer look. Note the huge difference between payback costs for the two identical loan amounts:

$142,000 at 8% for 30 years. Total payback amount: $375,096

$142,000 at 8% for 15 years. Total payback amount: $244,264

Difference: $130,832

Over the full term, this 15-year loan will save you $130,832! In fact, any time you select a shorter term fixed rate mortgage (FRM) you'll save money, typically thousands of dollars, often tens of thousands, sometimes more. And, even if you sell and move on after 5,

7, or 10 years, a bigger chunk of the sales price always goes into your pocket—not into the banker's! So, instead of opting automatically for a 30-year loan, have your lender also run the monthly repayment figures and the full payback figures for a 15-year FRM, and compare carefully.

### One More Option for Borrowers

To illustrate our final point in this section, let's stay with the Browns. Here's a brief recap of their position: They could afford to pay $1045 P+I per month. And, with that size payment they could borrow $142,000 for 30 years at 8 percent.

But, at the last minute, they have a change of mind. A 30-year financial commitment suddenly seems too long. Instead, they decide they'll go for a 15-year FRM. How will this affect their situation, and what they can do?

Well, they already know that their income limits them to a maximum P+I payment of $1045 per month, and that's not alterable. And they also realize that the same loan amount ($142,000) over 15 years will carry higher monthly payments than they can afford. Consequently, to stay within their budget, the 15-year loan will have to be for a smaller amount, which means they'll have to settle for a less expensive home.

They now must answer this question: Without exceeding the $1045 monthly P+I payment they're already qualified for, how much can they borrow if they go for a 15-year FRM at 8 percent?

Here's what they discover: Over 15 years at 8 percent, their $1045 (approximate) monthly P+I payment will qualify them for a smaller loan of $110,000. Let's see what has changed (figures are rounded off very slightly):

| Term of loan | 30 years | 15 years |
|---|---|---|
| Monthly payment | $1045 | $1045 |
| Interest Rate | 8% | 8% |
| Size of loan obtainable | $142,000 | $110,000 |

As you have seen, there are real advantages to 15-year loans. If you are sure your household budget will be able to handle the higher monthly payments, this loan is worth your serious consideration. However, if you are strongly set on the shorter-term mortgage but cannot afford its higher monthly payments, consider doing what the Browns did in this situation: Scale down and buy a less expensive home (with the same monthly payments), which you'll own in half the time.

But hold on. You still have another attractive option, perhaps the best one of all—a wealth-building "trick of the trade." This is a way to get all the benefits of a 15-year loan, without committing yourself to the higher monthly payments that go with it. Sounds almost too good to be true. But, unlike most things that sound that way, this one *is* true. And it's easy to do on your own, without paying anyone for assistance. It's called *accelerated payments,* or *pre-paying* your loan.

*Accelerated Payments*

Over the past few years the idea of pre-paying your mortgage has gained press and popularity. Almost always though, it seems that someone else wants to do it for you—your bank or mortgage company, or an Internet service—for a fee! In fact, it is simple to arrange, and you can do it yourself! All you need do is send in extra dollars with your monthly payment. The extra dollars go off your loan principal, reducing your debt to the lender. But why should you do this? To answer that, let's continue with the Browns. (Note: If you work out the math yourself you'll find slight variations from these figures due to rounding off of cents and fractions of cents):

We'll assume the couple are still considering the $142,000 30-year FRM at 8 percent. This loan, as we saw, would cost them close to $1045 per month (actually, $1041.95). Now they ask: How much extra would they have to send in each month to pay off the loan in 20 years instead of 30?

Here's what they discover: By sending in an extra $147.05 along with their $1041.95 monthly payment (total $1189), they'll pay off the loan in 20 years. But that's not all, not by a long shot! They will also save $90,475 in interest. Here's how:

$142,000 at 8%. Per month $1041.95.
Loan paid off after 30 years: Total paid:  $375,096

$142,000 at 8%. Per month $1189.00
Loan paid off after 20 years: Total paid:  <u>$284,621</u>

Interest saved:  $ 90,475

But perhaps paying an extra $147.05 per month is too steep. What if they sent in just an extra $57.05 each month, making a total payment of $1099 ($1041.95 plus $57.05)? Here's what they find:

$142,000 at 8%. Per month $1041.95.
Loan paid off after 30 years: Total paid:   $375,096

$142,000 at 8%. Per month $1099.00
Loan paid off after 25 years: Total paid:   $326,843

Interest saved:    $ 48,253

As you can see, the extra payment of $147.05 per month saved the Browns 10 years of payments in the first example, plus $90,475 in costs.

And in the second example, an extra payment of just $57.05 per month shortened the loan by 5 years and saved them $48,253. This is the miracle of pre-payment!

### The Advantages of Bi-Weekly Payments

Similar savings can be gained by making what is known as *bi-weekly* payments. Here's an example:

Suppose you have a $100,000 30-year FRM at 8 percent. Your monthly payment will be $733.77. Now divide $733.77 by 2 and you get $366.89. If you simply send in this amount bi-weekly (every two weeks) you'll make 26 such payments every year. This will save you $46,300.86 in interest charges, and will pay off this loan in just under 23 years (over seven years early). Yet your bi-weekly payments will cost you only $733.77 extra per year: that is $366.89 × 26 instead of $733.77 × 12 (figures are rounded off slightly).

If your lender does not offer a bi-weekly program (few do), or tells you they cannot accommodate your suggestion (most say they can't), you have yet another equally attractive alternative. Simply divide your regular payment of $733.77 by 12 and you get $61.15. Now add this $61.15 to the $733.77 to get $794.92. This will be your new monthly payment (twelve per year) and will bring you virtually the same saving as the bi-weekly method. Just send in your check for $794.92 each month. That's it! Note: With this option you'll be paying exactly the same amount each year as with the bi-weekly method ($794.92 × 12 versus $366.89 × 26).

### Some More Pre-Payment Options

Now, we'll look at some practical pre-payment variations using a loan at the historical average interest rate of 10%. We'll assume you are borrowing $100,000 on a 30-year FRM. Monthly payments will be $877.58. But you want to know what you can save by pre-paying

$25, $50, $100, and $200 per month, and how each will reduce the 30 year term:

To each monthly P+I Payment of $877.58, if you add a pre-payment of:

$25, you will save $36,659 and reduce the loan term by 4 years and 3 months

$50, you will save $60,323 and reduce the loan term by 7 years

$100, you will save $90,497 and reduce the loan term by 10 years and 9 months

$200, you will save $123,178 and reduce the loan term by 15 years and 1 month

Clearly, the figures make a very good case for pre-paying whatever extra monthly amount you can afford. Of course it doesn't have to be a consistent amount every month. You can pre-pay irregularly too, whenever your budget allows. There are no fees, costs, or applications involved. And you do *not* need anyone's permission. Your bank will simply credit the extra payment against the outstanding loan principal (which is exactly what you want them to do). If you feel more comfortable talking with your lender first, go ahead, but make sure you speak with the manager, or someone else who can understand what you are planning.

Even if your mortgage contract contains a pre-payment penalty clause (few do) this can often be waived if you request it. And even when you don't, the lender typically does not impose the penalty, which is usually too small anyway, and shouldn't cause you any worry.

It is worth restating here that it makes the most sense to pay off highest interest debts first. If, for example, you have credit card debt at, say, 15 percent interest, this should be paid off before you pre-pay a lower-interest-rate home loan. The same applies to higher-interest-rate car loans and college loans.

Remember, too, that you do not need anyone to set up a pre-payment program for you, nor need you pay anyone to do so. If your lender asks for a fee, as some do, request that it be waived. Most lenders will comply. Generally borrowers who pre-pay need do nothing more than write in the pre-payment amount on the *extra payment* line of the coupon from the mortgage payment book. For extra peace of mind, you might check to make sure your full payment is credited on the date it is received by your lender, not held until the end of the month (very unlikely).

## A Few High-Quality Resources

Finally, if you want to know more about home loan search strategies, I can recommend highly two books: *How to Save Thousands of Dollars on Your Home Mortgage* by Randy Johnson (John Wiley & Sons, 1998), and *How to Get the Best Home Loan* by W. Frazier Bell (John Wiley & Sons, 1992).

If you are interested in a clear explanation of the 'how-to' and benefits of pre-payment, and just about everything you could wish to know about this smart trick of the trade, I advise you to get a copy of *The Banker's Secret* by Marc Eisenson (Good Advice Press, 1984, 1-800-255-0899). The company's website, www.goodadvice-press.com, provides lots of useful money-saving information. This publisher also puts out a terrific software program that allows you to run all kinds of "what if" pre-payment scenarios on your home computer. Alternatively, the company will create a personalized pre-payment schedule for you.

And, after you've moved in, another truly excellent (and eye-opening) book that will show you how to use your household dollars in amazing and thoroughly rewarding ways is *Invest in Yourself* by Marc Eisenson, Gerri Detweiler, and Nancy Castleman (John Wiley & Sons, 1998, 1-800-255-0899).

And then ... then enjoy your new home. And each day ... each hour ... of life!

# FINAL NOTE

*Knowledge is fated to start out as heresy...*
—ALDOUS HUXLEY

When you succeed in pulling off a great buy—which you should now be capable of doing—don't expect to be acknowledged as a masterful negotiator, except by those closest to you.

By following what you have learned here, your finest and most profitable negotiation skills will be subtle—even *invisible.* They will not be recognized for what they are by the other side, therefore the advantage will be yours to steal. And steal it you will. That's precisely how it should be, for in this quiet strength you now have the power to positively manipulate. *That* is the secret of winning negotiation.

Alas, in the end, you'll likely be remembered as a stubborn buyer. But also, as someone who couldn't be talked out of—or into—anything. Such things, though, are irrelevant and insignificant. Your reward will be bigger, as will your exhilaration. And neither will come from a feeling that you have defeated the seller or real estate agent.

No. When it's all over—when you have negotiated well—you'll take deepest satisfaction from knowing that *you* protected *yourself* from loss and defeat. At least equal satisfaction will come from counting the money *you* saved. The thousands of dollars *you* earned the right to keep and spend as you please because *you* were prepared, *you* were willing, *you* were able—to negotiate.

These are the riches and the rewards *Not One Dollar More!* makes possible.

Take time to enjoy them.

# APPENDIX

*Success is a matter of buying your experience cheap
and selling it at a profit.*

—ANONYMOUS

## USEFUL RESOURCES

### Services of Benefit to Home Buyers and Sellers

This resources section is included to help you obtain further assistance with your goal of buying and selling real estate wisely, confidently, and profitably. The books, pamphlets, websites, services, and associations listed here can help in a variety of ways. If you feel one or more of these listings might provide for your needs or just answer questions, don't hesitate to make a call to the provider concerned, or log-on to the appropriate website. Resources are useful only to the degree that you use them!

First, though, let me repeat here what thousands of readers and dozens of critics have already said: *Not One Dollar More!* is in itself a uniquely valuable resource. Make use of it! It is the only book of its kind written exclusively for the benefit of the ordinary homebuyer, and it should be the *first* book you read when you decide to buy a home.

And finally, bear in mind that to handle homebuying decisions you do not need to become an expert, or to match your wits with the professionals in the industry. Certainly, though, you'll benefit greatly from being as knowledgeable as you can reasonably be about matters that relate to your goal. And you'll gain even more knowledge from using sources of genuine assistance that are always available to you.

The important point here is this: Don't take a back seat! Stay involved, ask questions, make sure you understand your situation and options, then take time to consider your best move. As an informed consumer, that's how you will best protect your money and other interests—and come away with a genuinely good deal!

## Online Loan Shopping and Related Services

Homebuyers connected to the Internet can access many very good sites offering all kinds of home-related help. While the majority of computer users seem not yet quite ready to switch over to electronic loan shopping, much early research and leg work can be accomplished efficiently online. Here is a list of highly recommended sites, along with brief notes on what you can expect to find (plus telephone numbers where appropriate):

**Home-Shark** (www.homeshark.com)
Excellent site with easy-to-navigate sections on many vital home buying and selling topics. Provides high-quality information on such things as schools, home-finding tips, loan shopping, neighborhoods, costs, demographics, and many more areas. Has links to lots of worthwhile sites, including sites with over 1 million home listings.

**Microsurf** (www.microsurf.com)
Provides mortgage rates, very useful information about lenders and loans, special reports on mortgage related topics, and more. One of the leading mortgage sites, highly consumer oriented. Will not display information from lenders and companies that do not play it straight. Has removed services from its site after investigation of consumer complaints. Great links to other sites.

**Home Advisor** (www.homeadvisor.msn.com)
Comprehensive information about most aspects of house hunting, including finding the right mortgage. The site offers a guided tour to help you understand the many types of useful information it offers. Even offers breakdowns of regional FBI crime statistics, among other things.

**Equifax** (www.equifax.com/1-800-685-1111)
Credit reporting agency. Good information on many credit issues. Here you can order a copy of your credit report.

**Trans Union** (www.tuc.com/1-800-916-8800)
Credit reporting agency. Directions for correcting credit report errors. Good tips. Here you can order a copy of your credit report.

**Experian** (www.experian.com/1-888-EXPERIAN)
Credit reporting agency. Solid advice on establishing, maintaining, and repairing your credit.

**QuickenMortgage** (www.quickenmortgage.com)
Internet mortgage broker. Many helpful areas. Financial calculators and credit report analyzer. Here you can order a merged credit report, the kind your lender will probably use in determining your credit worthiness. Excellent site all round.

**First American Credco** (www.confidentialcredit.com/1-800-443-9342)
Provides merged credit reports to consumers. A leading provider of credit reporting information. Interesting and informative website. Offers membership services and benefits to consumers.

**QSpace** (www.qspace.com/1-888-893-1002)
Provides merged credit reports to consumers.

**Realtor.com** (www.realtor.com)
Lists 1.3 million homes for sale all over the country. Provide lots of information on each home. Also lists National Association of Realtors agents. (Site is partly owned by NAR.)

**CyberHomes** (www.cyberhomes.com)
Extensive lists of homes for sale. Provides good advice on home-buying and figuring out your finances. Good tools for searching for a suitable home within a radius of designated geographic points. Also has finance calculators, with instructions on how best to use them. Will e-mail you updates on home listings according to criteria you provide.

**Owners.com** (www.owners.com)
Lists a huge number of homes for sale by owners (fisbos). Links to mortgage information sites.

**New Home Search Systems** (www.newhomesearch.com)
Lists builders and homes under construction. Shows floor plans and lets you search by budget.

## Online Mortgage Brokers and Information Services

**E-Loan** (www.e-loan.com)
Internet mortgage broker with lots of excellent advice on many topics. Will e-mail you with changing information matched to your specific needs. Offers mortgage finance calculators to help you figure costs, etc.

**Quicken Mortgage** (www.quickenmortgage.com)
Internet mortgage broker. Excellent easy-to-use tools for comparing mortgage rates and costs to determine the best value for money. Allows you to pre-qualify yourself, find out what you can afford, and calculate costs with online calculators.

**Loan Search** (www.loansearch.com/1-800-591-3279)
A model loan finding service (free) serving NY/NJ area. This service has much to recommend it.

**Microsurf** (www.microsurf.com)
One of the leading mortgage sites. Will not display information from companies that do not play it straight.

**LoanPage** (www.loanpage.com)
Comprehensive list of lenders, plus loan application forms.

**Federal Home Loan Mortgage Corporation** (www.freddiemac.com)
Current information on what mortgage loans and rates are available in the market.

**The Federal National Mortgage Association** (www.fanniemae.com)
A big resource of very useful information on loans and special programs.

**Mortgage Market Information Service** (www.interest.com)
Extensive information on mortgages.

**Home Price Check/Inpho, Inc.** (www.homepricecheck.com/1-800-IT-SOLD-4)
Home sales price information that is typically difficult to acquire. Covers 50 top metro areas and 73 percent of all disclosed U.S. home sales.

**Kiplinger's** (www.kiplinger.com)
Especially good for mortgage loan information, including rates for specific areas of the country. Kiplinger's is a monthly magazine on personal finance topics (highly recommended).

**HSH Associates** (www.hsh.com/1-800 UPDATES)
Indispensable information on mortgage rates and all aspects of homebuying. Offers excellent publications and many good articles and features on loan-shopping and related topics.

**The Internet Real Estate Directory** (www.ired.com)
Huge site with very good information, plus links to hundreds of lenders and loans. Rates other sites. Offers thousands of links.

**HouseMaster** (www.housemaster.com/1-800-526-3939)
Reputable nationwide home inspection group.

## Miscellaneous Recommended Services

**Buyer's Resource** (www.buyersresource.com/1-800-359-4092).
Leading nationwide multi-service exclusive buyer brokerage group. (See below for more information).

**Only Buyers—America: Real Estate**
(www.onlybuyersamerica.com/1-888-552-8937)
Exclusive buyer brokerage group. A leader in the field of equal buyer representation. Helpful, instructive. Nationwide network.

**The Buyer's Agent** (www.forbuyers.com/1-800-766-8728)
Excellent site of a leading Exclusive Buyer Agent group. Nationwide network.

**Bestagents** (www.bestagents.com/1-800-962-1313)
Nationwide network of agents working exclusively to represent homebuyers.

**NAEBA/National Association of Exclusive Buyer Agents**
(www.naeba.org/1-800-986-2322)
Top national network of buyer agents. Referrals to buyer agents around the country.

**RealSite** (www.realsites.com)
House listings in the United States and other countries.

**Kiplinger's Magazine** (www.kiplinger.com)
Superb site with a huge resource of good advice on homebuying and other money matters. Especially good for mortgage loan information, including rates for specific areas of the country.

**Money Magazine** (www.money.com)
Top site with loads of smart tools and advice to help you manage your finances. Well researched features on home buying and selling, mortgages, saving money, investing, and related topics.

**Consumer Reports** (www.consumerreports.org)
Reliable and detailed advice for consumers on many products and services.

**The National Financial Services Network** (www.nfsn.com)
Information on loans of various kinds, including mortgages. Financial advice.

**American Society of Home Inspectors**
(www.ashi.com/1-800-743-ASHI)
To find a qualified home inspector in any of the 50 states.

**Federal Trade Commission** (http://ftc.gov)
Good information on how to repair your credit.

**The Homebuyer's Fair** (www.fair.com)
Great tools for borrowers. Solid advice and opinions on many homebuying topics.

**Buyer's Resource, Inc.**
This dynamic group offers a range of excellent services to aid consumers in almost every area of home buying and selling. Except for FiSBO Registry (see below), which has a fee but saves consumers the usual high homeseller costs, all these services are generally provided at no cost to the consumer. In the group's nationwide network are the following:
    **Buyer's Resource** (www.buyersresource.com/1-800-359-4092). A nationwide franchise system, exclusively represents homebuyers in finding and buying homes.
    **Buyer's Homefinding Network** (www.finderhome.com/1-800-500-3569)
Helps homebuyers find a buyer agent in any community, regardless of whether there is a Buyer's Resource office available in the buyer's target area or not.
    **FiSBO Registry, Inc.** (www.fisbos.com/1-800-500-5520)
Provides a Homeseller Toolkit and related cost-saving moving and mortgage packages for homesellers selling their home on their own.
    **SellMyHouse Referral Service**
    (www.sellmyhouse.com/1-800-500-3569)

For those home sellers who would rather have a sales agent represent them, this service will locate and refer a top sales agent in their community.

## Recommended Publications and Software

**Good Advice Press** (www.goodadvicepress.com/1-800-255-0899)
For copies of two highly recommended books. First, *The Banker's Secret* shows how to save thousands of dollars on your mortgage, and contains a variety of easy-to-use amortization tables and payment tables (also available, *The Banker's Secret Loan Software Package*). And second, *Invest in Yourself: Six Secrets to a Rich Life* shows how to take charge of your life and make the most of your time, energy, and money. (Try also: www.investinyourself.com).

**Not One Dollar More! (Second Edition)** (www.notonedollar.com)
This best-selling book forced the U.S. real estate industry to reverse direction and support fair and equal representation for homebuyers. The website contains excerpts and solid advice from *Not One Dollar More!* You'll find reliable information on how to save thousands of dollars buying your next home. The site also has various newsletter articles by the author, including how-to features on negotiation (for anything you buy or trade) and related topics.

**How to Save Thousands of Dollars on Your Home Mortgage** (John Wiley & Sons.)
Comprehensive and well written, this book tells you all you'll probably want to know about mortgages, credit status, fees, points, how to get the loan that's right for you, and lots more. Author: Randy Johnson.

**How to Get the Best Home Loan** (John Wiley & Sons.)
Written by a banker, this book is a solid guide to the mortgage marketplace. It explains how to prepare for the loan-seeking process, the types of loans available, what to do when you run into questions or difficulties, and much more. Author: W. Frazier Bell.

## Resources of Special Benefit to Homebuyers

**Only Buyers—America (Real Estate)** (9101 East Kenyon Avenue, Suite 2300, Denver, CO 80237. Phone 1-888-552-8937)

Dynamic and highly service oriented buyer broker group led by Barry Miller, one of the pioneers of buyer brokerage in the United States. OBA agents offer homebuyers free, no-pressure consultations with absolutely no strings attached. Also provides a range of critical services, consumer advice, and other information. Services include assisting the buyer throughout the entire home finding, buying and negotiation processes, then right through to attending at the closing. Website: *www.onlybuyersamerica.com.*

**The Buyer's Agent, Inc.** (1225A Lynnfield Rd., Suite 273, Memphis, TN 38819. Phone 1-800-766-8728)
A leading group comprising buyer agent franchisees nationwide. All TBA agents represent homebuyers exclusively and work to a strict code of ethics. Provides quality assistance, consumer information, and referrals to local TBA franchisees. TBA works only in the buyer's best interests, and helps with finding suitable mortgages, insurance, attorneys, etc. Website: *www.forbuyers.com.*

**American Society of Home Inspectors, Inc. (ASHI)** (932 Lee Street, Suite 101, Des Plaines, IL 60016. Phone 1-800-743-ASHI)
This nonprofit group has members in most parts of the United States and is one of the largest and most reputable home inspection organizations. Provides a thorough, high-quality inspection service inside and outside the home. Members are held to a high standard of practice and a strict code of ethics. For information and a free booklet, *The Home Inspection and You,* call the toll-free number. Website: *www.ashi.com.*

**HouseMaster of America** (421 W. Union Av, Bound Brook, NJ 08805. Phone 1-800-526-3939)
A leading home inspection company with offices almost everywhere in the U.S., and in Canada. Provides comprehensive reports on all systems inside and outside the home. Inspectors report directly to the homebuyer and provide maintenance tips. Website: *www.housemaster.com.*

**Home Price Check/Inpho Inc.** (225 Fifth Street, Cambridge, MA 02142. Phone 1-617 868 7050)
Inpho Inc offers a unique Internet real estate information product, the Home Price Check. This Blue Book of Homes provides information-hungry consumers with U.S. home sales information that is typically difficult to acquire. Inpho continuously acquires data from 18 vendors, resulting in the largest home sale and property tax database available. Covers 50 top metro areas and 73 percent of all dis-

closed U.S. home sales. Access Home Price Check at 1-800-IT-SOLD-4 or on the web at *www.homepricecheck.com.*

**American Homeowners Foundation** (6776 Little Falls Road, Arlington, VA 22213-1213. Phone 1-703 536 7776. Order line 1-800-489-7776)
This is an independent, nonprofit educational and research organization serving the interests on 65 million homeowners and prospective homeowners. AHF offers model contracts that protect consumers who are considering a home purchase, remodeling, or home construction. Also offers good how-to books. AHF is dedicated to the concept of fair and equal representation for buyers and sellers, and to helping consumers make wise, well-informed decisions.

**Buyer's Resource, Inc.** (393 Hanover Center Road, Etna, NH 03750. Phone 1-800-359-4092)
This group has a nationwide network of affiliates providing many excellent services to aid consumers in almost every area of home buying and selling. Almost all services are generally provided at no cost to the consumer. The group's buyer agents represent homebuyers' interests exclusively. BR agents negotiate for the buyer, assist in finding a suitable mortgage, and help homebuyers find a buyer agent in any community. They also assist people selling their home on their own, and offer a range of additional services to homesellers. Website: *www.buyersresource.com.*

**HSH Associates** (1200 Route 23, Butler, NJ 07405. Phone 1-800-873-2837)
This is the nation's largest supplier of information on mortgages. National businesses and media rely on this company's data daily. Provides a valuable service for loan seekers, particularly *The Mortgage Kit, which* lists dozens of local lenders' interest rates and other important loan information such as points, fees, down-payment, etc for each. The kit also contains amortization tables and a very useful 56-page booklet *How to Shop for Your Mortgage: What Every Consumer Needs to Know* website: *www.hsh.com.*

## Additional Resources

Almost all the following information or advice services are free (except as noted):

*A Consumer's Guide to Mortgage Settlement Costs,* from the Federal Reserve Board, Publications Services, 20th and C Streets, NW, Washington, DC 20551.

*Settlement Costs: A HUD Guide.* Before you begin your search for a loan, ask any lender for a free copy of this.

*Fannie Mae's Consumer Guide to ARMs.* Write to: Federal National Mortgage Association, 3900 Wisconsin Av., NW, Washington, DC 20016.

*A Home of Your Own: Helpful Advice from HUD on Choosing and Buying a Home,* from U.S Department of Housing and Urban Development, Room 9170, Washington, DC 20410-8000. Or ask your local real estate professional.

*Facts for Consumers (series): Real Estate Brokers.* Federal Trade Commission, Washington, DC 20580.

*Buyers' and Sellers' Rights: Information brochures.* Obtainable from your local State Bar Association (most).

*Consumer's Resource Handbook.* U.S. Office of Consumer Affairs, Department of Commerce, Room 5718, Washington, DC 20230. Phone 1-202-377-5001.

*What Buyers and Sellers Need to Know About Real Estate Agents,* from American Association of Retired Persons, Box HOME, 601 E Street, Washington, DC 20049. Also available from Consumer Federation of America.

*Various Consumer Publications.* Consumer Information Center, Pueblo, CO 81009. Phone 1-719-948-4000. Various topics, including housing and homebuying. Some are free, some low cost.

*Various Types of Consumer Information and Services.* State, county and city government consumer protection offices. If you have a problem, your city or county consumer office will often investigate and try to resolve complaints. Check your local telephone directory.

# INDEX